The
Great Turkey
Cookbook

The Great Turkey Cookbook

385 Turkey Recipes for Every Day and Holidays

BY
VIRGINIA AND ROBERT HOFFMAN

Crossing Press
Freedom, CA 95019

WE WISH TO ACKNOWLEDGE . . .

Our appreciation for the help that we have received in the past three years, in the writing of this book.

Dr. Francine Bradley, Ph.D., Extension Poultry Specialist of the Avian Sciences Department, The University of California at Davis, for her many contributions, and The American Poultry Historical Society, for information on the early days of American turkey production.

The National Turkey Federation, who supplied us with recipes and material from which we prepared the sections on selection and preparation of turkey.

The California Poultry Industry Federation who generously shared many of their prize-winning recipes with us.

Ms. Anne Salisbury, of the R.C. Auletta Company, our source of recipes and cooking instructions from The Perdue Farms, Incorporated, one of America's leading turkey producers.

The Louis Rich Company, whose turkey products are found throughout the United States, for recipes and nutritional information.

Foster Farms, the leading poultry producer in California, who provided us with many "uniquely California" recipes.

Ms. Denise O'Meara of the British Turkey Information Service, who generously shared some of their best recipes with us.

Pinpoint Publishing, Santa Rosa, CA, for their nutritional analysis program "Micro Cookbook 4.0 for Windows © 1995."

Library of Congress Cataloging-in-Publication Data

The great turkey cookbook : 385 turkey recipes for every day and holidays
 by Virginia and Robert Hoffman.
  p. cm.
 Includes index.
 ISBN 0-89594-792-7 (paper)
  1. Cookery (Turkeys)   I. Hoffman, Virginia.   II. Hoffman, Robert.
TX750.5 T87G74 1995   95-19835
 641.6'6592—dc20   CIP

CONTENTS

Introduction 5
    How To Use This Cookbook 5
    What's So Special About Turkey 6
    There Are Many Kinds of Turkey Meat 7
    Nutritional Comparison 9
    Turkey, A Native American 10

Turkey Appetizers 13

Turkey Soups & Chilis 25

Turkey Salads 51

Asian & Indian 81

Italian & Mediterranean 109

Mexican & Southwestern..................................... 127

Casseroles & Meat Loaves 145

Pot Pies & Pastries 167

Sauté & Stir-Fry.. 187

Pot Roasts & Stews 217

Pastas & Grains 235

Roasting Breasts & Rolled Roasts 253

Roasting Whole & Half Turkeys 269

Barbecuing & Grilling... 283

Microwave Cooking 313

Sandwiches, Burgers, Hoagies & Sloppy Joes 335

More Stuffings & Sauces 367

Index.. 377

INTRODUCTION

How To Use This Cookbook

Each recipe is identified on the upper corner of the page as to the type of food (soup, salad, et cetera) and which part of the turkey can be used (leftovers, turkey breast, and so forth).

Ingredients in all the recipes are available in most grocery stores and/or supermarkets. In certain cases, we have named alternatives that are equally satisfactory.

Each recipe has a nutritional analysis based upon the larger number of servings noted. The editors and the publisher accept no responsibility for the accuracy of these analyses. There are many variations in ingredients, which can change these figures substantially.

What's So Special About Turkey

Today, nearly 60 percent of the U.S. population is made up of one- or two-person households. This is a dramatic change from the large families of previous generations. Now, career-minded singles, dual-income couples, single parents, "empty-nest" parents and seniors are the majority. Turkey is the right choice for today's lifestyle.

First, it is convenient. Turkey is available in more than thirty different forms at the market. You can buy it fresh, frozen, already cooked or smoked. It comes in portions for one or two, and for larger families.

Second, it is so easy and quick to prepare.

Third, it is delicious. Whether it be a slice of plain white breast of turkey, a drumstick or a plate of traditional roast turkey, it is moist, tender and rich in flavor.

Fourth, it is the most versatile of all meats. Turkey has the unique ability to take on and absorb seasonings and flavors, so you may use it instead of beef, pork and lamb in most, if not all, of your favorite recipes.

Fifth, it is good for you. Turkey has fewer calories, less fat and less cholesterol than beef, pork or lamb. See the Nutritional Comparison chart on page 9.

Sixth, it is much less expensive than beef, pork or lamb. It not only costs less per pound, but there is far less waste in the form of fat and bones.

Convenient, easy to prepare, delicious, versatile, healthy, economical—that's turkey!

There Are Many Kinds of Turkey Meat

Not so long ago, "turkey for dinner" meant buying and roasting a whole bird for Thanksgiving and Christmas. Today, you can choose from many different forms of turkey for any meal at any time of the year. Here's what is available, fresh or frozen:

Whole turkeys, ranging in size from 6 to 24 pounds. You can buy them pre-stuffed and pre-basted, even with a pop-out thermometer.

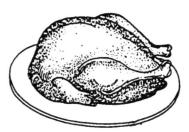

Whole Turkey

Half turkeys, with half breast, one drumstick, one thigh and one wing. Perfect for smaller families.

Whole or half breast. This is all white meat. Particularly good to substitute for pork.

Whole Turkey Breast

Thighs, the second joint of the leg, have juicy dark meat, are very simple to use and are low in price. Use them instead of beef, particularly in Italian dishes.

Drumsticks, the first joint of a turkey leg, are all dark meat and, like the thighs, are very versatile for a wide variety of dishes.

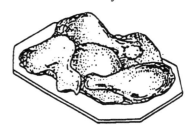

Turkey Thighs, Wings, Drumsticks

Wings, available whole or with the wing tip removed, are the least expensive turkey part. For many years, they were used only in making soups. Today, there are exciting recipes for turkey wings.

Roasts, both breast and hindquarters, are specially boned and bound with string, with a choice of white or dark meat, or both, in sizes from 2 to 8 pounds. The skin has been removed.

Turkey Hindquarter Roast

Turkey Breast Slices or Steaks

Ground Turkey

Turkey Ham, Bologna, Salami,
Pastrami, Franks and Weiners

Slices or steaks. These are cut from the tender white breast meat, to be used as you would use veal or tender beef steaks.

Tenderloin. The best cut of the turkey breast. Use as you would veal, pork or lamb.

Ground turkey. Probably the kind of turkey used most. Can be used in any recipe that calls for ground beef, pork or lamb.

Turkey sausage. Comes ground or as links. Like all turkey products, sausages are lower in fat content than their traditional source—pork. The giblets, which include the heart, liver, gizzard, necks and tails, are now available separately for making soups and stews. (The English make a fabulous pâté with the liver.)

Cooked turkey is also available. The white meat, available in both thick and thin slices, is ideal for sandwiches, salads and recipes calling for cooked turkey.

Turkey ham is boneless turkey thigh meat, rolled, cured and seasoned. It is available in the Deli section of your market.

Bacon-like turkey strips are fully cured and cooked and take just seconds to heat.

Turkey bologna, salami, pastrami, franks and corn dogs are available in most Deli departments. All have one-third less fat than the originals, and many people prefer them.

Smoked turkey, available as whole turkeys, breasts, wings, drumsticks and slices, is fully cooked and has a robust hickory smoked flavor.

NUTRITIONAL COMPARISON

Product	Calories	Total Fat	Saturated Fat	Cholesterol	Sodium	Protein	Iron
Whole Turkey Per 3-oz. Roasted, skinless	**129**	**2.6 gm**	**0.9 gm**	**64 mg**	**59 mg**	**25 gm**	**1.5 mg**
Beef Per 3-oz. Roasted, trimmed	192	9.4 gm	4.2 gm	73 mg	57 mg	25 gm	2.6 mg
Pork Per 3-oz. Roasted, trimmed	198	11.1 gm	3.8 gm	79 mg	59 mg	23 gm	1.1 mg
Lamb Per 3-oz. Roasted, trimmed	176	8.1 gm	3.0 gm	78 mg	71 mg	24 gm	1.7 mg
Ground Turkey Per 3-oz. Braised	**195**	**11 gm**	**3.2 gm**	**58 mg**	**70 mg**	**21 gm**	**1.6 mg**
Ground Beef 76% lean Per 3-oz. Broiled, trimmed	251	16.9 gm	6.5 gm	86 mg	71 mg	23 gm	2.6 mg
Ground Beef 82% lean Per 3-oz. Broiled, trimmed	233	14.4 gm	6.0 gm	86 mg	69 mg	24 gm	2.6 mg

Source: United States Department of Agriculture

Turkey, A Native American

Turkeys have played an important role in American and world history. Although popular American history places the discovery of turkey with the first Thanksgiving in America, the turkey was in the New World long before the Pilgrims.

Recent archaeological studies show that turkeys have roamed the Americas for ten million years. When Christopher Columbus came to the New World in 1492, turkeys were here to greet him. The name "turkey" came from Columbus, who, thinking that the New World was connected to India, named them "tuka," the East Indian Tamil language name for the peacock. (Actually, the turkey is a variety of pheasant.)

A few years later Cortez, the conqueror of Mexico, sent some turkeys to King Charles of Spain as part of his agreement to repay his Majesty with "One fifth of all the spoils taken in the New World." The turkeys then were called "tukki" by the Sephardic merchants of Spain, from their Hebrew word for the peacock.

By 1530, turkeys were being raised domestically in England, France and Italy, and soon were being exported to America, where the settlers bred them with the wild turkey to produce the magnificent Bronze and Narragansett breeds, which became the foundation of the American turkey industry.

Because wild turkeys were so plentiful in America, there were very few domesticated flocks. It was not until the early 1900s, when practically all wild turkeys had ceased to exist, that turkeys were raised domestically.

One of the few exceptions were the California missions, where as early as 1816 flocks of turkeys were being raised.

Transporting turkeys in those days was by herding a flock, sometimes as many as 500 birds, to market. In the late 1800s, turkey growers in Northern California herded their flocks to market, a 250-mile trip, which took 75 to 100 days.

Benjamin Franklin, who proposed the turkey as the official United States bird, was deeply disappointed when the bald eagle was chosen instead. In a letter to his daughter he wrote, "I wish the bald eagle had not been chosen as the Representative of our country! The Turkey is a much more respectable Bird, and therefore a true original native of America."

In England, turkeys raised in Suffolk were herded to London, and, in inclement weather, had their feet bound in cloth, over which leather shoes were laced. The 50-mile trip took three to four weeks and required five to ten persons and dogs.

Turkey production in the United States soared in the early part of the twentieth century. In the 1990s, nearly 300 million turkeys are raised in the U.S. each year.

Because turkey is now a year-round meat, no longer used only for Thanksgiving, Christmas and other special occasions, its consumption has risen to more than 20 pounds per person each year in the United States. (The French consume 13 pounds, Italians 11, Germans 8 and English 7, per person.)

J. A. Brillat-Savarin, in his book *The Physiology of Taste*, published in 1791, wrote of the American turkey as being "One of the most beautiful presents which the New World has made to the Old."

Now, on to the recipes . . . .

APPETIZERS

Ginger Turkey Wontons

Make and freeze up to 3 weeks ahead; do not thaw before frying.

1 1/4 pounds turkey breast
   tenderloins
2 cloves garlic
1 bunch green onions, chopped
2 tablespoons chopped fresh
   ginger

3 tablespoons Madeira wine or
   sherry
Salt and pepper to taste
1 package (14 ounces) wonton
   wrappers
3 cups oil, for frying

Put turkey, garlic, onion, ginger, Madeira, salt and pepper in food processor; process until smooth. Put 1 teaspoon of this filling in center of each wonton wrapper. Wet edges with water; fold to form triangle. Press around edges to seal. Wet both side points and pinch together over center. Freeze on baking sheet.

Heat oil to 375 degrees. Fry wontons a few at a time until golden brown, about 2 minutes. Drain on paper towels. Serve hot with dipping sauces.
Makes approximately 50 wontons.

SHERRY ORANGE SAUCE:
Combine 1 can (6 ounces) frozen orange juice concentrate, 1 tablespoon minced fresh ginger and 1/3 cup sherry in saucepan and bring just to a boil. Serve hot or cold.

SESAME SCALLION SAUCE:
Whisk together 1/2 cup rice vinegar, 2 tablespoons sesame oil, 2 tablespoons oyster sauce,* 5 green onions, chopped, and 2 tablespoons vegetable oil.

*Note: Oyster sauce can be found in the Oriental section of food stores.

Per Wonton (approx) excluding dipping sauces:

Calories 143	*Protein 3 gm*	*Fat 14 gm*
Carbohydrate 2 gm	*Sodium 32 mg*	*Cholesterol 9 mg*

Eggplant Turkey Stacks

Lining your baking sheet with aluminum foil makes cleanup easy.

8 ounces turkey ham, sliced
8 ounces provolone cheese,
   thinly sliced
1 large eggplant, sliced to
   1/8 inch thick

4 eggs, lightly beaten
1 cup seasoned bread crumbs
1/4 cup olive oil

Layer turkey ham and cheese on half the eggplant slices. Top with remaining eggplant slices. Dip "sandwiches" in eggs, then coat with bread crumbs. Place on foil-covered baking sheet. Drizzle with olive oil. Bake in 300 degree oven for 25 minutes; turn over halfway through cooking time. Cut into quarters to serve.   Makes about 86 appetizers.

Per Appetizer (approx):
Calories 26
Carbohydrate 1 gm

Protein 2 gm
Sodium 61 mg

Fat 2 gm
Cholesterol 13 mg

Smoked Turkey Quesadillas

Messy to eat, but so good! Serve with plenty of napkins.

2 cups shredded Cheddar cheese
12 flour tortillas (8 inches)
1 1/2 pounds smoked turkey breast,
   shredded

3/4 cup diced mild green chilies
Oil, for frying
1 1/2 cups guacamole
1 1/2 cups sour cream

Sprinkle cheese on half the tortillas. Top with turkey and chilies. Cover with remaining tortillas. Heat lightly oiled skillet over medium-high heat. Cook each quesadilla until golden brown and crisp, about 2 to 3 minutes per side. Cut into 8 wedges and serve with guacamole and sour cream.   Makes 48 appetizers.

Per Appetizer (approx):
Calories 123
Carbohydrate 11 gm

Protein 7 gm
Sodium 269 mg

Fat 6 gm
Cholesterol 14 mg

Country Pâté

3 pounds turkey drumsticks
Water or broth as needed
4 shallots, chopped
2 cloves garlic
1/4 teaspoon each ground
  allspice and mace
2 teaspoons fresh minced thyme
  or 1 teaspoon dried

1 teaspoon fresh minced
  marjoram or 1/2 teaspoon
  dried
2 tablespoons brandy
1 cup heavy cream
Salt and pepper to taste

Poach turkey drumsticks in water or broth to cover, gently simmering until meat is tender, about 1 1/2 hours. Pull turkey meat from bones; discard skin and bones.

Place turkey, shallots, garlic, spices, herbs and brandy in food processor; process for 1 minute. With motor running add cream slowly. Season with salt and pepper. Spoon into crock and refrigerate overnight. Serve with toasted baguette slices or crackers.   Makes approximately 3 cups.

Per 1/4-cup Serving (approx):
Calories 237
Carbohydrate 1 gm

Protein 23 gm
Sodium 101 mg

Fat 15 gm
Cholesterol 95 mg

Ginger-Orange Turkey Wings

If the Chinese had turkey (they didn't, until very recent times), they probably would have invented this zesty treatment of turkey wings, fit for an emperor.

4 turkey wings
1 bay leaf
1 clove garlic
3 1/2 cups orange juice
2 tablespoons grated orange
   zest

1/2 cup firmly packed brown
   sugar
2 tablespoons shredded fresh
   ginger
1 tablespoon soy sauce

Poach turkey wings in simmering water with bay leaf and garlic for 35 minutes. Drain water and arrange wings in baking dish. Combine juice, zest, sugar, ginger and soy sauce; bring to a boil. Simmer for 20 minutes. Pour over wings and bake at 350 degrees for 1 hour, basting occasionally.

Makes 4 servings.

Per Serving (approx):
Calories 680
Carbohydrate 62 gm

Protein 56 gm
Sodium 386 mg

Fat 23 gm
Cholesterol 145 mg

17

Turkey Liver Pâté

You'll probably have to order turkey livers from your market butcher a couple of days in advance. Very few butchers have them on hand, unless it is during a holiday period when they have lots of turkeys. If you think of it then, buy several pounds, freeze them and defrost when you are ready to make pâté.

8 tablespoons butter or margarine

1 large or 2 medium onions, very finely chopped

1 clove garlic, very finely minced

1 pound turkey livers, trimmed and quartered

1/4 teaspoon each black pepper, dried thyme, dried tarragon and salt

1/2 ounce brandy or Cognac

Melt 3 tablespoons of the butter in large frying pan over medium-low heat. Cook onions until soft and translucent, about 6 minutes. Add garlic and cook for another minute or two. Pour into blender or food processor. Puree for a minute.

Melt remaining butter in same pan and add livers. Sauté over medium-high heat until slightly browned on outside, rosy red on inside, about 4 to 5 minutes. Sprinkle livers with spices, herbs and brandy; cook for another minute or two. Be sure to scrape up browned residue in pan.

Add all this to onion-garlic puree in blender and puree until absolutely smooth.

Put in serving bowl, cover tightly and refrigerate for 8 hours or overnight. Serve with toast points or melba toast.   Makes 8 servings.

Per Serving (approx):
Calories 181
Carbohydrate 5 gm

Protein 9 gm
Sodium 226 mg

Fat 13 gm
Cholesterol 215 mg

Party Meatballs

1 pound ground turkey
1 egg, lightly beaten
1/3 cup finely chopped onion
1/3 cup dry bread crumbs

1 tablespoon dried parsley flakes
1 teaspoon instant beef bouillon
1/4 teaspoon salt
1/4 teaspoon black pepper

Combine all ingredients. Shape into 1-inch meatballs; place on shallow greased baking pan. Bake in 350 degree oven for 20 minutes.

Meanwhile, prepare Cranberry-Horseradish Sauce. Pour sauce over meatballs; serve hot.

Makes 3 dozen appetizers.

CRANBERRY-HORSERADISH SAUCE:
Combine 1 can (8 ounces) jellied cranberry sauce and 1 tablespoon prepared horseradish or 1 teaspoon grated orange zest in saucepan. Warm over medium heat, stirring until smooth.

Per Appetizer (approx):
Calories 34
Carbohydrate 3 gm

Protein 3 gm
Sodium 45 mg

Fat 1 gm
Cholesterol 15 mg

Crunchy Oven-Baked Turkey Drumettes

1 1/3 cups Grape-nuts
  cereal
2 teaspoons dried Italian seasoning
1/2 to 3/4 teaspoon red pepper
  flakes

1/2 cup buttermilk
2 pounds turkey drumettes

In food processor fitted with metal blade, process cereal, Italian seasoning and red pepper flakes for 30 seconds or until mixture is coarsely chopped. Transfer mixture into gallon-sized, self-closing plastic bag.

Pour buttermilk into 9-inch pie plate. Dip each turkey drumette into buttermilk, coating completely. One at a time, add drumettes to cereal mixture in plastic bag. Shake bag to completely coat drumette with cereal mixture. Remove drumette from bag. Repeat to coat remaining drumettes. Place drumettes in refrigerator for 30 to 45 minutes to allow coating to adhere better.

On 2- x 10- x 15-inch jelly-roll pan sprayed with nonstick spray, arrange drumettes. Bake, uncovered, at 400 degrees for 30 minutes. Cover drumettes loosely with foil and continue baking for 15 minutes or until meat thermometer reaches 170 degrees when inserted in thickest part of drumettes.

Makes 4 servings.

Per Serving (approx):
Calories 455
Carbohydrate 35 gm

Protein 44 gm
Sodium 370 mg

Fat 15 gm
Cholesterol 160 mg

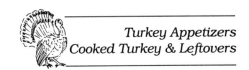

Parmesan Turkey Cubes

2 egg whites
2 tablespoons oil
1/3 cup seasoned bread crumbs
2 cloves garlic, minced
1 teaspoon dried parsley flakes

1 teaspoon dried dill, rosemary
  or basil
1 pound cooked turkey breast,
  cubed
1/4 cup grated Parmesan cheese
Pimiento-stuffed olives

Whisk egg whites and oil just to blend. Combine bread crumbs with garlic and herbs. Dip turkey in egg mixture, then coat with bread crumb mixture. Bake in preheated 450 degree oven until golden and crisp, about 8 to 10 minutes. Roll in Parmesan. Skewer with pimiento-stuffed olives.

Makes approximately 30 skewers.

Per Skewer (approx):
Calories 37
Carbohydrate 1 gm

Protein 5 gm
Sodium 35 mg

Fat 1 gm
Cholesterol 13 mg

Expenditures for Turkey Per Person	
Year	Dollar Amount
1986	14.21
1987	15.09
1988	15.04
1989	16.47
1990	17.35
1991	17.77
1992	17.40

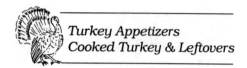

Cheese-n-Turkey Bundles

1 sheet puff pastry
Dijon-style mustard
Chopped fresh herbs
1/2 cup shredded cooked turkey
    breast

1 slice turkey ham
1 slice Swiss cheese
4 strands chives
1 egg, lightly beaten
1 1/2 teaspoons sesame seeds

Spread puff pastry sheet with mustard and sprinkle with herbs. Cut in quarters. Top each piece with 2 tablespoons shredded turkey and quarter slice of turkey ham and cheese. Bring edges of pastry together and tie each packet with chive. Brush with egg; sprinkle with sesame seeds and bake in preheated 425 degree oven until browned.

Makes 4 appetizers.

Per Appetizer (approx):
Calories 79
Carbohydrate 2 gm

Protein 9 gm
Sodium 126 mg

Fat 4 gm
Cholesterol 72 mg

Sesame Turkey Cubes

1/4 cup sesame seeds
1 cup dry bread crumbs
2 pounds smoked or oven-roasted
    turkey breast, cut in 3/4-inch cubes

5 eggs, lightly beaten
3 cups oil, for frying

Mix sesame seeds and bread crumbs together. Dip turkey in egg, then roll in bread crumb mixture. Heat oil to 375 degrees. Deep-fry turkey until golden brown, about 2 minutes. Serve with Honey Mustard.

Makes 60 appetizers.

HONEY MUSTARD:
Combine 3/4 cup Dijon-style mustard with 1/3 cup honey.

Per Appetizer (approx):
Calories 159
Carbohydrate 3 gm

Protein 5 gm
Sodium 101 mg

Fat 14 gm
Cholesterol 26 mg

Quick Turkey Appetizers

6 flour tortillas (10 inches)
4 teaspoons olive oil
1 cup salsa
1 pound deli smoked turkey, sliced
   and cut into 1/4-inch strips
1 medium tomato, chopped

2 tablespoons chopped cilantro
1 1/2 tablespoons chopped
   black olives
1/2 teaspoon crushed red
   pepper flakes
1 cup grated Monterey jack
   cheese

Place tortillas on two 12- x 14-inch baking sheets. Lightly brush both sides of tortillas with oil. Bake tortillas at 400 degrees for 3 minutes; remove from oven.

Spread salsa evenly over center of each tortilla, to within 1/2 inch of edge. Sprinkle turkey, tomato, cilantro, olives, red pepper and cheese evenly over salsa on each tortilla. Bake tortillas for 10 to 12 minutes longer or until cheese melts.

To serve, slice tortillas in eighths.   Makes 48 appetizers.

Per Appetizer (approx):
Calories 55
Carbohydrate 6 gm

Protein 4 gm
Sodium 163 mg

Fat 2 gm
Cholesterol 6 mg

Turkey Jack Appetizers

Turkey ham and turkey breast are combined in this recipe to make either appetizers or a main dish.

8 ounces turkey ham, sliced
8 ounces oven-roasted
   turkey breast, sliced
8 slices (1 ounce each)
   Monterey jack cheese
16 slices whole wheat bread

4 eggs, lightly beaten
2 tablespoons flour
3/4 cup milk
Oil, for deep-frying
1 cup sour cream
1 cup strawberry jam

Place 1 slice each turkey ham, turkey breast and cheese on 8 slices bread. Top with remaining bread; cut in quarters and secure with toothpicks. Whisk eggs, flour and milk together. Dip each minisandwich in batter. Deep-fry for 40 to 60 seconds at 375 degrees until golden brown, turning halfway through. Serve with sour cream and strawberry jam.

Makes 24 appetizers.

Per Appetizer (approx):
Calories 227
Carbohydrate 20 gm

Protein 10 gm
Sodium 268 mg

Fat 12 gm
Cholesterol 60 mg

SOUPS

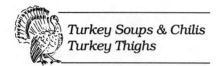

Golden Turkey Soup

Not too long ago the only way you could buy turkey for making soup was to buy a whole turkey and use the carcass. Now, you can buy turkey parts, such as thighs, wings or drumsticks, and simmer them to make a broth. Use your favorite turkey parts and yellow vegetables to make this golden turkey soup.

2 1/2 pounds turkey thighs
6 cups chicken broth
6 cups water
2 onions, sliced
4 carrots, chopped
2 pounds yams, thinly sliced
3 cloves garlic

1 cup yellow split peas
2 cups half-and-half
2 tablespoons curry powder
2 tablespoons brandy
Salt and pepper to taste
Croutons and chopped parsley,
    for garnish

Remove skin from turkey thighs. Combine broth, water, onions, carrots, yams, garlic and yellow split peas in large pot. Add turkey thighs. Bring to a boil; simmer for 1 hour. Remove turkey from pot. Cut meat from bones; discard bones and reserve meat.

Puree broth and vegetable mixture in batches in blender or food processor. Return puree to heat; add turkey meat and remaining ingredients except garnish. Simmer for 15 minutes or until heated through. Garnish with croutons and chopped parsley.   Makes 12 servings.

Per Serving (approx):
Calories 358
Carbohydrate 38 gm

Protein 27 gm
Sodium 875 mg

Fat 10 gm
Cholesterol 73 mg

Turkey Stock

There is probably no more useful item to have in your freezer than turkey soup stock. This stock becomes the base for many, many soups and stews. You may add noodles, rice, beans, potatoes, vegetables or bits and pieces of turkey. You may serve it piping hot to "cure" a cold, or chilled as a jellied aspic. The choices are endless and are limited only by your creativity.

5 pounds turkey backs, bones,
    necks, wings (but not liver)
    and/or any other turkey parts
2 large onions, coarsely chopped
3 large carrots, coarsely chopped
2 stalks celery with leaves,
    coarsely chopped

3 sprigs fresh thyme or
    1/2 teaspoon dried
5 sprigs parsley
2 bay leaves
12 black peppercorns

Put turkey pieces in stockpot or large pan with enough cold water to cover bones by an inch. Bring to a boil over medium heat. Skim off foam as it forms.

Reduce heat to medium-low, add remaining ingredients and simmer, partially covered, for 2 hours. If necessary, add more water to keep ingredients covered.

Strain through fine sieve or cheesecloth. When cool, skim off any fat from surface and store in freezer.   Makes approximately 1 quart.

Per Cup (approx):
Calories 187
Carbohydrate 38 gm

Protein 6 gm
Sodium 421 mg

Fat 0 gm
Cholesterol 0 mg

27

Amish Vegetable and Noodle Soup

1 turkey carcass with neck and
   giblets (except liver), chopped
   into large pieces (optional)
3 medium ribs celery, cut into
   1/2-inch slices
2 medium carrots, cut into
   1/4-inch rounds
1 large onion, chopped
1 can (46 ounces) chicken broth
   (about 6 cups)

1 tablespoon chopped parsley
1/2 teaspoon salt
1/2 teaspoon dried thyme
1 bay leaf
1/4 teaspoon black peppercorns
2 medium boiling potatoes,
   scrubbed and cut into 1-inch
   pieces
1/2 pound wide egg noodles
2 to 3 cups coarsely chopped
   cooked turkey

In large stockpot or Dutch oven over high heat, combine carcass pieces, celery, carrots, onion, broth and enough water to cover carcass; bring to a boil, skimming off foam. Reduce heat to low. Add parsley, salt, thyme, bay leaf and peppercorns. Simmer, partially covered, for 2 to 3 hours; if not using carcass, reduce to 30 minutes.

With tongs, remove pieces of carcass. Cut off meat and add to soup; discard bones. Increase heat to medium; add potatoes and cook for about 10 minutes or until almost tender. Add noodles; cook for about 10 minutes longer or until noodles are tender. Add turkey; cook for 2 minutes longer or until turkey is heated through.   Makes about 6 to 8 servings.

Per Serving (approx):
Calories 386
Carbohydrate 52 gm

Protein 30 gm
Sodium 801 mg

Fat 6 gm
Cholesterol 156 mg

Acorn Squash Soup

This rich, elegant soup is the perfect preface for a very special dinner, or as the main course for a luncheon.

3 cups cooked, peeled and diced
   acorn squash
2 cups turkey stock or chicken broth
1 cup whipping cream*
1/2 teaspoon ground nutmeg

2 cups cubed cooked turkey
1/4 cup dry sherry
Salt and pepper to taste
Minced parsley (optional)

Puree cooked squash in food processor or blender. Transfer squash to medium saucepan; stir in stock. Place over medium heat and cook for 5 to 10 minutes. Stir in cream and nutmeg. Reduce heat to medium-low. Add turkey and continue cooking for 5 to 6 minutes or until slightly thickened. Add sherry. Season with salt and pepper. To serve, sprinkle with parsley, if desired.   Makes 6 servings.

*Note: Half-and-half may be substituted for the heavier whipping cream.

Per Serving (approx):
Calories 258
Carbohydrate 9 gm

Protein 16 gm
Sodium 602 mg

Fat 18 gm
Cholesterol 90 mg

Turkey Corn Chowder

What's a tailgate picnic or after-game get-together without a mug of steaming hot soup? Add garlic French bread and fresh fruit to complete the menu.

1 large onion, chopped	1 1/2 teaspoons salt
3 tablespoons oil	1/2 teaspoon black pepper
1 pound ground turkey	2 teaspoons sugar
1 can (12 ounces) whole kernel corn	3 cups boiling water
1 large potato, diced	2/3 cup canned evaporated
1 can (16 ounces) tomatoes	milk

Sauté onion in oil in Dutch oven until transparent. Push to one side. Add turkey and cook, stirring, until lightly browned. Add remaining ingredients except canned milk.

Stir well. Cover and bring just to a boil; reduce heat and simmer for 30 minutes or until potatoes are tender.

Just before serving remove from heat and slowly stir in evaporated milk.
Makes 6 generous servings.

Per Serving (approx):
Calories 331
Carbohydrate 30 gm

Protein 19 gm
Sodium 695 mg

Fat 15 gm
Cholesterol 63 mg

Hearty Turkey-Vegetable Soup

Leftovers of turkey are the basis of this fall and winter standby. Double this recipe and freeze the extras.

2 cups turkey stock
1/4 cup regular pearl barley
Salt to taste
1/4 teaspoon black pepper
1 small onion, chopped
1/4 cup chopped parsley

1/2 cup chopped celery
1/2 cup sliced carrots
1/2 cup drained canned
 whole kernel corn
1 cup cubed cooked turkey

Combine stock, barley, salt, pepper, onion and parsley in 3-quart sauce-pan. Bring to a boil; reduce heat, cover and simmer for 40 minutes, stirring occasionally. Add more stock if necessary. Add celery and carrot; cook for an additional 20 minutes, stirring frequently. Add corn and turkey; bring to a boil. Boil for 2 minutes to heat through.

Makes 4 servings.

Per Serving (approx):
Calories 170
Carbohydrate 23 gm

Protein 14 gm
Sodium 878 mg

Fat 3 gm
Cholesterol 27 mg

Turkeys are fed a balanced diet of corn and soybean meal mixed with a supplement of vitamins and minerals. Fresh water is always available. It takes about 84 pounds of feed to raise a 30 pound tom turkey.

Wild Rice and Turkey Bacon Soup

1 pound turkey bacon, cooked
   to package directions and
   chopped
1 medium onion, chopped
1 medium carrot, chopped
1 medium potato, chopped
1 cup water

4 cups milk
2/3 cup wild rice, cooked and
   drained
1 can (10 3/4 ounces) cream of
   potato soup
1/2 cup shredded American
   cheese

In 3-quart saucepan over high heat, combine turkey, bacon, onion, carrot, potato and water; boil until vegetables are tender.

Reduce heat to medium-low; add milk, wild rice and potato soup. Simmer mixture for 6 minutes or until soup is heated through, stirring frequently.

Just before serving, fold in cheese. Garnish each serving with additional cheese, if desired.   **Makes 6 servings.**

Per Serving (approx):
Calories 435
Carbohydrate 40 gm

Protein 23 gm
Sodium 1026 mg

Fat 20 gm
Cholesterol 88 mg

New England Turkey Chowder

1 cup finely chopped celery
1/2 cup chopped onion
1 tablespoon margarine
2 cups turkey broth or
   reduced-sodium chicken bouillon
2 1/2 cups potatoes cut into
   1/2-inch cubes

1 teaspoon salt
1/4 teaspoon white pepper
Dash cayenne pepper
2 cups cooked turkey cut into
   1/2-inch cubes
2 cups cold skim milk
1/4 cup cornstarch

In 5-quart saucepan over medium-high heat, sauté celery and onion in margarine for 2 to 3 minutes, or until vegetables are tender-crisp.

Add broth, potatoes, salt, pepper and cayenne; bring to a boil. Reduce heat to low. Once mixture is at a simmer, cover and cook mixture for 8 to 10 minutes or until potatoes are tender. Stir in turkey.

In medium bowl gradually add milk to cornstarch. Stir mixture into soup. Increase heat to medium. Cook for 6 to 8 minutes or until mixture thickens.

Makes 4 servings.

Per Serving (approx):
Calories 316
Carbohydrate 32 gm

Protein 28 gm
Sodium 510 mg

Fat 8 gm
Cholesterol 56 mg

By the early 1800s, entire flocks were being wiped out by the hunters. By 1840, wild turkeys had become rare even in their former haven of New England.

Turkey Tortilla Soup

This hearty soup, which takes just a few minutes to prepare, has a base of leftover turkey.

1 cup chopped onion
2 teaspoons olive oil
1 can (4 ounces) chopped
  green chilies
1 package (1 1/4 ounces) taco
  seasoning mix
1 can (16 ounces) tomatoes,
  undrained
6 cups turkey broth or reduced-
  sodium chicken bouillon

1 package (10 ounces) frozen
  corn, thawed
2 cups cooked turkey cut into
  1/2-inch cubes
1/3 cup chopped cilantro
4 ounces unsalted tortilla chips,
  broken into pieces
1/2 cup shredded Monterey jack
  cheese

In 5-quart saucepan over medium heat, sauté onion in oil for 3 to 4 minutes or until translucent. Stir in chilies and taco seasoning mix; cook for 1 minute. Add tomatoes, breaking them up with spoon. Stir in turkey broth; bring to a boil. Add corn and turkey; reduce heat to low and simmer for 5 minutes. Add cilantro.

To serve, spoon 1 1/3 cups soup in each bowl. Top each serving with 1/2 ounce tortilla pieces and 1 tablespoon cheese.   Makes 8 servings.

Per Serving (approx):
Calories 244
Carbohydrate 24 gm

Protein 18 gm
Sodium 1053 mg

Fat 9 gm
Cholesterol 33 mg

Hot-n-Sour Turkey Soup

The Orient comes into your kitchen with this broth of drumsticks, Chinese vegetables and zestful seasonings.

2 turkey drumsticks
   (approximately 1 pound each)
2 1/2 quarts water
1 can (14 ounces) chicken broth
1 tablespoon coarsely chopped
   fresh ginger
1/4 cup soy sauce
2 green onions, chopped

1 ounce dry Chinese
   mushrooms,* soaked in
   1 cup water
1/2 cup sliced bamboo shoots
7 ounces tofu, diced
1/4 cup white vinegar
4 drops hot chile oil,* or to taste

In large pan over medium heat, cook turkey with 2 1/2 quarts water, broth, ginger, soy sauce and onions for 1 1/2 hours. Remove turkey meat from bones and return meat to pot.

When mushrooms have soaked for 20 minutes, slice and add to soup along with any remaining liquid. Add all remaining ingredients; cook for 20 minutes over medium-low heat.   Makes 8 servings.

*Note: Chinese mushrooms and hot chile oil may be found in Oriental section of grocery stores.

Per Serving (approx):
Calories 168
Carbohydrate 5 gm

Protein 20 gm
Sodium 866 mg

Fat 8 gm
Cholesterol 52 mg

Oriental "Flower" Soup

1 can (46 ounces) chicken broth
3 cups water
6 green onions, chopped
2 medium ribs celery, cut into
   1/2-inch slices
3 tablespoons minced fresh ginger
3 cloves garlic, crushed
2 to 3 cups coarsely chopped
   cooked turkey

16 ounces frozen Oriental vegetables, without sauce, thawed
1/2 cup sliced water chestnuts
   (optional)
2 tablespoons soy sauce,
   or to taste
3 large eggs, well beaten
Salt and pepper to taste

In large stockpot or Dutch oven, combine broth and water. Place over high heat and bring to a boil. Add onions, celery, ginger and garlic. Return to a boil. Reduce heat to low and simmer, partially covered, for 30 minutes.

Increase heat to medium and add cooked turkey, Oriental vegetables, water chestnuts and soy sauce. Bring to a boil and simmer for 2 minutes.

Stirring soup, slowly add eggs. Remove from heat immediately and let stand for 1 minute or until "egg flowers" form. Season with salt and pepper to taste.

                                                              Makes 6 to 8 servings.

Per Serving (approx):
Calories 210
Carbohydrate 17 gm

Protein 22 gm
Sodium 1327 mg

Fat 6 gm
Cholesterol 120 mg

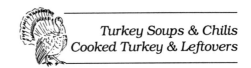

Turkey Divan Soup

Classic Turkey Divan makes an elegant entree. But if all you have are bits of leftover turkey or drumsticks, you can make this main-dish soup, duplicating the same flavors and providing the same elegance, for far less money.

1/2 cup chopped onion
1 tablespoon butter
2 1/2 cups chicken or turkey stock
   or 2 cans (10 1/2 ounces each)
   chicken broth
1 clove garlic, minced
2 cups heavy cream
1/8 teaspoon each white pepper
   and ground nutmeg

2 1/2 cups shredded Cheddar
   cheese
2 stalks broccoli, blanched and
   cut up
2 cups leftover cooked turkey
   turkey chunks*
4 ounces turkey ham, cut into
   strips

Sauté onion in butter; add stock and garlic. Stir in cream and seasonings. Heat for 10 minutes without boiling. Add cheese, broccoli, turkey and turkey ham; warm over low heat until cheese melts Serve immediately. Top with additional shredded cheese, if desired.

Makes 4 servings.

*Note: Two turkey drumsticks could be substituted for leftover turkey. Poach in simmering water until tender, about 1 hour. Remove meat from bones and cut up.

Per Serving (approx):
Calories 729
Carbohydrate 9 gm

Protein 39 gm
Sodium 1406 mg

Fat 60 gm
Cholesterol 247 mg

Moroccan Crockpot Soup

For Moroccans, a favorite meal includes the hearty, spicy soup they call Harira, served with honey cakes and dates. This crockpot version could simmer through any busy day, ready for a sunset supper.*

2 pounds turkey thighs
1 1/2 cups lentils, rinsed and
   picked over
1 cup chopped onion
1 cup chopped celery
   with leaves

2 tablespoons tomato paste
1 teaspoon ground turmeric
3/4 teaspoon ground cinnamon
7 cups chicken broth or water
2 to 3 tablespoons lemon juice
Salt and pepper to taste

Place thighs in crockpot. Add lentils, onion, celery, tomato paste, turmeric, cinnamon and chicken broth; stir. Place lid on pot and set temperature to high or low. Allow soup to cook until thighs are tender, 3 to 5 hours on high, or 7 to 9 hours on low.

Transfer thighs from soup to cutting board; remove and discard skin and bones. Cut meat into bite-sized pieces; return to soup. Season to taste with lemon juice, salt and pepper. Serve hot.   Makes 6 servings.

*Note: For a special treat, serve with oranges and cinnamon. Peel and section 6 small oranges. Add 2 teaspoons lemon juice and sprinkle with sugar and ground cinnamon to taste. Chill and serve.

Per Serving (approx):
Calories 380
Carbohydrate 33 gm

Protein 45 gm
Sodium 478 mg

Fat 8 gm
Cholesterol 93 mg

Turkey Vegetable Chowder

1 1/2 pounds boneless turkey thighs
2 medium onions, chopped
3 cups chicken broth
2 tablespoons dry sherry
  (optional)
1 bay leaf
1 teaspoon dried thyme

Salt to taste
1/4 teaspoon black pepper
3 carrots, thickly sliced
  (about 1 cup)
2 ribs celery, thickly sliced
  (about 3/4 cup)
2 potatoes, cubed (about 2 cups)

In Dutch oven combine thighs, onions, broth, sherry, bay leaf, thyme, salt and pepper. Over high heat bring to a boil. Reduce heat to low; cover and simmer for 35 minutes.

Remove turkey and cut into chunks; return to pot and add carrots, celery and potatoes. Over high heat bring to a boil. Reduce heat to low; cover and simmer for 20 to 25 minutes longer or until turkey and vegetables are tender. Makes 6 servings.

Per Serving (approx):
Calories 198
Carbohydrate 16 gm

Protein 22 gm
Sodium 849 mg

Fat 5 gm
Cholesterol 71 mg

Portuguese Sopa

The Portuguese love soup! And you will, too, with their recipe of a delightful blending of herbs and garlic, which transforms smoked turkey breast, simmered in chicken broth, into a culinary adventure.

1 onion, chopped
2 stalks celery with leaves,
   chopped
1 clove garlic, minced
2 tablespoons oil
1 pound smoked or cooked
   turkey breast, cubed
4 cups water

2 cans (14 1/2 ounces each)
   chicken broth
1 teaspoon dried summer savory
Salt and pepper to taste
2 cans (15 1/2 ounces each)
   garbanzo beans, drained
1/4 head cabbage, chopped

Sauté onion, celery and garlic in oil for 3 minutes. Add turkey, water, broth and seasonings; simmer for 30 minutes. Add garbanzo beans and cabbage; cook for 15 minutes.   Makes 8 servings.

Per Serving (approx):
Calories 360
Carbohydrate 45 gm

Protein 25 gm
Sodium 1034 mg

Fat 9 gm
Cholesterol 22 mg

Year	Whole Body	Parts & Cut-up	Total
1986	7.0	18.5	25.5
1987	7.9	25.2	33.1
1988	7.4	43.5	50.9
1989	8.9	31.7	40.6
1990	13.7	40.2	53.9
1991	16.6	86.8	103.4
1992	20.3	150.3	170.6
1993**	21.0	166.0	187.0

U.S. Turkey Exports*

*In millions of pounds
**Estimated

Harvest Soup

2 pounds turkey wings
6 cups water
2 tablespoons instant chicken
  bouillon
1 teaspoon dried poultry seasoning

Salt to taste
1/4 teaspoon black pepper
1 package (16 ounces) frozen
  vegetable blend, thawed
1/4 cup uncooked pasta

Place turkey in stockpot or Dutch oven with water, bouillon and seasonings. Bring to a boil; reduce heat, cover and simmer for 2 hours. Remove turkey and add vegetables and pasta. Bring to a boil; reduce heat, cover and simmer for 10 minutes more. Meanwhile, remove turkey skin and discard. Remove turkey from bones and cut into bite-sized pieces. Add turkey to soup before serving.   Makes 6 servings.

SLOW-COOKER METHOD:
Place turkey in slow cooker with bouillon, seasonings and 4 1/2 cups water. Cover. Cook on low setting for 10 hours. Remove turkey. Add vegetables and pasta. Cover and cook on high setting for 30 minutes. Meanwhile, remove turkey skin and discard. Remove turkey from bones and cut into bite-sized pieces. Add turkey to soup before serving.

Per Serving (approx):
Calories 296
Carbohydrate 12 gm

Protein 32 gm
Sodium 340 mg

Fat 14 gm
Cholesterol 88 mg

Rich Turkey Soup

Use economical turkey parts for this low-cost, tasty soup.

2 pounds turkey necks and backs	3 onions
1 teaspoon salt	4 stalks celery
1 bay leaf	1 1/2 cups diced or sliced carrot
1 sprig parsley	1 1/2 cups diced potato
	1 1/2 cups sliced zucchini

Place turkey necks and backs in large kettle. Add water to cover, salt, bay leaf, parsley, 2 onions (quartered) and 2 stalks celery. Bring to a boil; cover, reduce heat and simmer for 2 hours.

When cool enough to handle, strain and measure broth (there should be at least 2 quarts); discard cooked vegetables. Pick meat from turkey bones and add to strained broth. Chop remaining onion and celery stalks. Add to broth along with diced carrot and potato.

Simmer for 15 minutes. Add zucchini and continue simmering until vegetables are tender. Taste, and add a little additional salt, if needed.

Makes about 2 1/2 quarts, 6 servings.

Per Serving (approx):
Calories 403
Carbohydrate 44 gm

Protein 38 gm
Sodium 991 mg

Fat 9 gm
Cholesterol 93 mg

Santa Fe Chili

2 tablespoons oil
2 pounds ground turkey
1/2 cup chopped onion
2 cloves garlic, minced
2 tablespoons chili powder,
  or to taste
1 tablespoon paprika

2 teaspoons ground cumin
1/2 teaspoon salt
Freshly ground pepper to taste
1 can tomatoes (28 ounces),
  drained
2 cans red kidney beans
  (15 ounces each), drained

In large skillet over medium heat, warm oil. Add turkey and onion; cook, stirring, for about 4 to 5 minutes or until turkey is no longer pink.

Stir in garlic, chili powder, paprika, cumin, salt, pepper and tomatoes; cover. Increase heat to high and bring to a boil. Reduce heat and simmer for 1 to 2 hours. Add beans and cook until heated through. May be prepared a day ahead.   Makes 8 servings.

Per Serving (approx):
Calories 344
Carbohydrate 24 gm

Protein 28 gm
Sodium 641 mg

Fat 16 gm
Cholesterol 76 mg

California Turkey Chili

Californians have been using turkey in everything since the 1700s, when wild turkeys were domesticated by the Franciscan monks at the monasteries. We use canned tomatoes and kidney beans instead of fresh, for your convenience.

1 cup chopped green bell pepper
1 1/4 cups chopped onion
2 cloves garlic, minced
3 tablespoons oil
1 can (28 ounces) kidney beans, drained
1 can (28 ounces) stewed tomatoes
1 cup red wine or water
3 cups cubed cooked turkey

1 tablespoon chili powder
1 tablespoon chopped cilantro or 1 teaspoon dried coriander
1 teaspoon crushed red pepper flakes
1/2 teaspoon salt
Grated cheese, chopped onion or chopped cilantro, for garnish (optional)

Sauté bell pepper, onion and garlic in oil until soft. Add beans, tomatoes, wine, turkey and seasonings. Simmer for 25 minutes. Serve topped with grated cheese, chopped onion or cilantro, if desired.

Makes 6 servings.

Per Serving (approx):
Calories 718
Carbohydrate 93 gm

Protein 55 gm
Sodium 610 mg

Fat 11 gm
Cholesterol 53 mg

The first authenticated reference to turkey production in California is in a letter from Fray Pedro Munoz at Mission San Fernando to Fray Antonio Ripoll at Mission Santa Barbara. He wrote that he could not send any turkeys to Santa Barbara for all his hens were sitting on nests. The letter was dated May 9, 1816.

Texas Turkey Chili

2 pounds turkey thighs
2 teaspoons oil
1 cup water
2 large onions, cut into chunks
2 medium green bell peppers, cut
   into chunks
1 can (28 ounces) tomatoes,
   with liquid

2 cloves garlic, minced
2 tablespoons chili powder
2 teaspoons ground cumin
1 teaspoon salt
1/4 teaspoon cayenne pepper
1/4 cup shredded Cheddar
   cheese

Remove skin from turkey thighs. Cut the meat away from the bones using a sharp knife. Cut into 1-inch chunks. Brown in oil in stockpot or Dutch oven over medium heat.

Add remaining ingredients except cheese. Bring to a boil; reduce heat, cover and simmer for 1 hour. Remove cover and simmer for about 15 minutes more or to desired thickness. Ladle into bowls; sprinkle with cheese.   Makes 4 servings.

Per Serving (approx):
Calories 452
Carbohydrate 23 gm

Protein 51 gm
Sodium 815 mg

Fat 17 gm
Cholesterol 147 mg

Easy Turkey Chili

1 pound ground turkey
1 medium onion, chopped
1/2 medium green bell pepper,
   chopped
1/4 cup sliced celery
1 tablespoon vegetable oil
1 can (15 1/2 ounces)
   kidney beans, with liquid
1 can (14 1/2 ounces) stewed
   tomatoes

1 can (12 ounces) tomato juice
1 can (6 ounces) tomato paste
1 tablespoon Worcestershire
   sauce
1 teaspoon ground cumin or
   chili powder
1/2 teaspoon salt
1/4 teaspoon garlic powder

Place turkey and fresh vegetables in large skillet with oil. Cook over medium heat for 10 minutes, stirring and separating turkey as it cooks. Add remaining ingredients. Bring to a boil; reduce heat and simmer for at least 30 minutes, stirring occasionally.   Makes 6 servings.

Per Serving (approx):
Calories 460
Carbohydrate 61 gm

Protein 35 gm
Sodium 673 mg

Fat 9 gm
Cholesterol 55 mg

Crockpot Chili

Chili fans, like chili, run from mild to volcanic. This is a medium-to-hot dish meant to be prepared early and left to perk as a warm welcome at the end of the day.

1 to 1 1/2 pounds turkey thigh cutlets
1 can (16 ounces) pinto, red kidney or black beans, drained
1 can (14 ounces) Italian plum tomatoes, undrained*
1/2 cup chopped onion
1/2 cup chopped green bell pepper

3 tablespoons chili powder
1 tablespoon ground cumin
2 cloves garlic, minced
1/2 to 1 teaspoon hot pepper sauce (optional)
Salt and pepper to taste
Sour cream (optional)
Chopped green onion (optional)

Trim turkey cutlets and cut into 1-inch pieces. Add turkey, beans, undrained tomatoes, onion, bell pepper, chili, cumin, garlic and hot pepper sauce to crockpot; stir to combine. Cover crockpot and set temperature control to high or low. Allow chili to cook until meat is tender, 3 to 5 hours on high, or 7 to 9 hours on low. Season with salt and pepper to taste.

Serve chili topped with dollop of sour cream and chopped green onion, if desired. Makes 4 to 6 servings.

*Note: For thicker chili, use only half the juice from the tomatoes.

Per Serving (approx):
Calories 244
Carbohydrate 18 gm

Protein 28 gm
Sodium 483 mg

Fat 7 gm
Cholesterol 70 mg

Black Bean Chili

1/4 cup oil
3/4 cup chopped onion
2 cloves garlic, minced
4 to 6 tablespoons chili powder,
   or to taste
1 tablespoon dried oregano
2 teaspoons ground cumin
1 teaspoon salt
3 cups chopped cooked turkey

1 can (28 ounces) crushed
   tomatoes
1/2 to 1 cup water
2 cans (16 ounces each) black
   beans, drained
Shredded Monterey jack cheese,
   chopped onion and sour cream
   (optional)

In large skillet or Dutch oven over medium heat, warm oil. Add onion, garlic, chili powder, oregano, cumin and salt. Sauté for 5 minutes or until onion is tender. Stir in turkey, tomatoes and 1/2 cup water. Simmer, uncovered, for 15 minutes, adding water if needed.

Stir in beans; cook for 15 minutes longer or until slightly thickened. Serve chili topped with shredded Monterey jack cheese, chopped onion and sour cream, if desired.

Makes 6 servings.

Per Serving (approx):
Calories 462
Carbohydrate 48 gm

Protein 36 gm
Sodium 1150 mg

Fat 14 gm
Cholesterol 53 mg

White Turkey Chili

The name of this recipe comes from the white cannellini beans, which are used instead of the customary red kidney beans.

1 1/2 cups coarsely chopped onion
2 cloves garlic, minced
1 tablespoon olive oil
1 jalapeño pepper, minced
1 can (4 ounces) chopped mild
    green chilies
1 teaspoon ground cumin
1/2 teaspoon dried oregano
1/4 teaspoon cayenne pepper
1/4 teaspoon salt

1 cup reduced-sodium chicken
    bouillon
1 can (19 ounces) white kidney
    beans (cannellini), drained
    and rinsed
2 cups cooked turkey cut into
    1/2-inch cubes
1/4 cup coarsely chopped
    cilantro
1/2 cup reduced-fat Monterey
    jack cheese

In 3-quart saucepan over medium-high heat, sauté onion and garlic in oil for 5 minutes or until onion is tender. Add jalapeño pepper, chilies, cumin, oregano, cayenne pepper and salt. Cook for 1 minute.

Stir in bouillon, beans and turkey. Bring to a boil; reduce heat and simmer, uncovered, for 20 to 25 minutes or until slightly thickened. Stir in cilantro.

To serve, ladle into bowls and top each with 2 tablespoons cheese.

Makes 4 servings.

Per Serving (approx):
Calories 323
Carbohydrate 23 gm

Protein 34 gm
Sodium 798 mg

Fat 10 gm
Cholesterol 65 mg

Vintner's Turkey Chili

The red wine is essential to the success of this chili—and a glass or two with it is nice, too!

1 cup chopped green bell pepper
1 1/4 cups chopped onion
2 cloves garlic, minced
3 tablespoons oil
2 cans (15 1/2 ounces each) kidney beans, drained
1 can (28 ounces) stewed tomatoes, crushed
1 cup red wine

3 cups cooked turkey cut into 1/2-inch cubes
1 tablespoon chili powder
1 tablespoon cilantro or 1 teaspoon dried
1 teaspoon crushed red pepper flakes
1/2 teaspoon salt

In 3-quart saucepan over medium-high heat, sauté bell pepper, onion and garlic in oil for 5 minutes or until vegetables are tender-crisp.

Add beans, tomatoes, wine, turkey, chili powder, cilantro, red pepper and salt. Increase heat to high and bring mixture to a boil; reduce heat to low and simmer mixture, uncovered, for 25 minutes.

To serve, garnish with additional chopped onion or cilantro, if desired.

Makes 6 servings.

Per Serving (approx):
Calories 356
Carbohydrate 35 gm

Protein 30 gm
Sodium 1094 mg

Fat 11 gm
Cholesterol 54 mg

SALADS

Curried Turkey Pasta Salad

A colorful presentation and well worth the effort.

1 pound turkey breast cutlets
   or tenderloins, cut into
   1/2- by 2-inch strips
2 teaspoons peanut oil
1/4 teaspoon garlic powder
1/4 teaspoon curry powder
1/8 teaspoon ground ginger
Nonstick vegetable cooking spray
2 ounces fresh snow peas,
   blanched

1/2 cup sliced mushrooms
8 cherry tomatoes, halved
1/4 cup red bell pepper cut
   into 1/4- by 2-inch strips
1/4 cup green bell pepper
   cut into 1/4- by 2-inch strips
2 cups rotini pasta, cooked
   to package directions and
   drained

In medium bowl combine turkey, oil, garlic powder, curry powder and ginger. Cover and refrigerate for 30 minutes. Coat large nonstick skillet with vegetable cooking spray. Over medium-high heat, sauté turkey mixture for 4 to 5 minutes or until turkey is no longer pink in center.

Prepare Chutney Salad Dressing. In large bowl combine cooked turkey mixture, snow peas, mushrooms, tomatoes, bell peppers, pasta and Chutney Dressing. Cover and refrigerate for 20 minutes to allow flavors to blend.
                                     Makes 6 servings.

CHUTNEY SALAD DRESSING:
In blender combine 1/3 cup peanut oil, 1/3 cup mango chutney, 2 tablespoons fresh lemon juice, 1 1/2 teaspoons curry powder, 1/2 teaspoon salt and 1/2 teaspoon hot pepper sauce. Blend until mixture is smooth.

Per Serving (approx):
Calories 387
Carbohydrate 37 gm
           Protein 23 gm
           Sodium 242 mg
                 Fat 16 gm
                 Cholesterol 42 mg

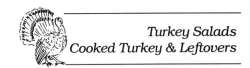

Mandarin Salad

1/3 cup mayonnaise
1 tablespoon Dijon mustard
1/2 teaspoon ground ginger
1/2 teaspoon sesame seeds
1 can (11 ounces) mandarin
   orange segments, drained
   (liquid reserved)
2 cups chopped cooked turkey

1 cup diagonally sliced celery
1/4 cup thinly sliced green
   onion
1/2 cup coarsely chopped
   pecans
Spinach or lettuce leaves
Toasted coconut, for garnish

In small bowl stir together mayonnaise, mustard, ginger, sesame seeds and 1/4 cup reserved mandarin orange liquid.

In large bowl mix turkey, celery, green onion and chopped pecans. Pour mayonnaise mixture over turkey mixture; stir to combine. Add mandarin orange segments, tossing well. Refrigerate until well chilled. Serve on bed of greens and top with coconut.   Makes 4 servings.

Per Serving (approx):
Calories 428
Carbohydrate 18 gm

Protein 24 gm
Sodium 328 mg

Fat 29 gm
Cholesterol 60 mg

Many precocial birds, such as the turkey, experience a short period of rapid learning just after hatching. This is called the imprinting sensitive period. During this short time the animal forms a long-lasting memory or template of its immediate environment. It earns the characteristics of its mother and hence its species. This information directs the animal's behavior in later life. It may choose to mate with an animal that resembles this "mother" even if the "mother" has been a human keeper. Also, the mature bird may later prefer the kind of environment he was exposed to during this early imprinting period.

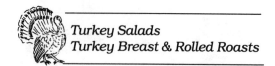
Salad Niçoise #1

3 to 4 pounds boneless turkey
   breast
7 tablespoons extravirgin olive
   oil
2 tablespoons dried *herbs de*
   Provence*
1 tablespoon lemon juice
1 tablespoon balsamic vinegar
1 tablespoon red wine vinegar
1 teaspoon Dijon mustard
1 clove garlic, minced

1 teaspoon anchovy paste
   (optional)
Salt and pepper to taste
Romaine lettuce leaves
10 red new potatoes, boiled
   until tender, cooled and sliced
6 tomatoes, cut into wedges
1 1/4 pounds fresh green beans,
   cooked until tender-crisp
1 cup Niçoise olives

Prepare outdoor grill for cooking or preheat broiler. Pat turkey dry and rub with 1 tablespoon of the olive oil and the *herbs de Provence*. Grill or broil turkey 6 to 8 inches from heat source for about 20 minutes per pound or until cooked through, turning occasionally.

Meanwhile, in small bowl combine lemon juice, vinegars, mustard, garlic, anchovy paste, salt and pepper to make dressing. Slowly whisk in remaining 6 tablespoons oil.

To assemble salad, line large platter with lettuce. Slice grilled turkey and arrange on lettuce. Surround turkey with sliced potatoes, tomatoes, green beans and olives. Drizzle with dressing and serve.

Makes 12 servings.

*Note: Herbs de Provence are the herbs typical of southern France: thyme, summer savory, basil and rosemary. Commercial blends are available.

Per Serving (approx):
Calories 418
Carbohydrate 32 gm

Protein 44 gm
Sodium 244 mg

Fat 12 gm
Cholesterol 106 mg

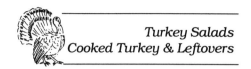

Salad Niçoise #2

This version of salad Niçoise has no garlic.

1/4 cup olive oil
3 tablespoons wine vinegar
1 to 2 cloves garlic, minced
2 tablespoons minced fresh
  basil
2 teaspoons Dijon mustard
1/2 teaspoon salt
1/4 teaspoon black pepper
2 cups diced cooked turkey

3 cups cooked, peeled and diced
  potato
2 cups green beans, cooked
  tender-crisp
1/3 cup sliced red onion
1/2 cup pitted Niçoise or
  oil-cured olives
2 tomatoes, quartered
Lettuce leaves (optional)

In small bowl combine oil, vinegar, garlic, basil, mustard, salt and pepper to make dressing; mix well and set aside. In salad bowl combine turkey, potato, beans, onion and olives; toss gently. Garnish with tomatoes, drizzle with dressing and serve on bed of lettuce, if desired.

Makes 4 to 6 servings.

Per Serving (approx):
Calories 318
Carbohydrate 26 gm

Protein 17 gm
Sodium 696 mg

Fat 16 gm
Cholesterol 35 mg

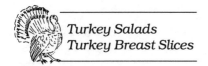

Nouvelle Salade

This should be served really hot so the dressing, turkey and greens are properly blended.

1 pound turkey breast slices	2 tablespoons chopped green
8 cups mixed greens	onion
2 medium tomatoes, cut into	1 medium green bell pepper, cut
wedges	into thin strips
1 tablespoon oil	

Cut turkey slices into thin strips; set aside. Arrange 2 cups greens and the tomatoes on each of 4 dinner plates. Warm oil in skillet over medium-high heat. Add turkey strips, onion and bell pepper. Stir-fry for about 8 minutes. Place hot turkey mixture over greens.

Combine dressing ingredients; add to skillet. Heat for about 1 minute or until boiling. Drizzle over salads.

Makes 4 servings.

DIJON SALAD DRESSING:
Combine 1/3 cup oil, 1/3 cup red wine vinegar, 1/3 cup water, 2 tablespoons Dijon mustard, 1 tablespoon sugar, 1/4 teaspoon garlic powder and 1/4 teaspoon black pepper.

Per Serving (approx):
Calories 426	*Protein 27 gm*	*Fat 29 gm*
Carbohydrate 11 gm	*Sodium 256 mg*	*Cholesterol 61 mg*

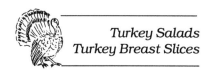

Minted Turkey Salad

The cuisine of Southeast Asia lends mint to turkey in this delightful salad. It is worthy of being served to your most discriminating guest or family member for lunch or as a light supper entree!

1 pound turkey breast slices
1/3 cup lemon juice
1/4 cup soy sauce
1/4 cup oil
1/4 teaspoon garlic powder
Salt and pepper to taste
1 can (15 1/2 ounces) garbanzo
    beans, drained

1 can (14 ounces) artichoke
    hearts, drained and
    quartered
3 green onions, chopped
1 red bell pepper, chopped
1 head butter lettuce

Marinate turkey slices in mixture of lemon juice, soy sauce, oil, garlic powder, salt and pepper for about 1 hour. In shallow pan bake marinated turkey for 15 minutes at 350 degrees, turning halfway through. Let cool. Meanwhile, prepare Minted Mayonnaise.

Slice turkey into strips; combine with garbanzo beans, artichoke hearts, onion, bell pepper and Minted Mayonnaise. Serve on bed of lettuce.

Makes 6 to 8 servings.

MINTED MAYONNAISE:
In blender, mix 3 egg yolks with 1/4 cup lemon juice. With blender running, slowly drizzle in 1 cup olive oil or vegetable oil. Stir in 2 tablespoons chopped fresh mint and salt to taste.

Per Serving (approx):
Calories 709
Carbohydrate 30 gm

Protein 33 gm
Sodium 1074 mg

Fat 50 gm
Cholesterol 165 mg

Turkey Taco Salad

1 pound ground turkey
1 package (1 1/4 ounces)
  taco seasoning mix
3/4 cup water
1 small head lettuce, torn into
  bite-sized pieces
1 cup corn chips

1 cup (4 ounces) shredded
  Cheddar cheese
1 tomato, chopped
1/4 cup sour cream
Sliced ripe olives, chopped
  onion, chopped avocado and
  taco sauce (optional)

Cook turkey in skillet over medium heat for 8 to 10 minutes or until no longer pink, stirring and separating turkey as it cooks. Stir in seasoning mix and water. Bring to a boil; reduce heat and simmer for 10 minutes, stirring occasionally.

Place lettuce on 4 plates. Top each with corn chips, cheese, turkey mixture, tomato, sour cream and other toppings as desired.

Makes 4 servings.

Per Serving (approx):
Calories 525
Carbohydrate 16 gm

Protein 30 gm
Sodium 973 mg

Fat 26 gm
Cholesterol 118 mg

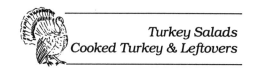

Pasta Primavera Salad

This makes a spectacular dish, especially for a buffet. The green, white and red of the ingredients are particularly cheery on a dark fall or winter evening.

4 cloves garlic, minced
1 medium zucchini, cut in thin
   2-inch sticks
2 cups snow peas, stringed
   and stemmed
1/2 cup chopped red onion
4 green onions, chopped
Approximately 1/2 cup plus 2
   tablespoons olive oil
1 pound pasta (shell, macaroni
   or corkscrew), cooked and well
   drained

1/4 cup chopped sun-dried
   tomatoes
1 cup chopped parsley
1/2 cup chopped fresh basil or
   2 tablespoons dried
1 package (10 ounces) frozen
   petite peas, thawed
2 cups cubed roasted turkey
   breast
Salt and pepper to taste

Sauté garlic, zucchini, snow peas, red onion and green onions in the 2 tablespoons olive oil until tender-crisp. In large bowl, toss pasta with sautéed vegetables, tomatoes, parsley, basil, petite peas, the 1/2 cup olive oil, turkey, salt and pepper. Add more olive oil if needed. Serve at room temperature. Makes 8 to 10 servings.

Note: If you like a bit of tartness or a sharper flavor in this salad, try adding balsamic or red wine vinegar, a bit at a time, to this salad.

Per Serving (approx):
Calories 320
Carbohydrate 34 gm
   Protein 14 gm
   Sodium 107 mg
   Fat 14 gm
   Cholesterol 48 mg

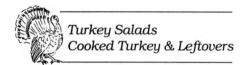

Gingery Stir-Fry Salad

1/3 cup chicken broth or water
1 tablespoon dry sherry
1 teaspoon cornstarch
3 tablespoons oil
1 1/2 tablespoons minced
  fresh ginger
2 green onions, finely chopped
1 clove garlic, minced

1 cup broccoli florets
1 carrot, sliced diagonally
  1/4 inch thick
1 medium zucchini, halved
  lengthwise and sliced
  diagonally 1/2 inch thick
2 cups cooked turkey cut into
  thick strips
Chinese cabbage leaves

In small bowl combine broth and sherry. Add cornstarch; stir to dissolve and set aside.

In large skillet or wok over high heat, warm oil. Add ginger, onion and garlic; stir-fry until fragrant, about 30 seconds. Add broccoli and carrot; stir-fry for 1 minute. Add zucchini; stir-fry for 1 minute longer. Add turkey strips; stir-fry for 1 minute.

Stir broth mixture to blend. Add to skillet and stir for about 30 seconds until vegetables are coated with sauce. Serve warm on cabbage leaves.

Makes 4 servings.

Per Serving (approx):
Calories 348
Carbohydrate 20 gm

Protein 32 gm
Sodium 511 mg

Fat 15 gm
Cholesterol 53 mg

New Potato and Turkey Ham Salad

This is a terrific salad for a potluck because it holds up well. Keep it chilled until ready to serve.

1/4 cup herbed wine vinegar
3 tablespoons salad oil
1/2 teaspoon each salt and
 dried basil
1/8 teaspoon black pepper
2 pounds small red potatoes,
 cooked and cubed
1 1/4 cups diced celery

1 cup chopped red or green
 bell pepper
1/4 cup chopped green onion
3 hard-cooked eggs, chopped
1/4 cup each mayonnaise and
 sour cream
2 cups cubed turkey ham

Whisk together vinegar, oil, salt, basil and black pepper. Add potatoes, celery, bell pepper and green onion; let marinate for 1 hour. Combine eggs, mayonnaise and sour cream; add to potato mixture and fold in gently. Fold in turkey ham. Serve immediately or refrigerate for up to a day. Serve on lettuce-lined platter.   Makes 6 to 8 servings.

Per Serving (approx):
Calories 420
Carbohydrate 40 gm

Protein 16 gm
Sodium 784 mg

Fat 22 gm
Cholesterol 139 mg

Only one of every six turkeys is sold whole, for roasting. The other five are sold as parts, or processed into turkey products such as ham, sausages, frankfurters, salami, etc.

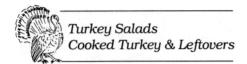

Colorful Turkey Pasta Salad

This is one of those dishes that you can prepare a day or two in advance, refrigerate, and have ready as soon as you get home from work or play. Looks great, too, for a buffet.

2 cups cubed oven-roasted turkey
    breast
2 1/2 cups tricolored rotini
    pasta, cooked and drained
1/2 cup thinly sliced onion
1/4 cup thinly sliced celery
1/4 cup chopped parsley

1 tablespoon oil
1 1/2 teaspoons chopped fresh
    tarragon or 1/2 teaspoon dried
2 tablespoons tarragon vinegar
1 tablespoon lemon juice
2 tablespoons reduced-calorie
    mayonnaise

In large bowl combine turkey, pasta, onion, celery, parsley, oil, tarragon, vinegar, lemon juice and mayonnaise. Mix thoroughly; cover and refrigerate for 1 to 2 hours or overnight.

Makes 4 servings.

Per Serving (approx):
Calories 458
Carbohydrate 60 gm

Protein 30 gm
Sodium 119 mg

Fat 10 gm
Cholesterol 56 mg

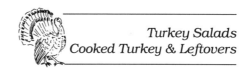

Waldorf Turkey Salad

The Waldorf part of the name comes from a salad that originated at the Waldorf Hotel in New York City many years ago. The salad became a regular item on the menu of hundreds of diners and restaurants in small towns across America in the 1940s and '50s. It's an easy way to feed a lot of people because you can make it ahead. The turkey mixture will keep up to four days in the refrigerator.

6 ounces cubed cooked turkey
   breast
1/2 cup diced celery
1 small Red Delicious apple,
   cut into small cubes
2 tablespoons chopped walnuts

1 tablespoon reduced-calorie
   mayonnaise
1 tablespoon nonfat yogurt
1/8 teaspoon ground nutmeg
1/8 teaspoon ground cinnamon
4 lettuce leaves

In medium bowl combine turkey, celery, apple, walnuts, mayonnaise, yogurt, nutmeg and cinnamon. Cover and refrigerate for at least 1 hour or overnight to allow flavors to blend.

To serve, arrange lettuce leaves on 4 plates. Spoon 3/4 cup turkey mixture over each lettuce leaf. This makes a good sandwich on raisin bread.

Makes 4 servings.

Per Serving (approx):
Calories 130
Carbohydrate 10 gm

Protein 14 gm
Sodium 59 mg

Fat 4 gm
Cholesterol 36 mg

Smoked Turkey and Fresh Vegetable Salad

If salt is a problem in your diet, use oven-roasted turkey instead of smoked turkey.

1/2 pound smoked turkey breast, cut into 1/2-inch cubes	1/3 cup reduced-calorie mayonnaise
1 cup broccoli florets	1 teaspoon Dijon-style mustard
1/2 cup thinly sliced yellow squash	1 teaspoon lemon juice
1/2 cup coarsely grated carrot	1/2 teaspoon dried dill weed
1/4 cup thinly sliced red bell pepper	1/4 teaspoon dried parsley flakes
1/4 cup thinly sliced green onion	1/8 teaspoon garlic powder

In medium bowl combine turkey, broccoli, squash, carrot, bell pepper and onion. In small bowl combine mayonnaise, mustard, lemon juice, dill, parsley and garlic powder. Fold mayonnaise mixture into turkey and vegetables. Cover and chill for at least 1 hour.

Makes 2 servings.

Per Serving (approx):
Calories 269
Carbohydrate 13 gm

Protein 27 gm
Sodium 1378 mg

Fat 13 gm
Cholesterol 48 mg

White Bean and Smoked Turkey Salad

Substitute canned white beans, rinsed and drained, for dried beans if you prefer. You could also make this salad with garbanzo beans.

1 pound dried white beans
1 pound smoked turkey breast, cubed
1 cup thinly sliced red onion

1 cup chopped Italian parsley
Salt and pepper to taste
1 1/2 cups chopped tomato
1 cup imported black olives

Soak beans overnight in cold water to cover; drain. Place beans in saucepan and add cold water to cover. Bring to a boil. Cook until tender, about 45 minutes, skimming any scum that forms on surface. Meanwhile, prepare Mustard Garlic Dressing. Drain beans and combine with 1 cup dressing.

To bean mixture add turkey, onion, parsley, salt and pepper. Refrigerate, covered, for at least 2 hours. To serve, bring to room temperature; toss with chopped tomato and with more dressing if necessary. Garnish with olives.   Makes 8 servings.

MUSTARD GARLIC DRESSING:
Combine 1 egg yolk, 1/4 cup Dijon-style mustard and 1/2 cup red wine vinegar in food processor or blender. Process for 1 minute. While motor is running, add 4 cloves garlic and then 1 1/2 cups olive oil in slow, steady stream. Season to taste with salt and pepper. Refrigerate until ready to use.

Per Serving (approx):
Calories 584
Carbohydrate 21 gm

Protein 18 gm
Sodium 1106 mg

Fat 46 gm
Cholesterol 50 mg

Tuscany Bean Salad

1 pound turkey ham, diced
1 pound white beans, cooked and
   cooled
3 cups diced tomato
1 cup chopped parsley
1/3 cup chopped fresh mint

6 green onions, chopped
1 teaspoon salt
1/2 teaspoon black pepper
1/2 teaspoon dry mustard
1/3 cup Champagne vinegar
2/3 cup olive oil

In large bowl combine turkey ham, beans, tomato, parsley, mint and onions. In small bowl mix together salt, pepper, mustard and vinegar for dressing. Whisk in oil. Pour dressing over salad; mix well. Refrigerate for 30 minutes before serving.   Makes 12 servings.

Per Serving (approx):
Calories 229
Carbohydrate 13 gm

Protein 11 gm
Sodium 674 mg

Fat 14 gm
Cholesterol 21 mg

Chutney Turkey Salad

1 1/2 pounds smoked or
   oven-roasted turkey, cubed
2 cups seedless red or green
   grapes
1 1/2 cups chopped celery
1 cup slivered almonds,
   lightly toasted

1/2 cup sour cream
1/2 cup mayonnaise
1/2 cup mango chutney,
   chopped
1/2 teaspoon curry powder,
   or to taste)
Salt and pepper to taste

In large bowl combine turkey, grapes, celery and almonds. In medium bowl whisk together sour cream and mayonnaise; stir in chutney, curry powder, salt and pepper; toss gently with turkey mixture.
                          Makes 6 to 8 servings.

Per Serving (approx):
Calories 539
Carbohydrate 26 gm

Protein 28 gm
Sodium 1344 mg

Fat 36 gm
Cholesterol 63 mg

Pizzeria Salad

1 package (10 ounces)
   tagliarini pasta
2 cups cubed turkey ham or
   turkey pastrami
1 cup chopped tomato

1 cup sliced mushrooms
1 cup cubed mozzarella cheese
1/2 cup sliced ripe olives
1/4 cup sliced green onion

Prepare Italian Dressing. Cook tagliarini according to package directions; drain and transfer to a bowl. Pour Italian Dressing over pasta while still warm. Add remaining ingredients; toss gently. Serve immediately or chill.

Makes 6 to 8 servings.

ITALIAN DRESSING:
Whisk together 1/2 cup red wine vinegar, 1/2 cup oil, 1 clove garlic, minced, 1 teaspoon sugar, 1 teaspoon Dijon-style mustard, 1/2 teaspoon dried Italian seasoning, 1/2 teaspoon seasoned salt and 1/4 teaspoon black pepper.

Per Serving (approx):
Calories 371
Carbohydrate 30 gm

Protein 15 gm
Sodium 769 mg

Fat 20 gm
Cholesterol 31 mg

Arizona Turkey Salad

Smoked turkey is the key to this easy-to-make salad because the turkey is precooked and ready to use. The dressing is something special.

1 pound smoked turkey breast,
    cut in 1/2-inch strips
1 head red leaf lettuce, torn
    into bite-sized pieces

1/2 bunch watercress
1 cup halved red seedless grapes
1/2 cup walnuts, toasted

Toss all ingredients together. Serve with Creamy Cheese Dressing.

Makes 6 servings.

CREAMY CHEESE DRESSING:
In blender whirl together 1 egg yolk, 2 ounces Roquefort or blue cheese, 2 tablespoons Champagne vinegar and 1 teaspoon Dijon-style mustard. Slowly add 1/3 cup oil while blender is running. Stir in 1/4 cup cream and salt and pepper to taste.

Per Serving (approx):
Calories 349
Carbohydrate 6 gm

Protein 19 gm
Sodium 978 mg

Fat 27 gm
Cholesterol 82 mg

The wild turkey roamed from the Atlantic coast to as far west as Arizona, from the Great Lakes down south into Central America.

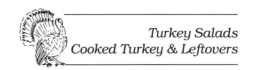

Curried Turkey Salad Amandine

Those Thanksgiving turkey leftovers earn a place for themselves in this crisp and crunchy salad, with a dressing lightly sparked by curry.

2 to 3 cups cooked turkey pieces

2 cups sliced celery

1/3 cup sliced green onion

1/2 cup blanched almonds, toasted

Lettuce

Toasted coconut chips

Raisins

Toss turkey, celery, onion and almonds together. Add Curry Mayonnaise and mix well. Serve on crisp lettuce. Top with coconut chips and raisins.

Makes 4 servings.

CURRY MAYONNAISE:

Combine 1/2 cup mayonnaise, 1 teaspoon lemon juice, 1/2 teaspoon curry powder and 1/2 teaspoon salt; mix well.

Per Serving (approx):

Calories 482

Carbohydrate 8 gm

Protein 30 gm

Sodium 572 mg

Fat 37 gm

Cholesterol 77 mg

Getting Enough z z Z's

Many people report drowsiness after eating Thanksgiving dinner. Recent studies suggest that the composition of a meal (particularly the ratio of carbohydrate to protein) influences the production of brain neurotransmitters which are involved in sleep, mood and depression.

Neurotransmitters in the brain are produced by the amino acid, tryptophan. A carbohydrate-rich–not a protein-rich–meal increased the level of tryptophan in the brain.

Since many people eat an unusually large, many-coursed, carbohydrate-rich meal at Thanksgiving, they often associate the drowsiness they feel with the turkey. To be more accurate, they should associate their sleepy feelings to the increased amount of carbohydrates consumed.

Fruitful Turkey Salad

3 tablespoons oil
1 pound turkey breast slices,
   cut into 1-inch strips
1/2 cup mayonnaise
1/4 cup sour cream
2 tablespoons honey
1 tablespoon lime juice

1 teaspoon chopped fresh dill,
   plus more for garnish
1 cup seedless grapes, halved
1 red Delicious apple, chopped
1/2 cup chopped pecans
Lettuce leaves

Warm oil in medium skillet over medium heat. Add turkey and cook for 5 to 7 minutes or until turkey is no longer pink; stir occasionally. Drain and chill.

In large bowl combine mayonnaise, sour cream, honey, lime juice and dill. Add turkey, grapes, apple and pecans; toss. Serve turkey mixture over lettuce leaves. Garnish with dill.   Makes 4 servings.

Per Serving (approx):
| *Calories 671* | *Protein 26 gm* | *Fat 52 gm* |
| *Carbohydrate 24 gm* | *Sodium 219 mg* | *Cholesterol 77 mg* |

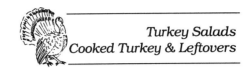

Szechuan Turkey Salad

A spicy peanut dressing makes this cabbage salad special.

4 ounces snow peas, stringed
  and stemmed
4 ounces bean sprouts
1 pound oven-roasted turkey
  breast

1 red bell pepper, cut in long
  thin strips
1 1/2 cups shredded Chinese
  cabbage
1/2 cup sliced cucumber

Blanch snow peas and bean sprouts in boiling salted water for about 30 seconds. Drain in sieve under cold running water; drain again and pat dry. Combine all salad ingredients; toss with Szechuan Dressing.

                                        Makes 6 servings.

SZECHUAN DRESSING:
Whisk together 1/3 cup oil, 1/4 cup white vinegar, 1/4 cup soy sauce, 3 tablespoons peanut butter and 2 teaspoons red pepper flakes.

Per Serving (approx):
Calories 300
Carbohydrate 8 gm

Protein 21 gm
Sodium 734 mg

Fat 21 gm
Cholesterol 41 mg

Hollywood Turkey Salad

Belgian endive or spinach could take the place of some of the leaf lettuce.

1 pound smoked turkey breast,
   cut in 1/2-inch strips
1/2 head red leaf lettuce
1/2 head green leaf lettuce
1/2 bunch watercress

1 cup each red and green
   seedless grapes
2/3 cup slivered almonds
   or chopped walnuts, toasted

Toss all ingredients together. Serve with Blue Cheese Dressing.

Makes 6 servings.

BLUE CHEESE DRESSING:
In blender puree 1 ounce blue cheese, 2 tablespoons white white wine vinegar and 1 teaspoon Dijon-style mustard. With motor running, slowly add 1/3 cup salad oil. Transfer to bowl; whisk in 1/4 cup heavy cream and salt and pepper to taste.

Per Serving (approx):
Calories 375
Carbohydrate 10 gm

Protein 20 gm
Sodium 912 mg

Fat 29 gm
Cholesterol 50 mg

Affluent, traditional families are the most likely to consume turkey at least once in a two-week period. Double-income families with no children, affluent empty-nesters and working parents also head the list of those who have made turkey a regular part of their lifestyles.

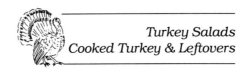

Chinese Turkey Salad

4 cups shredded cooked
  turkey
1 head lettuce, shredded
4 green onions, thinly sliced
1 bunch cilantro, chopped
  (reserve a few leaves for garnish)
1/4 cup sesame seeds, toasted
1 cup chopped peanuts,
  cashews or slivered almonds

2 cups seedless red or green
  grapes, halved or whole
3 cups bean threads or rice
  sticks, fried in salad or
  sesame oil* (cooked white
  rice may be used)
1 carrot, thinly sliced diagonally
Additional whole nuts (optional)
Small clusters of grapes

Mix together turkey, lettuce, onions, cilantro, seeds, nuts and grapes. Pour Lemon Dressing over top and toss to coat. Place a nest of bean threads on each plate. Spoon turkey mixture over top.

Garnish with reserved cilantro, a few carrot slices, additional nuts, if desired, and small clusters of grapes.   Makes 4 to 6 servings.

LEMON DRESSING:
Blend together 1/2 teaspoon dry mustard, 1 teaspoon sugar, 3 tablespoons lemon juice, 1 clove garlic, minced, 1 teaspoon soy sauce and 1/4 cup sesame oil or salad oil.

*Note: Deep-fry bean threads or rice sticks, a bunch at a time, until light and puffy. Do not burn. Drain on paper towels.

Per Serving (approx):
Calories 691
Carbohydrate 20 gm

Protein 54 gm
Sodium 353 mg

Fat 44 gm
Cholesterol 106 mg

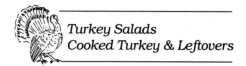
Rice Salad with Pesto Dressing

If you like pesto with pasta, you'll love pesto with rice.

3 tablespoons chopped fresh
    basil or 1 tablespoon dried
1/4 cup grated Parmesan cheese
3 tablespoons lemon juice
1/2 cup olive oil
1 pound turkey breast, cooked
    and shredded

3 cups cooked long-grain rice
1 cup cooked wild rice
1 green bell pepper, chopped
1 red bell pepper, chopped
1/2 cup chopped red onion
3/4 cup sliced ripe olives
Salt and pepper to taste

In blender combine basil, Parmesan and lemon juice. With motor running, slowly add olive oil to make a creamy dressing. Combine remaining ingredients in bowl. Add dressing and toss gently with fork to blend.

Makes 6 to 8 servings.

Per Serving (approx):
Calories 561
Carbohydrate 85 gm

Protein 6 gm
Sodium 316 mg

Fat 22 gm
Cholesterol 3 mg

Kansas City Salad

3 cups diced cooked turkey
1/2 cup bottled French dressing
2 tablespoons mayonnaise
1 tablespoon lemon juice
1/4 cup thinly sliced green onion

4 to 6 Bibb or iceberg lettuce
    cups
4 to 6 slices bacon, cooked crisp
    and crumbled

In medium bowl combine turkey and dressing. Cover and let marinate in refrigerator for 1 to 2 hours. Drain excess marinade; fold in mayonnaise, lemon juice and onion. To serve, spoon salad into lettuce cups; top with bacon.

Makes 4 to 6 servings.

Per Serving (approx):
Calories 292
Carbohydrate 5 gm

Protein 23 gm
Sodium 564 mg

Fat 20 gm
Cholesterol 74 mg

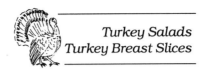

Turkey Spinach Salad

1 pound turkey breast slices,
   cut into 1-inch strips
3 tablespoons oil
2 bunches spinach, torn and chilled

1 cup sliced mushrooms
  (optional)
1/2 cup chopped walnuts
1 tomato, chopped

Prepare Apple-Soy Marinade; marinate turkey for at least 15 minutes. Cook turkey in medium skillet in hot oil for 5 to 7 minutes or until no longer pink, stirring occasionally. Drain and set aside.

Prepare Sweet & Sour Dressing. Mix remaining ingredients with cooked turkey and toss with dressing. Serve immediately.

Makes 6 to 8 servings.

APPLE-SOY MARINADE:
Combine 1/4 cup soy sauce, 1/4 cup apple juice, 2 sliced green onions and 1 clove garlic, minced.

SWEET & SOUR DRESSING:
Combine 1/3 cup oil, 1/4 cup cider vinegar, 2 tablespoons brown sugar and 1/2 teaspoon onion powder.

Per Serving (approx):
Calories 288
Carbohydrate 7 gm

Protein 15 gm
Sodium 554 mg

Fat 22 gm
Cholesterol 31 mg

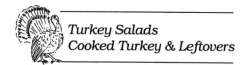

Apple Pie Turkey Salad

2 1/4 cups cubed cooked turkey
2 cups diced celery
2 cups diced unpeeled Granny Smith
   apples
1/4 cup raisins
2 tablespoons reduced-calorie
   mayonnaise

2 tablespoons plain low-fat
   yogurt
1/4 teaspoon ground nutmeg
1/4 teaspoon ground cinnamon
Salt and pepper to taste
Lettuce leaves
Grated Cheddar cheese, for
   garnish (optional)

In large bowl combine turkey, celery, apples and raisins. In small bowl combine mayonnaise, yogurt, nutmeg and cinnamon; fold into turkey mixture. Season to taste with salt and pepper. Serve on lettuce leaves and garnish with grated Cheddar cheese, if desired.   Makes 6 servings.

Per Serving (approx):
Calories 157
Carbohydrate 14 gm
Protein 16 gm
Sodium 115 mg
Fat 4 gm
Cholesterol 42 mg

Turkey and Corn Bread Salad

2 cups cooked turkey cut into
   1/2-inch cubes
1 cup corn bread stuffing mix
1/2 cup drained whole kernel
   corn
1/4 cup coarsely chopped
   green bell pepper

1/4 cup finely chopped onion
1 jar (2 ounces) chopped
   pimiento, drained
1/2 cup reduced-calorie
   cucumber or buttermilk
   salad dressing

In large bowl combine turkey, 3/4 cup of the corn bread stuffing mix, turkey, the corn, bell pepper, onion, pimiento and dressing. Cover and refrigerate for 4 hours or overnight. To serve, top salad with remaining 1/4 cup stuffing mix.   Makes 4 servings.

Per Serving (approx):
Calories 294
Carbohydrate 26 gm
Protein 24 gm
Sodium 728 mg
Fat 10 gm
Cholesterol 54 mg

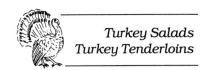

Tender-ness Turkey Stir-Fry Salad

1 pound turkey breast tenderloins
6 tablespoons peanut oil
1 small bunch green onions, cut
  diagonally into 1-inch pieces
1 red bell pepper, julienned
1 medium zucchini,
  julienned
1 can (8 ounces) water
  chestnuts, drained and sliced
1 clove garlic, minced

1 tablespoon reduced-sodium
  soy sauce
2 cups shredded Chinese
  cabbage
4 cups cooked Asian noodles
  or other pasta (8 ounces
  uncooked)
1/3 cup light teriyaki sauce
Cilantro sprigs (optional)

Slice tenderloins lengthwise in half along natural crease. Cut into 1-inch chunks. In wok or large nonstick skillet over medium-high heat, warm 2 tablespoons of the oil. Add turkey and stir-fry for 2 to 3 minutes.

Add onions and bell pepper; cook for 1 minute longer, stirring constantly.

Add zucchini, water chestnuts and garlic; stir-fry for 1 minute longer or until vegetables are tender-crisp and turkey is cooked through. Stir in soy sauce and set aside.

In large bowl combine shredded cabbage and noodles. In small bowl whisk together remaining peanut oil and teriyaki sauce. Add turkey mixture to bowl; toss with teriyaki mixture. Garnish with cilantro and serve with Oriental-style corn or rice chips and iced tea.   Makes 6 servings.

Per Serving (approx):
Calories 457
Carbohydrate 33 gm

Protein 24 gm
Sodium 1168 mg

Fat 26 gm
Cholesterol 46 mg

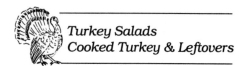
Curried Salad Bombay

1/2 cup reduced-calorie
   mayonnaise
1/2 cup plain low-fat yogurt
1 tablespoon peach or mango
   chutney
2 to 3 teaspoons curry powder
Salt and pepper to taste
1 1/2 pounds cubed cooked turkey
   breast

1 red apple, unpeeled and sliced
1 green apple, unpeeled
   and sliced
3/4 cup red and/or green
   seedless grapes
2 tablespoons snipped chives
Curly green or Bibb lettuce

In medium bowl combine mayonnaise, yogurt, chutney, curry, salt and pepper. Add turkey, then add apples, grapes and chives; toss gently to coat ingredients with dressing. Serve salad on bed of lettuce.

Makes 6 servings.

Per Serving (approx):
Calories 241
Carbohydrate 14 gm

Protein 28 gm
Sodium 263 mg

Fat 8 gm
Cholesterol 78 mg

Deluxe Turkey Salad

1 cup cubed cooked turkey
2 cups crisp lettuce torn in
   bite-sized pieces
1/4 cup golden raisins
1/2 cup red grapes, halved
   and seeded if necessary
1 sweet gherkin, chopped

1/4 cup chopped pecans
2 tablespoons chopped red
   onion
1/4 cup cubed mild Cheddar
   cheese
1/2 cup salad dressing or
   mayonnaise

In large bowl combine turkey, lettuce, raisins, grapes, gherkin, pecans, onion and cheese. Toss with salad dressing.   Makes 2 servings.

Per Serving (approx):
Calories 776
Carbohydrate 31 gm

Protein 27 gm
Sodium 704 mg

Fat 60 gm
Cholesterol 68 mg

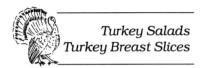

Fruit and Turkey Medley

4 cups torn mixed greens (Bibb, Romaine, leaf lettuce, spinach or cilantro)
1 orange, peeled and sliced crosswise
1/2 cantaloupe, cubed
1 cup seedless grapes
1 apple, thinly sliced into wedges and dipped in lemon juice

1 pear, cubed
1/4 cup chopped pecans or pecan halves
1 tablespoon margarine
1 pound turkey breast slices
Enoki mushrooms, for garnish (optional)

Arrange greens, fruit and pecans on 4 large plates. Combine dressing ingredients; set aside. Warm half the margarine in skillet over medium heat. When margarine begins to bubble, add half the turkey. Cook for 3 minutes; turn turkey over and cook for 2 minutes more. Remove from pan and repeat with remaining margarine and turkey.

Arrange warm turkey evenly among salads. Add Orange-Mint Dressing to skillet; bring to a boil. Pour hot dressing over salad; garnish with mushrooms, if desired. Serve immediately.   Makes 4 servings.

ORANGE-MINT DRESSING:
Combine 1/2 cup orange juice, 1/4 cup olive oil, 1 tablespoon Dijon mustard and 1 teaspoon dried mint.

Per Serving (approx):
Calories 452
Carbohydrate 35 gm

Protein 38 gm
Sodium 209 mg

Fat 23 gm
Cholesterol 94 mg

Caesar Turkey Salad

Here is our version of one of today's most popular salads.

Nonstick vegetable cooking spray
1 pound turkey breast slices,
  cut in strips
4 cups torn Romaine lettuce
1/2 cup thinly sliced red onion

1/2 cup croutons (Caesar salad
  or Parmesan cheese flavored)
2 tablespoons freshly grated
  Parmesan cheese
1 hard-cooked egg, cut into
  wedges (optional)

Spray large skillet with nonstick vegetable cooking spray. Warm over medium-high heat for about 30 seconds. Add turkey breast strips. Cook and stir for 2 to 4 minutes or until lightly browned. Remove from skillet and let cool slightly. Prepare dressing; set aside.

In large bowl combine lettuce, onion and warm turkey. Add dressing; toss gently to coat. Add croutons and toss gently. Sprinkle with cheese. Top with egg, if desired. Serve immediately.   Makes 6 servings.

CAESAR DRESSING:
In small bowl combine 3 tablespoons each fresh lemon juice and water, 2 teaspoons each Worcestershire sauce and olive oil, 2 cloves garlic, crushed, 1 teaspoon anchovy paste, 1/2 teaspoon grated lemon zest and 1/8 teaspoon black pepper. Mix well. Stir in 4 tablespoons low-fat sour cream 1 tablespoon at a time until smooth.

Per Serving (approx):
Calories 192
Carbohydrate 7 gm

Protein 21 gm
Sodium 148 mg

Fat 9 gm
Cholesterol 79 mg

ASIAN & INDIAN

Steaks Shanghai

Add stir-fried vegetables, a steaming bowl of rice and a wedge of melon or a scoop of sherbet for dessert, and you have a "company-quality" meal with a Chinese accent.

4 to 8 turkey breast steaks
   (1 1/2 pounds total),
   cut 1/4 to 1/2 inch thick
1/2 teaspoon salt
1/4 teaspoon black pepper
3 tablespoons peanut oil
1 1/2 tablespoons cornstarch
1 1/2 teaspoons chicken
   seasoned stock base

1/2 teaspoon ground ginger
1 teaspoon brown sugar
2 tablespoons sherry
1 tablespoon wine vinegar
1/4 cup soy sauce
1 1/2 cups water
Hot cooked rice (optional)
1/4 cup sliced green onion
   (optional)

Season steaks with salt and pepper. Cook in heated oil in skillet until golden brown, turning once. Turkey steaks cook quickly, so be careful not to overcook. Remove steaks from pan.

Combine all remaining ingredients except rice and onion in pan. Cook and stir until sauce clears and thickens. Return turkey steaks to sauce and reheat for a few minutes. Serve plain or with rice, and sprinkle with green onion, if desired.   Makes 4 servings.

Per Serving (approx):

Calories 328	*Protein 42 gm*	*Fat 15 gm*
Carbohydrate 6 gm	*Sodium 1422 mg*	*Cholesterol 94 mg*

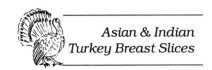
Ginger Turkey Stir-Fry

2 cups boiling water
1 cup bulgur
1/3 cup water
2 tablespoons fresh lemon juice
2 tablespoons honey
1 teaspoon fresh grated ginger,
    or 1/2 teaspoon
    ground ginger
1 tablespoon reduced-sodium
    soy sauce

1 large clove garlic, minced
2 tablespoons cornstarch
1 tablespoon oil
2 cups diagonally sliced carrot
2 cups broccoli florets
2 cups sliced mushrooms
1 can (8 ounces) water
    chestnuts, drained and sliced
1 pound turkey breast slices or
    cutlets, cut in strips

Pour boiling water over bulgur and let stand for 1 hour; drain and set aside.

Combine the 1/3 cup water, lemon juice, honey, ginger, soy sauce and garlic. Dissolve cornstarch in mixture; set aside.

Heat oil over high heat in wok or large skillet. Add carrot; stir-fry for 3 minutes or until tender-crisp. Add broccoli, mushrooms and water chestnuts; stir-fry for about 2 minutes more. Remove from pan.

Stir-fry turkey until lightly browned. Add soy sauce mixture and cook, stirring constantly, until thickened and translucent. Add reserved vegetables; heat through. Serve over drained bulgur.

Makes 6 servings.

Per Serving (approx):
Calories 303
Carbohydrate 45 gm

Protein 23 gm
Sodium 180 mg

Fat 4 gm
Cholesterol 47 mg

*Asian & Indian
Cooked Turkey & Leftovers*

Turkey Chow Mein

*Leftover turkey is the key to this familiar Chinese recipe for chow mein,
American style.*

2 to 3 cups cooked turkey pieces
1 can (13 3/4 ounces)
   chicken broth
3 tablespoons soy sauce
1/8 teaspoon ground ginger
1/8 teaspoon black pepper
1 cup sliced onion
1 clove garlic, minced
2 tablespoons oil
1 cup sliced celery

1/2 cup slivered bell pepper
2 tablespoons cornstarch
2 cups fresh bean sprouts
   or 1 can (16 ounces), drained
1 cup sliced fresh mushrooms
   or 1 can (4 ounces), drained
1 1/2 cups fresh Chinese pea
   pods or 1 package (6 ounces)
   frozen and thawed

Toss turkey with 1/2 cup of the broth, the soy sauce, ginger and black
pepper; set aside. Sauté onion and garlic in oil for 3 minutes in large
skillet with cover. Add celery, bell pepper and remaining broth. Bring to
a boil, cover and cook over moderate heat for 2 to 3 minutes.

Drain turkey, saving marinade, and add to celery mixture. Mix cornstarch with drained marinade. Add to skillet and cook, stirring, until
sauce thickens. Stir in bean sprouts, mushrooms and pea pods. Cover
and cook for 2 to 3 minutes longer. Serve with rice.

Makes 6 servings.

Per Serving (approx):
Calories 336
Carbohydrate 42 gm

Protein 23 gm
Sodium 973 mg

Fat 8 gm
Cholesterol 44 mg

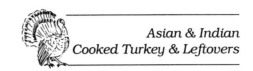

Curried Turkey Dinner

1 package (10 ounces) frozen
   broccoli spears, cooked
   and drained
2 cups cubed cooked turkey
1 can (10 1/2 ounces)
   reduced-sodium cream of
   mushroom soup

1/4 cup reduced-calorie
   mayonnaise
1 1/2 teaspoons lemon juice
1 teaspoon curry powder
1 cup seasoned croutons

In 8-inch-square baking dish, layer broccoli and turkey.

In small bowl, combine soup, mayonnaise, lemon juice and curry powder. Pour over turkey and top with croutons. Bake in preheated 350 degree oven for 20 to 25 minutes or until bubbly.

Makes 4 servings.

Per Serving (approx):
Calories 321
Carbohydrate 21 gm

Protein 24 gm
Sodium 720 mg

Fat 16 gm
Cholesterol 63 mg

Shanghai'd Turkey

1 pound skinless turkey
   tenderloins
1/2 cup white wine
3 tablespoons reduced-sodium
   soy sauce
1 tablespoon cornstarch
Black pepper to taste
1 tablespoon sugar
2 teaspoons rice vinegar or
   white vinegar
1 1/2 tablespoons oil
1 clove garlic, minced

1 teaspoon minced fresh ginger
2 carrots, shredded
1/3 pound green beans, split
   lengthwise and lightly steamed
1/2 cup thinly sliced green
   onion
2 cups hot cooked Chinese
   noodles (optional)
Carrots cut in flower shapes
   (optional)
Chopped green onion and
   cilantro sprigs (optional)

Slice turkey in thin strips and place in medium bowl. Sprinkle with 1/4 cup of the wine, 1 tablespoon of the soy sauce, the cornstarch and pepper. Toss to coat with mixture, then let marinate at room temperature for 15 minutes. In small bowl combine remaining 1/4 cup wine, remaining 2 tablespoons soy sauce, sugar and vinegar. Set aside.

Warm wok or large, heavy nonstick skillet over medium-high heat. Slowly add oil. Stir in garlic, ginger and turkey. Stir-fry for 3 to 4 minutes until turkey is cooked through. Add carrots, beans, green onions and reserved wine mixture. Cook for 1 to 2 minutes longer. Serve over Chinese noodles, garnished with carrot flowers, chopped green onion and cilantro sprigs, if desired.

Makes 4 servings.

Per Serving (approx):
Calories 246
Carbohydrate 13 gm

Protein 28 gm
Sodium 393 mg

Fat 7 gm
Cholesterol 70 mg

Asian & Indian
Turkey Cutlets

Sesame Turkey Cutlets

2 teaspoons lemon juice
1 teaspoon soy sauce
1 teaspoon honey
1/8 teaspoon black pepper

1 1/2 pound turkey breast
  cutlets or slices
1 tablespoon margarine
1 tablespoon sesame seeds,
  toasted*

In small bowl combine lemon juice, soy sauce and honey; set aside.

Lightly sprinkle pepper over cutlets. In skillet over medium-high heat, sauté cutlets in margarine for 1 to 2 minutes per side or until turkey is no longer pink in center. Pour lemon juice mixture over cutlets; heat through.

Serve cutlets garnished with sesame seeds.   Makes 2 servings.

*Note: To toast sesame seeds, warm large nonstick skillet over medium heat; toast sesame seeds until golden brown. Stir frequently. Do not allow to scorch.

Per Serving (approx):
Calories 220
Carbohydrate 5 gm

Protein 28 gm
Sodium 316 mg

Fat 10 gm
Cholesterol 70 mg

87

Armenian Turkey Dumplings

The cuisine of Armenia coupled with ground turkey results in a dumpling soup whose aroma alone will warm your heart on a cold, wet winter day.

1 pound ground turkey
2/3 cup Tabbouleh Salad Mix*
1/3 cup chopped parsley
  (reserve 1 tablespoon for garnish)
2 tablespoons chopped fresh
  mint or 1 teaspoon dried
1 teaspoon paprika

1/4 teaspoon ground cinnamon
Salt and cayenne to taste
3 cans (14 1/2 ounces each)
  beef broth
1 1/2 cups water
3 tablespoons tomato paste
1/2 cup plain yogurt

Knead turkey with tabbouleh mix, spices and seasonings. Form into 12 balls and chill.

Combine beef broth, water and tomato paste and bring to a boil. Drop dumplings in boiling broth about six at a time; cook for 5 minutes. Remove with slotted spoon; repeat with remaining dumplings. Serve dumplings in broth garnished with dollop of yogurt and sprinkle of parsley.

Makes 6 servings.

*Note: Prepare 1 box (7 ounces) Tabbouleh Salad Mix without tomato; retain unused portion for other use.

Per Serving (approx):
Calories 201
Carbohydrate 15 gm

Protein 19 gm
Sodium 799 mg

Fat 7 gm
Cholesterol 57 mg

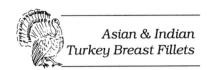

Turkey Fillets with Chutney Sauce

Ten minutes to make, twenty minutes to bake—what could be nicer for a busy yet hungry person?

4 turkey breast fillets
1 cup chicken broth
1 onion, chopped
1/2 cup mango chutney

2 cloves garlic, minced
2 teaspoons curry powder
Shredded coconut, chopped
   green onions and raisins,
   for garnish

Arrange turkey fillets in 9- x 12-inch baking dish. In small bowl mix broth, onion, mango chutney, garlic and curry powder; spoon over turkey. Cover and bake at 350 degrees for 20 minutes or more depending on thickness of the fillets. Meanwhile, prepare rice. Garnish turkey with shredded coconut, chopped green onion and raisins.

Makes 4 to 6 servings.

RICE:
Combine 1 1/2 cups basmati or white rice, 1 1/2 cups water, 4 green onions, chopped, and 1/2 cup chopped mushrooms. Cover, bring to a boil, reduce heat and simmer for 20 minutes. Add 1/2 cup frozen peas during last 5 minutes of cooking time.

Per Serving (approx) including rice:
Calories 408   *Protein 12 gm*   *Fat 2 gm*
Carbohydrate 86 gm   *Sodium 407 mg*   *Cholesterol 12 mg*

Asian & Indian
Turkey Breast Fillets

Mideast Fajitas

This marriage of two cuisines produces a new gourmet offspring.

1/4 cup oil
3/4 teaspoon ground ginger
3/4 teaspoon ground coriander
3/4 teaspoon ground cumin
Salt and coarsely ground black
   pepper to taste
3 pounds turkey breast fillets

18 lightly toasted pita breads
   (6 inches)
3 small cucumbers, thinly sliced
2 cups shredded Romaine
   lettuce
3 medium red onions, thinly
   sliced

In wide, shallow bowl combine oil, ginger, coriander, cumin, salt and pepper. Add turkey fillets; turn to coat with seasonings. Cover and let marinate in refrigerator for at least 1 hour. Meanwhile, prepare Mango Salsa and set aside.

Prepare outdoor grill for cooking or preheat broiler. Grill or broil fillets 5 to 6 inches from heat source for 3 to 5 minutes on each side or until cooked through. Remove fillets to cutting board and slice into 1/4-inch strips. To serve, split pita breads open to form pockets. Divide turkey, cucumbers, lettuce and onion among pita pockets. Serve with Mango Salsa.

Makes 12 to 14 servings.

MANGO SALSA:
In large bowl combine 3 large, ripe mangoes or peaches, peeled and diced, 1 can (4 ounces) chopped mild green chilies, 1/2 cup diced red bell pepper, 1/3 cup chopped green onion, 1/4 cup finely chopped cilantro, 3 tablespoons fresh lemon juice, 3/4 teaspoon ground ginger and salt and pepper to taste. Mix well. Makes 3 cups salsa.

Per Serving (approx):
Calories 473
Carbohydrate 70 gm

Protein 36 gm
Sodium 682 mg

Fat 5 gm
Cholesterol 70 mg

90

Turkey Satay with Peanut Sauce

1 pound turkey tenderloins
3 tablespoons low-fat milk
1 tablespoon olive oil
1 teaspoon reduced-sodium
  soy sauce
1 tablespoon dried onion

1/2 teaspoon red pepper flakes
1/2 teaspoon lemon zest
1/4 teaspoon ground ginger
1/8 teaspoon coconut extract

Cut turkey tenderloins in half lengthwise. Between two 12-inch pieces of waxed paper, using a meat mallet, flatten each turkey half. Cut each turkey half into 1-inch-wide strips.

In self-closing plastic freezer bag, combine milk, oil, soy sauce, onion, pepper flakes, lemon zest, ginger and coconut extract. Add turkey strips; seal bag and turn bag to coat strips. Refrigerate for at least 4 hours. Meanwhile, prepare Peanut Sauce.

Remove grill rack from charcoal grill and lightly coat with vegetable cooking spray; set aside. Prepare grill for direct-heat cooking.

Soak bamboo skewers in water for 15 minutes. Weave turkey strips onto bamboo skewers. Discard marinade. Position grill rack over hot coals. Grill turkey for 2 to 3 minutes per side or until turkey is no longer pink in center. Serve with Peanut Sauce.   Makes 4 servings.

PEANUT SAUCE:
In food processor fitted with metal blade and motor running, drop in 1 small clove garlic and 1 tablespoon chopped onion. Process for 10 seconds or until chopped. Add 1/4 cup creamy peanut butter, 1 1/2 teaspoons lemon juice, 1/4 teaspoon reduced-sodium soy sauce, 1/8 teaspoon cayenne pepper and dash of coconut extract. Process for 20 seconds or until blended. With motor running, slowly add 1/4 cup low-fat milk. Process sauce until smooth and well blended, scraping sides often. Heat until slightly thickened.

Per Serving (approx):
Calories 250
Carbohydrate 5 gm

Protein 33 gm
Sodium 180 mg

Fat 11 gm
Cholesterol 171 mg

Bombay Turkey

1/2 pound turkey tenderloins
   or slices, cut into 1/2-inch strips
1/2 cup cubed red Delicious apple

3/4 teaspoon curry powder
1 1/2 teaspoons margarine
1/4 cup mango chutney

In small bowl combine turkey, apple and curry powder; let stand for 10 minutes. In medium nonstick skillet over medium-high heat, stir-fry turkey mixture in margarine for 2 to 3 minutes or until turkey is no longer pink. Stir in chutney and continue to cook until heated through. Serve over rice, if desired. **Makes 2 servings.**

Per Serving (approx):
Calories 256
Carbohydrate 26 gm

Protein 27 gm
Sodium 178 mg

Fat 5 gm
Cholesterol 70 mg

Chinese Simmered Turkey Strips

1 pound turkey tenderloins,
   cut into strips
1 tablespoon oil
1/3 cup firmly packed brown sugar
3/4 cup water
1/3 cup soy sauce
2 tablespoons catsup
1 tablespoon cider vinegar

1/8 teaspoon ground ginger
1 green onion, sliced
1 clove garlic, finely chopped
1 tablespoon cornstarch
   dissolved in 1 tablespoon
   cold water

In medium skillet over medium-high heat, cook turkey in hot oil, stirring occasionally, for 5 to 8 minutes or until turkey is no longer pink. Add remaining ingredients except cornstarch and rice. Bring to a boil; cover, reduce heat and simmer for 10 minutes, stirring occasionally. Stir in cornstarch mixture; heat until thickened. Serve with hot cooked rice. **Makes 4 to 6 servings.**

Per Serving (approx):
Calories 173
Carbohydrate 11 gm

Protein 17 gm
Sodium 1008 mg

Fat 7 gm
Cholesterol 41 mg

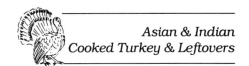

Quick Curry

1/4 cup oil
1 carrot, thinly sliced
1 small onion, thinly sliced
1 apple, thinly sliced
3 tablespoons flour
2 tablespoons curry powder
1/2 to 3/4 teaspoon cayenne
  pepper (optional)
1/4 teaspoon black pepper

1 can (13 3/4 ounces) chicken
  broth
1/2 cup whipping cream
3 cups chopped or shredded
  cooked turkey
Salt to taste
Hot cooked rice or baked
  pastry shells
Chutney, raisins and slivered
  almonds (optional)

In large skillet over medium heat, warm oil. Add carrot, onion and apple; sauté for 1 minute. Stir in flour, curry powder, cayenne and black pepper. Blend well; cook 1 to 2 minutes. Stir in broth and cream; cook 1 to 2 minutes until thickened, stirring often. Stir in turkey and heat through. Season to taste with salt.

Serve over rice or in baked pastry shells. Garnish with chutney, raisins and almonds, if desired.   Makes 6 servings.

Per Serving (approx):
Calories 534
Carbohydrate 28 gm

Protein 26 gm
Sodium 326 mg

Fat 36 gm
Cholesterol 80 mg

Madras Turkey with New Delhi Rice

This dish becomes a special event when served with chopped banana, toasted coconut and peanuts.

3 pounds turkey drumsticks
2 green apples, chopped
2 stalks celery, chopped
1 onion, sliced
2 tablespoons butter
3 tablespoons curry powder
1 cup chicken broth

1 cup whipping cream
Salt and pepper to taste
3 green onions, chopped
Toasted coconut, chopped peanuts, chopped banana and chopped cucumber

Poach turkey drumsticks in enough water to cover for 1 1/2 hours or until tender. Remove meat from bones; cut meat in bite-sized pieces and reserve.

Sauté apples, celery and onion in butter. Add curry, turkey meat, broth and cream. Simmer for 30 minutes. Season to taste with salt and pepper. Top each serving with chopped green onion. Serve with New Delhi Rice and condiments.

Makes 6 to 8 servings.

NEW DELHI RICE:
Combine 4 cups water, 2 cups rice, 3/4 cup currants and 3/4 teaspoon ground cardamom. Bring to a boil; cover and reduce heat to low. Simmer for 20 minutes.

Per Serving (approx):
Calories 819
Carbohydrate 81 gm

Protein 53 gm
Sodium 751 mg

Fat 31 gm
Cholesterol 180 mg

Asian & Indian
Turkey Steaks

Cantonese Turkey Steaks

1 1/2 pounds turkey breast
    steaks, cut 1/2 to 3/4 inch
    thick*
2 teaspoons oil
1 can (6 ounces) pineapple juice
1/2 cup chicken or turkey broth
1 large clove garlic, mashed
2 1/2 tablespoons soy sauce
Pinch of fennel or anise seed

1/2 teaspoon light brown or
    granulated sugar
1 large Spanish onion, halved
and thinly sliced
1 medium green bell pepper,
    quartered and sliced 1/8 inch
    thick
2 tablespoons sliced pimientos

Rinse and pat turkey dry with paper towels. Warm oil over medium-high heat in skillet. Sear steaks quickly on both sides. Remove to plate. Add juice, broth and garlic. Boil about 8 minutes to reduce by half. Add soy sauce, fennel seed, sugar, vegetables and pimientos. Simmer for about 2 minutes or until vegetables start to soften.

Return steaks to pan. Spoon mixture over them and simmer over low heat for an additional few minutes or just until steaks are no longer pink. Serve steaks dressed liberally with vegetable mixture.

Makes 6 servings.

*Note: Steaks may be bone in or boneless. Your meat clerk may cut steaks for you from a whole, frozen or fresh turkey breast.

Per Serving (approx):
Calories 165
Carbohydrate 9 gm

Protein 25 gm
Sodium 721 mg

Fat 3 gm
Cholesterol 58 mg

Szechuan Stir-Fry

Some like it hot—and if you're one of them, this dish is for you.

1/4 cup soy sauce
1 teaspoon sugar
1 teaspoon cornstarch
1/2 teaspoon red pepper flakes
   (optional)
1/4 teaspoon ground ginger
1 clove garlic, finely chopped
1 pound turkey breast slices,
   cut into strips

2 tablespoons oil
1 red bell pepper, thinly sliced
4 green onions, cut into
   1/2-inch pieces
6 ounces pea pods (fresh, or
   frozen and thawed)

In medium bowl combine soy sauce, sugar, cornstarch, red pepper flakes, ginger and garlic. Add turkey; let marinate for at least 15 minutes. In large skillet or wok over medium-high heat, stir-fry turkey in 1 tablespoon of the oil for about 5 minutes or until turkey is no longer pink. Remove turkey from skillet.

Heat remaining 1 tablespoon oil in skillet and stir-fry vegetables until tender-crisp, 1 to 2 minutes. Return turkey to skillet; mix with vegetables. Serve over hot cooked rice. Makes 4 to 6 servings.

Per Serving (approx):
Calories 175
Carbohydrate 5 gm

Protein 18 gm
Sodium 721 mg

Fat 9 gm
Cholesterol 41 mg

Modern turkeys have much more white breast meat than earlier turkeys; this makes them easier to carve.

Asian & Indian
Turkey Thighs

Taj Kabobs

This classic recipe from India calls for chicken. We changed it to turkey and, quite honestly, like it better.

15 large cloves garlic
1 cup plain low-fat yogurt
3 tablespoons lemon juice
3 tablespoons minced fresh ginger
1 tablespoon curry powder
1 1/2 teaspoons ground
    coriander

1 1/2 teaspoons cayenne pepper
3 to 4 pounds skinless and
    boneless turkey thighs,
    cut into 2-inch cubes

Finely mince 3 cloves garlic. In wide, shallow bowl, combine yogurt, lemon juice, ginger, curry, coriander, minced garlic and cayenne. Add turkey to yogurt mixture, turning to coat well. Cover and let marinate in refrigerator for at least 1 hour.

Prepare outdoor grill for cooking or preheat broiler. On metal skewers, alternately thread turkey cubes and remaining 12 cloves garlic. Grill or broil 6 to 8 inches from heat source for 20 to 30 minutes or until turkey is cooked through, turning once or twice during grilling. Serve kabobs on bed of hot couscous or brown rice pilaf.   Makes 12 servings.

Per Serving (approx) excluding couscous or pilaf:
Calories 189   *Protein 29 gm*   *Fat 6 gm*
Carbohydrate 3 gm   *Sodium 122 mg*   *Cholesterol 107 mg*

Chinese Skillet Dinner

2 tablespoons oil
2 tablespoons minced fresh ginger
1 clove garlic, minced
1 cup chicken broth
1/4 cup soy sauce
2 tablespoons rice wine or
   dry sherry
5 teaspoons cornstarch
1 tablespoon wine vinegar

1 tablespoon sugar
Crushed red pepper flakes
   (optional)
3 cups shredded cooked turkey
2 cups shredded carrot
2 cups thinly sliced green onion
8 ounces water chestnuts,
   drained and sliced
8 ounces Chinese rice noodles,
   cooked

In large skillet over medium-high heat, warm oil. Add ginger and garlic; sauté briefly. In small bowl combine broth, soy sauce, rice wine, cornstarch, vinegar, sugar and red pepper flakes (if desired); pour into skillet and cook until sauce is slightly thickened.

Stir in turkey, carrot, green onion and water chestnuts. Sauté for 1 to 2 minutes longer. Add rice noodles; toss and serve hot.

Makes 6 to 8 servings.

Per Serving (approx):
Calories 330
Carbohydrate 29 gm

Protein 20 gm
Sodium 701 mg

Fat 15 gm
Cholesterol 40 mg

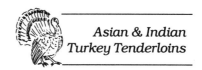

Turkey Teriyaki Tidbits with Pennies and Rice

1 pound turkey breast tenderloins
3 tablespoons reduced-calorie,
   cholesterol-free mayonnaise

3/4 cup crushed chow mein
   noodles

Prepare Light Teriyaki Sauce. Slice tenderloins lengthwise in half along natural crease; cut into 1-inch chunks. In shallow bowl combine mayonnaise and 2 tablespoons Light Teriyaki Sauce; dip turkey chunks into mixture, then roll in crushed noodles. Place turkey on baking sheet. Bake in preheated 375 degree oven for 15 to 18 minutes or until crisp and cooked through. Serve with Pennies and Rice.

Makes 4 to 6 servings.

LIGHT TERIYAKI SAUCE:
Place 1/3 cup lemon juice in small bowl. Using garlic press, squeeze 1 piece (1 inch) diced fresh ginger over bowl to collect extract. Discard pulp. Press 1 clove garlic into bowl, then add 1 teaspoon Oriental chile paste (if used), pinch of sugar, 1 tablespoon reduced-sodium soy sauce and 2 teaspoons sesame oil. Stir well. Cover and store in refrigerator up to 1 week. Use as marinade, dipping sauce or salad dressing. Once used as marinade, discard sauce; do not reuse.   Makes about 1/2 cup.

PENNIES AND RICE:
In wok or large nonstick skillet over medium heat, melt 2 tablespoons margarine. Add 1/4 cup thinly sliced green onion; sauté briefly. Add 2 cups cooked brown or white rice and 2/3 cup thinly sliced, lightly steamed carrot pennies. Toss until heated through. Season to taste with salt, black pepper and a few drops of reduced-sodium soy sauce, if desired.

Makes 4 to 6 servings.

Per Serving (approx):
Calories 287
Carbohydrate 27 gm

Protein 19 gm
Sodium 639 mg

Fat 12 gm
Cholesterol 43 mg

Teriyaki Turkey

3 tablespoons brown sugar
3 tablespoons soy sauce
1 tablespoon lemon juice
1/4 teaspoon ground ginger
1 clove garlic, finely chopped
2 teaspoons cornstarch
1 can (20 ounces) pineapple
   chunks, juice reserved

1 pound turkey breast fillets
2 tablespoons oil
3 green onions, cut into
   1-inch pieces
1 red bell pepper, cut into
   1-inch pieces

In medium bowl combine brown sugar, soy sauce, lemon juice, ginger, garlic, cornstarch and 2 tablespoons of the reserved pineapple juice. Add turkey; let stand for at least 15 minutes. Drain; reserve marinade.

In large skillet warm oil until hot; add turkey, cover and cook for 8 to 10 minutes on each side. Add onions, bell pepper, pineapple chunks and reserved marinade. Cook for 2 minutes more or until turkey is no longer pink. Serve with rice.   Makes 4 servings.

Per Serving (approx):
Calories 342
Carbohydrate 29 gm

Protein 26 gm
Sodium 825 mg

Fat 14 gm
Cholesterol 61 mg

Turkey with Orange

2 turkey thighs or drumsticks
  (2 to 3 pounds)*
1/2 teaspoon paprika
1 medium onion, sliced
1/2 cup orange juice
  concentrate
1/3 cup water

2 tablespoons brown sugar
2 tablespoons chopped parsley
2 teaspoons soy sauce
1/2 teaspoon ground ginger
Orange twists, for garnish

Place turkey under broiler to brown. (If using only thighs, remove skin.) Transfer to Dutch oven or roasting pan; and sprinkle with paprika. Arrange onion slices over turkey. Combine juice concentrate, water, brown sugar, parsley, soy sauce and ginger. Pour over turkey and onion.

Cover and bake in pre-heated 400 degree oven for approximately 1 hour or until turkey is tender. Baste once or twice. Slice meat, coat with sauce and garnish with orange twists. Serve with rice or pasta.

Makes 4 servings.

*Note: Thighs may be boned before cooking.

Per Serving (approx):
Calories 152
Carbohydrate 11 gm

Protein 17 gm
Sodium 210 mg

Fat 5 gm
Cholesterol 56 mg

Turkey meat is extremely rich in riboflavin, niacin and calcium.

Thai Turkey and Mango Stir-Fry

1 1/4 pounds skinless and
  boneless turkey thighs
2 tablespoons reduced-sodium
  soy sauce
3 teaspoons rice wine
2 teaspoons cornstarch

4 teaspoons peanut oil
2 ripe mangoes, cut into
  1/4-inch slices
1/4 cup thinly sliced green
  onion
1 tablespoon grated fresh ginger

Slice turkey into thin strips. In shallow bowl combine 1 tablespoon of the soy sauce, 2 teaspoons of the rice wine and the cornstarch. Add turkey to mixture and toss to coat evenly. Let stand for 5 minutes.

Warm wok or large, heavy nonstick skillet over medium-high heat. Slowly add oil. Add turkey and stir-fry for 6 to 8 minutes or until cooked through. Add remaining 1 tablespoon soy sauce and 1 teaspoon rice wine. Stir-fry for 30 seconds. Add mango slices, green onion and ginger. Stir-fry for 2 to 3 minutes longer. Serve with hot rice. Makes 5 servings.

Per Serving (approx):
Calories 324
Carbohydrate 34 gm

Protein 26 gm
Sodium 337 mg

Fat 9 gm
Cholesterol 85 mg

Japanese-Style Turkey Steaks

1/2 teaspoon reduced-sodium
   chicken bouillon granules
2 tablespoons boiling water
2 tablespoons reduced-sodium
   soy sauce

2 tablespoons dry sherry
1 teaspoon ground ginger
1 garlic clove, crushed
1 pound turkey breast steaks,
   sliced 3/4 inch thick

In large shallow bowl, dissolve bouillon in boiling water. Add soy sauce, sherry, ginger, garlic and turkey. Refrigerate turkey mixture for 35 to 45 minutes.

Preheat grill for direct-heat cooking.* Drain marinade from turkey and discard. Grill turkey for 15 minutes or until turkey meat is no longer pink in center, turning every 5 minutes.   Makes 4 servings.

*Note: For information on direct-heat cooking, see page 284.

Per Serving (approx):
Calories 142
Carbohydrate 2 gm

Protein 27 gm
Sodium 381 mg

Fat 2 gm
Cholesterol 70 mg

Teriyaki Turkey Wings

2 pounds turkey wings
1 cup water
2/3 cup soy sauce
1/2 cup sherry

2 tablespoons brown sugar
2 tablespoons honey
1 teaspoon ground ginger
1/4 teaspoon garlic powder

Place turkey wings in casserole with water; cover and bake in 350 degree oven for 2 hours. Pour off liquid. Combine remaining ingredients and pour over turkey. Bake uncovered for 15 minutes; turn turkey over and bake for 15 minutes more. Serve turkey with sauce.

Makes 2 servings.

Per Serving (approx):
Calories 934
Carbohydrate 36 gm

Protein 92 gm
Sodium 943 mg

Fat 40 gm
Cholesterol 256 mg

Firecracker Rolls

1 pound turkey breast slices
1 head bok choy
  (about 1 1/2 pounds)*
Peanut oil
2 tablespoons bottled
  Szechuan chile sauce or chile
  paste with garlic**

4 ounces sliced turkey ham
1/2 cup diagonally sliced
  green onion
1 red bell pepper, slivered

Pound turkey with mallet to flatten slightly; set aside.

Trim off green leafy parts from bok choy, leaving leaves whole. Slice up remaining bok choy crosswise; set aside. Add leafy bok choy to oil in hot skillet; cover and cook over medium-high heat for 2 minutes, shaking pan often to prevent sticking.

To make rolls, spread turkey slices with a little more than half the chile sauce, then top with turkey ham and leafy bok choy. Roll up meat into long rolls, starting from long side, and fasten rolls with picks. Coat rolls with remaining chile sauce.

To cook, sauté rolls in 2 tablespoons oil in skillet over medium-high heat, turning to brown all sides. Cook for 4 to 5 minutes or just until done. Remove picks and transfer rolls to platter; keep warm. Add a little oil to pan; heat pan and add reserved bok choy, green onion and red bell pepper. Stir-fry over high heat for 5 minutes or until tender-crisp. Spoon alongside meat, arranging grilled green onion as firecracker "fuses."

Makes 4 servings.

*Note: If bok choy is not available, use 8 leaves Swiss chard; stir-fry chard stems and 2 cups sliced celery.

**Note: This sauce is quite spicy. For a milder approach, substitute bottled American-style barbecue sauce.

Per Serving (approx):
Calories 276
Carbohydrate 4 gm

Protein 31 gm
Sodium 431 mg

Fat 15 gm
Cholesterol 77 mg

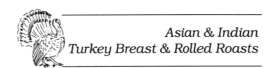

Oriental Turkey Breast Dinner

1/4 cup soy sauce
1 tablespoon honey
1 teaspoon sesame oil
1 teaspoon minced garlic
1 teaspoon minced fresh ginger
1 turkey half breast, boned and
  skinned (1 to 1 1/2 pounds)
4 small leeks, split lengthwise
4 ounces shiitake mushrooms,
  cut in halves

2 crookneck squash, quartered
  lengthwise
2 Japanese eggplant, quartered
1 red bell pepper, quartered
3 tablespoons white wine,
  chicken stock or water
Salt and pepper to taste
2 tablespoons chopped cilantro

Combine soy sauce, honey, sesame oil, garlic and ginger; brush over turkey breast, reserving some for vegetables. Let stand 1 hour, then remove breast from marinade and brown both sides of breast under broiler. Brown under broiler.

Place browned breast in center of double layer of heavy-duty foil about 18 inches square. Surround with vegetables. Brush vegetables with remaining marinade; spoon wine over breast. Season with salt and pepper, seal foil and bake in 350 degree oven for about 35 minutes. Sprinkle with cilantro and serve with rice. Makes 4 servings.

Per Serving (approx):
Calories 397
Carbohydrate 81 gm

Protein 11 gm
Sodium 1167 mg

Fat 3 gm
Cholesterol 3 mg

Turkey Vegetable Tempura

This dish was actually invented by Spanish and Portuguese missionaries in Japan in the sixteenth century, and we brought it up to date using turkey.

1 pound turkey breast slices, cut in
    bite-sized pieces
1 cup cornstarch
2 eggs, lightly beaten
1 cup Japanese-flavored or plain
    bread crumbs

Oil, for deep-frying
3 cups assorted bite-sized
    pieces of broccoli, mush-
    rooms, zucchini and green
    onions

Dip pieces of turkey in cornstarch, then in egg. Coat with bread crumbs. Deep-fry in oil at 375 degrees for 2 to 3 minutes. Repeat dipping procedure for vegetables, then cook for 1 minute or until tender-crisp. Serve with Ginger-Sherry Dipping Sauce.   Makes 4 servings.

GINGER-SHERRY DIPPING SAUCE:
Combine 1/4 cup each soy sauce and water, 2 tablespoons sherry, 1 tablespoon each grated fresh ginger and brown sugar and 1 minced green onion. Mix well.

Per Serving (approx):
Calories 770
Carbohydrate 69 gm

Protein 36 gm
Sodium 1346 mg

Fat 38 gm
Cholesterol 169 mg

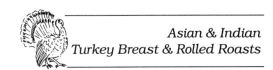

Turkey Yakitori

1/2 teaspoon reduced-sodium
   chicken bouillon granules
2 tablespoons boiling water
1 pound boneless turkey breast,
   cut into 1-inch cubes
2 tablespoons reduced-sodium
   soy sauce
2 tablespoons dry sherry or
   white wine

1 teaspoon ground ginger
1 clove garlic, pressed
3 green onions, cut into
   2-inch lengths
3/4 cup cubed green bell
   pepper

Dissolve bouillon granules in boiling water; mix in plastic bag with turkey, soy sauce, sherry, ginger and garlic. Prop bag in container so that all turkey is submerged. Allow to marinate for at least 4 hours in refrigerator.

Thread turkey onto skewers with green onion and bell pepper cubes. Grill over hot coals (or broil) 6 inches from heat, for 4 to 5 minutes on each side. Brush with remaining marinade while cooking. If desired, prepare additional marinade as dipping sauce. Do not use original marinade as dip when serving.   Makes 4 servings.

Per Serving (approx):
Calories 143
Carbohydrate gm

Protein 27 gm
Sodium 350 mg

Fat 1 gm
Cholesterol 56 mg

Hunan Salad

Hunan cuisine's fiery flavors are captured in this zesty salad. No, we do not know of any way to make it milder. It is spicy!

2 turkey drumsticks
  (1 pound each)
2 ounces mung bean threads*
4 ounces snow peas, blanched

1 cup shredded Chinese cabbage
1/2 cup sliced cucumber
1/2 red bell pepper, sliced

Poach turkey in water to cover for 1 1/2 hours or until done and tender. Remove meat from bones; shred and chill.

Soak bean threads in enough cold water to cover for 15 minutes. Drain and plunge into boiling water for 3 minutes; drain and chill.

Toss all ingredients with Hunan Dressing.   Makes 6 servings.

HUNAN DRESSING:
Whisk 1/3 cup oil, 1/4 cup soy sauce, 1/4 cup white vinegar, 3 table-spoons peanut butter, 1 1/2 teaspoons chile paste, or 4 drops hot chile oil.

*Note: Bean threads are thin dry noodles made from mung bean flour; they may be found in Chinese markets or the Oriental food section of grocery stores.

Per Serving (approx):
Calories 346
Carbohydrate 6 gm

Protein 26 gm
Sodium 768 mg

Fat 24 gm
Cholesterol 69 mg

ITALIAN &
MEDITERRANEAN

Turkey Cacciatore

Chicken is the traditional meat for cacciatore, but we think you'll like this as well—possibly better.

1/2 cup thinly sliced onion	1/4 cup red wine
1/2 cup cubed green bell pepper	1 bay leaf
2 tablespoons margarine	2 teaspoons sugar
1/4 pound mushrooms, quartered	1/2 teaspoon dried basil
2 cloves garlic, minced	1/2 teaspoon dried thyme
1 can (8 ounces) stewed tomatoes	1/2 teaspoon dried oregano
	1/4 teaspoon salt
1 can (8 ounces) tomato sauce	4 turkey thighs (about 3 pounds)

In 3-quart saucepan over medium heat, sauté onion and bell pepper in margarine until onion is transparent and pepper is tender-crisp. Add mushrooms and garlic; cook for 2 to 3 minutes.

Stir in tomatoes, tomato sauce, wine, bay leaf, sugar, basil, thyme, oregano and salt. Bring to a boil. Add turkey thighs. Reduce heat to low; cover and cook for 1 to 1 1/2 hours or until turkey is tender and internal temperature of center of each turkey thigh reaches 180 to 185 degrees.

Serve over spaghetti, if desired.   Makes 4 to 6 servings.

Per Serving (approx):
Calories 297	*Protein 38 gm*	*Fat 11 gm*
Carbohydrate 10 gm	*Sodium 605 mg*	*Cholesterol 134 mg*

Only tom turkeys (males) gobble. Hen turkeys (females) make a clicking noise.

Italian Turkey

*If you are interested in economy, this recipe calls for one turkey thigh to
serve four people, which it does, very generously.*

1 tablespoon corn oil
1 turkey thigh, boned and skinned,
　cut into 1-inch cubes
1 ripe tomato, peeled and cut into
　chunks
1 green bell pepper, thinly sliced
1 clove garlic, minced
2 tablespoons lemon juice

1 teaspoon dried basil or
　dried Italian seasoning
Salt and pepper to taste
2 teaspoons cornstarch dis-
　solved in 3 tablespoons water
Cooked vermicelli
Grated Parmesan cheese
　(optional)

Heat oil in Dutch oven over high heat. Brown turkey thigh cubes. Reduce heat to low and add tomato, bell pepper, garlic, lemon juice, basil,
salt and pepper. Cover and cook until meat is fork tender, about 45 minutes.

Stir cornstarch mixture into sauce and bring to a boil, stirring until
sauce is thickened.

To serve, place turkey over cooked vermicelli and top each serving with 1
teaspoon Parmesan cheese, if desired. Makes 4 servings.

Per Serving (approx):
Calories 268
Carbohydrate 5 gm

Protein 33 gm
Sodium 89 mg

Fat 12 gm
Cholesterol 112 mg

Sicilian Turkey Braciola

In Sicily, cooking is often sweet and savory, tempered by refreshing fruits and fruit ice desserts. Braciola is typically prepared with rolled flank steak.

1 to 1 1/4 pounds ground turkey
3 teaspoons dried Italian
   seasoning, divided
2 packages (10 ounces each) frozen
   chopped spinach, thawed and
   squeezed dry
1 clove garlic, minced
1/2 teaspoon salt
1/4 teaspoon black pepper

1/2 cup raisins
3 hard-cooked eggs, sliced
1 tablespoon olive oil
3/4 cup chopped onion
1 can (28 ounces) crushed
   tomatoes
Salt and pepper to taste
1 tablespoon honey
1/2 teaspoon ground cinnamon

In medium bowl combine turkey with 1/2 teaspoon of the Italian seasoning. Place on 15-inch sheet of aluminum foil and spread to form rectangle approximately 8 by 10 inches.

In small bowl combine spinach, garlic, salt and pepper. Spread mixture over turkey, leaving 1-inch border around sides. Scatter raisins on top. Place eggs on short end of rectangle and roll up, jelly-roll style, pressing ends together to seal in stuffing.

In large, deep skillet over medium heat, warm oil. Add onion and sauté until translucent. Add tomatoes, remaining Italian seasoning and salt and pepper to taste. Stir in honey and cinnamon. Carefully lift turkey roll into skillet; spoon sauce over top. Reduce heat to medium-low; cover and cook for 30 to 35 minutes or until turkey springs back to the touch. Slice and serve with sauce.   Makes 4 to 6 servings.

Per Serving (approx):
Calories 325
Carbohydrate 28 gm

Protein 25 gm
Sodium 587 mg

Fat 12 gm
Cholesterol 175 mg

Turkey Parmigiana

2 egg whites
1 tablespoon skim milk or water
1/2 cup seasoned bread crumbs
2 tablespoons Parmesan cheese

1 pound turkey breast cutlets,
 1/4 inch thick
1 cup Italian spaghetti sauce
4 ounces part-skim mozzarella
 cheese, sliced

In shallow bowl beat egg whites with milk. In another shallow bowl, combine bread crumbs and Parmesan cheese.

Dip cutlets into egg mixture, then into bread crumb mixture. Arrange on greased 10- x 15- x 1-inch baking pan. Bake cutlets for 4 to 5 minutes in preheated 400 degree oven.

Pour spaghetti sauce evenly over cutlets. Top each cutlet with slice of mozzarella cheese. Bake for 4 to 5 minutes more to heat sauce and melt cheese.   Makes 4 servings.

Per Serving (approx):
Calories 301
Carbohydrate 15 gm

Protein 39 gm
Sodium 679 mg

Fat 8 gm
Cholesterol 90 mg

Creamy Turkey Piccata

1 pound turkey breast fillets
4 tablespoons butter
2 tablespoons flour
1 cup whipping cream or milk
1/2 cup white wine

1 tablespoon lemon juice
1/4 cup drained capers
Lemon slices and parsley sprigs,
 for garnish

In large skillet over medium heat, cook fillets in 2 tablespoons of the butter for 8 to 11 minutes on each side or until lightly browned and no longer pink in center. Remove from pan and keep warm.

Melt remaining butter in pan; stir in flour and whisk in cream. Simmer until sauce thickens slightly. Slowly stir in wine, lemon juice and capers; heat through. Serve sauce over fillets. Garnish with lemon slices and parsley.   Makes 4 servings.

Per Serving (approx):
Calories 339
Carbohydrate 7 gm

Protein 27 gm
Sodium 319 mg

Fat 20 gm
Cholesterol 101 mg

113

Country Parmigiana

No, we didn't convert this parmigiana recipe for you. This recipe came to us from Italy, where turkey is now widely used in place of veal and pork. Try it.

3 tablespoons milk
1 egg, lightly beaten
1/3 cup seasoned dry bread crumbs
1/3 cup grated Parmesan cheese
1 pound turkey breast slices

1 tomato, sliced
1 teaspoon crushed dried
 oregano
1 cup grated mozzarella cheese
Chopped parsley, for garnish

Whisk together milk and egg. On sheet of waxed paper, mix bread crumbs and Parmesan cheese. Dip turkey breast slices into egg mixture and then bread crumb mixture, coating both sides.

Place slices in single layer on greased shallow baking pan. In preheated 450 degree oven, bake for 8 to 10 minutes or until turkey is golden brown and no longer pink in center. Top turkey with tomato slices; sprinkle with oregano and mozzarella. Place under broiler until cheese bubbles. Garnish with parsley.   Makes 4 servings.

Per Serving (approx):
Calories 331
Carbohydrate 8 gm

Protein 36 gm
Sodium 366 mg

Fat 17 gm
Cholesterol 144 mg

Turkey Consumption	
Country	Pounds/Capita
U.K.	8.2
Ireland	8.8
Italy	10.4
Canada	10.4
France	12.3
United States	18.4
Israel	22.0

According to USDA 1990 data, the above countries consumed the most turkey.

Italian & Mediterranean
Turkey Tenderloins

Turkey Medallions Piccata

This is a classic Italian veal piccata. We changed only the meat, from veal to turkey.

1 pound turkey breast tenderloins,
   cut in 3/4-inch-thick medallions
Salt and pepper to taste
1 large clove garlic, crushed

1 teaspoon olive oil
1 teaspoon margarine
1 tablespoon lemon juice
4 teaspoons drained capers

Lightly sprinkle one side of each medallion with salt and pepper.

In large nonstick skillet over medium-high heat, sauté turkey and garlic in oil and margarine for approximately 1 to 1 1/2 minutes per side, turning each medallion over when edges have turned from pink to white. Continue cooking medallions until meat thermometer reaches 170 to 175 degrees and centers of medallions are no longer pink.

Remove skillet from heat. Pour lemon juice over medallions and sprinkle capers over top; serve immediately.   Makes 4 servings.

Per Serving (approx):
Calories 150
Carbohydrate 1 gm

Protein 27 gm
Sodium 162 mg

Fat 4 gm
Cholesterol 70 mg

Turkey Perugia

This is another example of a great Italian veal dish being changed to turkey by the Italians. You'll see why when you prepare it.

1 1/2 tablespoons olive oil
1 small clove garlic, minced
1 teaspoon dried Italian
　seasoning
Salt and pepper to taste
1 pound turkey breast tenderloins
1 1/2 cups thinly sliced fennel
3 tablespoons Marsala wine

1/2 cup reduced-sodium
　chicken broth
Juice and grated zest from 1
　small lemon
1 tablespoon minced parsley
2 cups hot cooked rice
Lemon wedges (optional)
Parsley sprigs (optional)

In small bowl combine 1 1/2 teaspoons of the olive oil, the minced garlic and seasonings. Brush mixture evenly on all sides of tenderloins.

In large nonstick skillet over medium-high heat, warm remaining 1 tablespoon oil. Add turkey and sauté until lightly browned. Remove turkey from skillet and set aside. Add fennel to skillet and sauté for 2 to 3 minutes. Remove fennel and set aside with turkey.

Add Marsala and broth to skillet; bring to a boil, scraping up browned bits from bottom of skillet. Return turkey and fennel to skillet; reduce heat to low. Sprinkle with lemon juice, lemon zest and minced parsley. Cover and simmer for 15 to 20 minutes or until turkey is cooked through.

Serve with rice and garnish with lemon wedges and parsley sprigs, if desired. 　　　　　　　　　　　　　　　　　　　　　　　Makes 4 servings.

Per Serving (approx):
Calories 328
Carbohydrate 33 gm

Protein 30 gm
Sodium 213 mg

Fat 7 gm
Cholesterol 70 mg

Milano Turkey Roll
with Tomato Basil Salsa

This recipe from Milan, Italy, was created originally with veal. Nowadays it's made with turkey.

6 boneless turkey breast slices
   (2 to 3 ounces each)
Salt and pepper to taste
2 cloves garlic, minced
1/2 cup chopped onion
1 each green and red bell
   pepper, chopped
3 tablespoons oil

Additional oil for brushing
   turkey
2 cups cooked rice
2/3 cup sliced ripe olives
3 tablespoons chopped fresh
   basil or 1 1/2 teaspoons dried
1 cup shredded Cheddar cheese

Pound turkey breast slices to 1/4 inch thick. Overlap to make large rectangle. Sprinkle with salt and pepper.

Sauté garlic, onion and bell peppers in the 3 tablespoons oil until soft. Combine with cooked rice, olives and basil. Spread rice mixture on turkey, leaving 1/2-inch border. Top with cheese. Roll up from long side; transfer to greased baking sheet. Brush with oil.

Bake in preheated 350 degree oven for 30 to 35 minutes. Let stand for 15 minutes before slicing. Serve warm or at room temperature with Tomato Basil Salsa.

TOMATO BASIL SALSA:
Combine 4 peeled, seeded and chopped tomatoes, 1/2 cup sliced green onion, 2 cloves garlic, minced, 3 tablespoons chopped fresh basil (or 1 1/2 teaspoons dried) and 1 1/2 tablespoons olive oil. Let stand for 1 hour for flavors to blend.

Makes 6 main-course servings, or 10 appetizer servings.

Per Main-Course Serving (approx) excluding Salsa:
| *Calories 339* | *Protein 19 gm* | *Fat 18 gm* |
| *Carbohydrate 24 gm* | *Sodium 353 mg* | *Cholesterol 50 mg* |

Florentine Turkey Bundles

The French call anything cooked with spinach "florentine," which is how this recipe got its name.

4 ounces mushrooms, thinly
   sliced
5 tablespoons olive oil
1/4 cup plus 2 tablespoons dry
   Marsala wine
3/4 cup whipping cream
1/4 cup shredded Swiss cheese
1/4 cup grated Parmesan cheese

1/4 cup ricotta cheese
1 package (10 ounces) frozen
   spinach, thawed and
   squeezed dry
Salt and pepper to taste
6 turkey breast cutlets
2 tablespoons unsalted butter

Sauté mushrooms in 2 tablespoons of the oil. Add 1/4 cup each Marsala and whipping cream. Simmer and reduce until thick. Mix in cheeses and spinach; season to taste with salt and pepper.

Pound each turkey cutlet until about 1/4 inch thick. Spread 1/4 cup stuffing over each, leaving 1/2-inch border. Roll up and tie securely with string. Sauté bundles in remaining olive oil until well browned. Add 1 tablespoon water; cover and cook over low heat for about 10 minutes or until cooked through.

Remove bundles from pan, slice and keep warm. Add remaining 1/2 cup cream and 2 tablespoons Marsala to pan, scraping up browned bits. Reduce until sauce coats spoon; swirl in butter and serve immediately with bundles. Makes 6 servings.

Per Serving (approx):
Calories 334
Carbohydrate 5 gm

Protein 7 gm
Sodium 212 mg

Fat 30 gm
Cholesterol 64 mg

Italian Stir-Fry

1 teaspoon cornstarch
1/2 teaspoon dried Italian seasoning
1/8 teaspoon salt
Dash of red pepper flakes
1/4 cup reduced-sodium chicken
   bouillon
1/4 cup white wine

1/2 pound turkey breast cutlets
   or slices, cut into 1/2-inch
   strips
1/4 cup green onion, thinly
   sliced
1 clove garlic, minced
1 1/2 teaspoons margarine

In small bowl combine cornstarch, Italian seasoning, salt, pepper flakes, bouillon and wine; set aside.

In medium nonstick skillet over medium-high heat, stir-fry turkey, onion and garlic in margarine for 2 minutes or until meat is no longer pink. Add bouillon mixture; cook and stir until sauce is thickened.

Serve over cooked spaghetti, if desired.   Makes 2 servings.

Per Serving (approx):
Calories 172
Carbohydrate 3 gm

Protein 27 gm
Sodium 261 mg

Fat 5 gm
Cholesterol 70 mg

By 1530, turkeys were being raised domestically in Italy, France and England. So when the Pilgrims and other early settlers arrived on the American shores, they were already familiar with eating turkey.

Florentine Turkey Roll

1 1/4 pounds ground turkey
1 small yellow onion,
   finely chopped
2 cloves garlic, minced
1 egg white
1/4 cup tomato juice
1/2 teaspoon dried basil
1/4 teaspoon cayenne pepper

1 package (10 ounces) frozen
   chopped spinach, thawed and
   squeezed dry
1 medium red bell pepper, cut
   into 1/2-inch-wide strips
1/2 cup grated part-skim mozzarella cheese
Fresh basil (optional)

In large bowl combine turkey, onion, garlic, egg white, juice, dried basil and cayenne. On 11- by 12-inch piece of waxed paper, pat turkey mixture into 10-inch square. Top mixture with spinach, bell pepper strips and cheese. Carefully lift waxed paper and roll up turkey mixture jelly-roll fashion. Seal edges.

On 2- x 10- x 15-inch jelly-roll pan, bake turkey roll, uncovered, at 350 degrees for 40 to 45 minutes or until meat thermometer registers 165 degrees in center of turkey roll.

Remove turkey roll from oven and let stand for 5 minutes before slicing. Place on serving platter and garnish with fresh basil, if desired.

Makes 6 servings.

Per Serving (approx):
Calories 181
Carbohydrate 4 gm

Protein 22 gm
Sodium 207 mg

Fat 9 gm
Cholesterol 74 mg

Turkey and Prosciutto Cordon Bleu

The classic French chicken Cordon Bleu is the mother of this recipe.

1 pound turkey breast cutlets,
   about 1/4 inch thick
2 tablespoons Dijon-style mustard
2 ounces prosciutto ham,
   very thinly sliced
2 ounces Gruyère, Jarlsberg
   or Samsoe cheese, sliced
   (low-fat Gruyère works well)

2 tablespoons chopped Italian
   parsley
1 tablespoon melted butter or
   olive oil
2 tablespoons freshly squeezed
   lemon juice
1 clove garlic, minced
Freshly ground black pepper
   to taste

Pound turkey slices lightly to flatten. Cut turkey into approximately 2-inch by 5-inch rectangles to make 16 pieces, allowing 4 turkey pieces per serving. Lay turkey flat on board and spread lightly with mustard. Cut prosciutto and cheese into 16 strips each. Lay slice of prosciutto and slice of cheese on top of each strip of turkey. Sprinkle with parsley. Roll up and thread bundles onto skewers, allowing 4 per skewer.

Mix together melted butter, lemon juice, garlic and pepper. Brush over turkey bundles. Place skewers on foil-lined rack in broiling pan.

Broil about 4 to 6 inches from heat until golden; turn and baste with butter mixture, broil the other side, allowing 4 to 5 minutes per side to cook through. Makes 4 servings.

Per Serving (approx):
Calories 275
Carbohydrate 2 gm

Protein 32 gm
Sodium 477 mg

Fat 15 gm
Cholesterol 89 mg

*Italian & Mediterranean
Ground Turkey*

Mediterranean Turkey and Eggplant Stir-Fry

1 pound ground turkey
1 cup thinly sliced onion
2 cloves garlic, minced
1 1/2 teaspoons crushed dried, oregano
1 teaspoon crushed dried mint
3/4 teaspoon salt
1/4 teaspoon black pepper
1 tablespoon olive oil

4 cups eggplant cut into 1/2-inch cubes
1 cup green bell pepper cut into 1/2-inch cubes
1 teaspoon sugar
1 medium tomato, peeled and cut into wedges
2 tablespoons crumbled feta cheese

In large nonstick skillet over medium-high heat, sauté turkey, onion, garlic, oregano, mint, salt and pepper in oil for 5 to 6 minutes or until meat is no longer pink. Remove turkey mixture from skillet and set aside.

In same skillet, sauté eggplant and bell pepper for 4 minutes or until vegetables are tender-crisp.

Combine turkey mixture with vegetable mixture. Stir in sugar and tomato. Cook mixture over medium-high heat for 4 to 5 minutes or until heated through. To serve, top turkey mixture with feta cheese.

Makes 4 to 6 servings.

Per Serving (approx):
Calories 257
Carbohydrate 13 gm

Protein 22 gm
Sodium 573 mg

Fat 13 gm
Cholesterol 87 mg

The early settlers brought domesticated turkeys from Europe and soon began cross breeding them with the larger wild turkeys they found here.

Scallopini #1

The name "scallopini" comes from the Italian word for a small square of veal. Turkepini?

1 turkey quarter breast
   (1 3/4 to 2 pounds) or
   equivalent turkey breast slices
1/4 cup flour
1 teaspoon salt
1/4 teaspoon paprika
1/8 teaspoon white pepper
2 tablespoons butter
2 tablespoons oil

6 ounces small mushrooms,
   halved (1 1/2 cups)
1/4 teaspoon minced garlic
3/4 cup dry white wine
1 tablespoon finely chopped
   parsley
1 1/2 teaspoons lemon juice
1/4 teaspoon crumbled dried
   Italian seasoning

Bone and skin turkey breast. Place meat in freezer for about 1 hour or until surface of meat is thoroughly chilled and slightly firm. Cut meat in 1/4-inch slices. Combine flour, salt, paprika and pepper; flour meat slices, shaking off excess.

Heat 1 tablespoon each butter and oil in large skillet. Add layer of meat and brown lightly on both sides. As meat is browned, remove and keep warm. Brown remaining turkey, adding remaining butter and oil as needed.

When all meat is browned, add mushrooms and garlic to skillet and sauté lightly. Return browned turkey to skillet. Combine wine, parsley, lemon juice and Italian seasoning. Pour over all and simmer rapidly for 5 to 10 minutes or until liquid is reduced and turkey is tender.

Makes about 6 servings.

Per Serving (approx):
Calories 336
Carbohydrate 6 gm

Protein 34 gm
Sodium 499 mg

Fat 18 gm
Cholesterol 92 mg

Scallopini #2

This is one of two different scallopini recipes in this cookbook. We've included both because scallopini is such a popular entree, and because turkey adapts so well to it.

4 tablespoons margarine
1/2 pound mushrooms,
   thinly sliced
1/4 cup flour
1/8 teaspoon black pepper

1 pound turkey breast slices or
   breast cutlets
1/4 cup dry sherry
1 tablespoon water
Chopped parsley, for garnish

Melt 2 tablespoons of the margarine in large skillet over medium heat. Add mushrooms and sauté until tender. Remove from pan.

Combine flour and pepper. Coat turkey with flour mixture, shaking off excess. Melt remaining margarine in skillet over medium-high heat; brown turkey on both sides, a few pieces at a time. Allow 1 to 2 minutes per side. Remove from pan.

Slowly add sherry and water to skillet, stirring until liquid is slightly thickened and smooth. Return turkey and mushrooms to pan until just heated through. Arrange on serving platter and garnish with chopped parsley.

Makes 4 servings.

Per Serving (approx):
Calories 253
Carbohydrate 8 gm

Protein 24 gm
Sodium 188 mg

Fat 12 gm
Cholesterol 56 mg

Turkey Shish Kabobs

Turkey is easy to cube and skewer with chunks of vegetables and fruit for the "meat on a stick" that is popular throughout the eastern Mediterranean area.

1 1/4 pounds boneless turkey thighs
3 tablespoons lemon juice
2 cloves garlic, minced
3 tablespoons fresh chopped oregano
   or 1 tablespoon dried
1 1/2 teaspoons fresh chopped basil
   or 2 teaspoons dried

1/4 teaspoon black pepper
1 small red bell pepper, cut
   into 2-inch cubes
1 small green bell pepper, cut
   into 2-inch cubes
1 medium sweet yellow onion,
   cut into 8 wedges

Cut turkey thighs into 2-inch pieces. In large bowl combine lemon juice, garlic and seasonings. Add turkey, bell peppers and onion; toss well to coat with marinade. Cover and refrigerate for 1 hour or longer, turning occasionally.

Prepare lightly greased outdoor grill for cooking. Thread meat and vegetables on skewers, alternating ingredients. Grill, uncovered, 5 to 6 inches over medium-hot coals for 30 to 40 minutes or until meat is cooked through and vegetables are tender, turning occasionally.

Makes 4 or 5 servings.

Per Serving (approx):
Calories 177
Carbohydrate 8 gm

Protein 24 gm
Sodium 68 mg

Fat 6 gm
Cholesterol 70 mg

Turkey meat is one of the very lowest of all meats in caloric content.

Moroccan Turkey Wings

Inexpensive turkey wings achieve elegance when immersed in this Moroccan marinade of vinegar, cumin, mace, sage and other exotic spices, and blended with dried apricots! The cuisine of the Casbah is yours with this exotic dish.

1/3 cup red wine vinegar
2 tablespoons olive oil
3 cloves garlic, minced
1 teaspoon each dried thyme, dried
   sage and ground ginger
1/2 teaspoon ground cumin

1/4 teaspoon ground mace
1 cup quartered dried apricots
Salt and pepper to taste
3 pounds turkey wings
1/4 cup firmly packed
   brown sugar
1/2 cup Madeira wine

In 2-quart shallow ovenproof casserole, combine vinegar, oil, garlic, herbs and spices, apricots, salt and pepper. Add turkey wings and let marinate overnight.

Sprinkle brown sugar and Madeira wine into marinade, then cover and bake for 45 minutes at 350 degrees. Uncover and bake for 45 minutes more or until turkey is tender; turn wings several times during baking. Cut turkey wings in half and serve with rice, if desired.

Makes 4 or 5 servings.

Per Serving (approx):
Calories 783
Carbohydrate 35 gm

Protein 67 gm
Sodium 253 mg

Fat 37 gm
Cholesterol 193 mg

MEXICAN &
SOUTHWESTERN

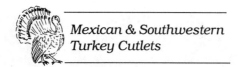

San Antonio Turkey Fajitas

*Traditionally, these fajitas are served with a background of mariachi music
coming from a flat-bottomed boat that is drifting by on the San Antonio River.*

1 pound turkey breast cutlets
   or slices, cut into 1/2-inch
   strips
1/2 cup chopped cilantro
1 clove garlic, minced
1/2 teaspoon ground cumin
1/4 teaspoon chili powder
1/8 teaspoon reduced-sodium
   soy sauce
1/8 teaspoon Worcestershire
   sauce
2 teaspoons oil

1 red bell pepper, cut into slices
   1/8 inch by 2 inches
1 green bell pepper, cut into
   slices 1/8 inch by 2 inches
2 cups thinly sliced onion
   separated into rings
3 tablespoons lime juice
8 flour tortillas
Reduced-calorie sour cream
   (optional)
Guacamole (optional)
Pico de Gallo sauce or salsa
   (optional)

In 1-quart bowl combine turkey, cilantro, garlic, cumin, chili powder,
soy sauce and Worcestershire sauce. Cover and refrigerate for 1 hour.

In large nonstick skillet over medium-high heat, stir-fry turkey mixture
in 1 teaspoon of the oil for 4 minutes or until turkey is no longer pink.
Remove from skillet and set aside.

Add remaining 1 teaspoon oil to skillet. Stir-fry bell peppers for 2 minutes or until slightly softened. Add onion; cook, stirring constantly, until vegetables are tender-crisp.

Return turkey strips to skillet. Pour lime juice over mixture and stir to
combine. Remove from heat and serve immediately wrapped in flour tortillas. Garnish with sour cream, guacamole and Pico de Gallo sauce, if
desired.

Makes 4 servings.

Per Serving (approx):
Calories 420
Carbohydrate 57 gm

Protein 35 gm
Sodium 509 mg

Fat 5 gm
Cholesterol 70 mg

Pavo Fajitas

1 tablespoon each Worcestershire
  sauce, soy sauce and vinegar
1 teaspoon chili powder
1 pound turkey breast slices,
  cut into 1-inch strips
1 clove garlic, finely chopped

1 tablespoon oil
1 medium onion, sliced
1 green bell pepper, sliced
Flour tortillas, avocado slices,
  sour cream and chopped
  cilantro

In medium bowl combine Worcestershire sauce, soy sauce, vinegar and chili powder. Add turkey; let marinate for 15 minutes. In medium skillet over medium-high heat, cook turkey in hot oil for 5 to 7 minutes or until turkey is no longer pink.

Remove turkey from skillet. Cook onion and bell pepper until tender-crisp. Return turkey to skillet; heat through. Serve with tortillas, avocado, sour cream and cilantro.   Makes 4 servings.

> *Per Serving (approx):*
> Calories 454   Protein 34 gm   Fat 15 gm
> Carbohydrate 47 gm   Sodium 595 mg   Cholesterol 61 mg

Veracruz Turkey Slices

1 pound turkey breast slices
1 tablespoon oil
2 tomatoes, chopped
2 green onions, sliced
1 garlic clove, finely chopped
1 can (4 ounces) diced green chiles

1 teaspoon chopped cilantro
1/2 teaspoon dried crushed
  oregano leaves
Salt and pepper to taste
1 avocado, sliced

In large skillet over medium heat, cook turkey slices in hot oil for 4 to 6 minutes on each side or until turkey is no longer pink. Remove slices and keep warm.

In skillet simmer tomatoes, onions, garlic, chilies, cilantro, oregano, salt and pepper over medium-high heat for 7 minutes or until tomatoes soften and liquid evaporates; stir frequently. Spoon sauce over turkey slices. Garnish with avocado.   Makes 4 servings.

> *Per Serving (approx):*
> Calories 303   Protein 26 gm   Fat 18 gm
> Carbohydrate 9 gm   Sodium 490 mg   Cholesterol 61 mg

Mexican & Southwestern
Turkey Cutlets

Turkey Fajitas

1 cup thinly sliced onion
3 tablespoons oil
2 tablespoons lime juice
2 cloves garlic, minced
1/2 teaspoon dried oregano
1/2 teaspoon ground cumin
1/2 teaspoon chili powder

1 pound turkey breast cutlets,
   cut into strips
1/2 cup green or yellow bell pepper cut into strips
1/4 cup chopped cilantro or
   parsley
8 small flour tortillas, warmed
Sour cream (optional)

In shallow dish combine onion, 2 tablespoons of the oil, the lime juice, garlic, oregano, cumin and chili powder. Add turkey; cover and let marinate for 1 hour.

In large skillet over medium-high heat, warm remaining oil. Add turkey and marinade, bell pepper and cilantro. Sauté for 5 minutes, stirring often, until turkey is no longer pink and vegetables are tender-crisp. To serve, roll turkey mixture in warmed tortillas; garnish with sour cream, if desired.   Makes 4 servings.

Per Serving (approx):
Calories 383
Carbohydrate 29 gm

Protein 31 gm
Sodium 363 mg

Fat 16 gm
Cholesterol 70 mg

The turkey is a native of Mexico, and was introduced into Europe by the expedition of Cortez to the new world, and called by his followers the 'American' or 'Mexican' peacock from its habit of strutting.

Baked Chilies Rellenos

Mexico has been cooking with turkey for several thousand years, so they should know how to do it.

4 cans (4 ounces each) whole
   green chilies, drained, rinsed,
   seeds removed, slit on one
   side and opened flat
Nonstick vegetable cooking spray
1 package (4 ounces) reduced-
   fat Monterey jack cheese, cut
   into 1/2-inch strips
2 cups cooked turkey cut into
   1/2-inch strips (about 3/4 pound)

1/2 cup flour
1/2 teaspoon baking powder
Salt to taste
1/2 cup skim milk
3 eggs
2/3 cup shredded nonfat
   Cheddar cheese

Arrange chilies in 11- x 7 1/2- x 1 1/2-inch baking dish lightly coated with vegetable cooking spray. Fill each chile half with cheese and turkey. Fold over edges of chilies and place seamside down in dish.

In medium bowl combine flour, baking powder and salt. Whisk together milk and eggs. Slowly add egg mixture to flour mixture, beating until smooth. Pour over prepared chilies.

Bake at 450 degrees for 15 minutes. Turn off oven and remove casserole. Sprinkle cheddar cheese over top and return to hot oven for 1 minute to melt cheese. Serve immediately. Makes 6 servings.

Per Serving (approx):
Calories 238
Carbohydrate 12 gm

Protein 30 gm
Sodium 434 mg

Fat 7 gm
Cholesterol 145 mg

Turkey Leg Tacos with Green Sauce

3 1/2 pounds turkey
  drumsticks (about 6)
1 medium onion, chopped
1 cup chopped celery with leaves
1 clove garlic, crushed

Salt to taste
1 teaspoon black pepper
18 corn tortillas
Sour cream, for accompaniment

In large soup pot, combine turkey drumsticks, onion, celery and garlic. Cover with water and add salt and pepper. Bring to a low boil; reduce heat to low and cover pot. Cook until drumsticks are fork tender, about 1 1/2 hours. Remove from heat and strain off broth. (Freeze broth for another use.)

When turkey is cool enough to handle, remove meat from bones. Discard bones and skin. Shred meat and set aside. Prepare Green Sauce.

Add turkey to Green Sauce. Heat through and add salt to taste.

To make tacos, wrap tortillas in foil and heat in oven. Spoon a little turkey mixture in middle of each soft, warm tortilla and fold over. Serve sour cream at the table. Allow 3 tacos per person.

Makes 6 servings.

GREEN SAUCE:
In blender or food processor, combine 2 cans (18 ounces each) Mexican green tomatoes (tomatillos), 3 or 4 fresh serrano chilies, seeded, and 1/3 cup well-packed cilantro leaves. Blend or process until smooth; set aside. In 12-inch skillet, heat 2 tablespoons corn oil; sauté 1 small diced onion with 2 large cloves minced garlic until onion is transparent. Pour in tomatillo mixture.

Per Serving (approx):
Calories 744	*Protein 62 gm*	*Fat 31 gm*
Carbohydrate 55 gm	*Sodium 354 mg*	*Cholesterol 165 mg*

Rio Grande Turkey

This is a super burrito!

2 pounds turkey thighs
1 can (8 ounces) tomato sauce
1 can (4 ounces) chopped green
   chilies
1/4 cup chopped onion
2 tablespoons chili powder

2 tablespoons Worcestershire
   sauce
1/4 teaspoon garlic powder
8 flour tortillas, warmed
Chopped lettuce
1/2 cup sour cream

Place turkey in skillet with tomato sauce, chilies, onion, chili powder, Worcestershire sauce and garlic powder. Bring to a boil; reduce heat, cover and simmer for 2 hours. Remove cover; cook for 15 minutes more.

Remove turkey from bones; shred, using 2 forks. Return turkey to tomato mixture and stir to combine. Spoon on tortilla with chopped lettuce; roll up to serve. Top with sour cream.   Makes 4 servings.

SLOW-COOKER METHOD:
Rinse turkey; remove skin. Place in slow cooker with tomato sauce, chilies, onion, chili powder, Worcestershire sauce and garlic powder. Cover. Cook on low setting for 10 hours. Remove turkey and continue cooking, uncovered, on high setting for 30 minutes more. Shred turkey and return to tomato mixture. Serve as above.

Per Serving (approx):
Calories 858
Carbohydrate 89 gm

Protein 65 gm
Sodium 1493 mg

Fat 27 gm
Cholesterol 151 mg

Empanadas Grande

These are traditionally made with tortillas, but this version uses pie crust, so if you wish, you can call them meat pies. Regardless of what you want to call them, make them.

1 pound ground turkey
1 clove garlic, minced
1 cup chopped onion
1/2 cup chopped green bell pepper
1 tablespoon oil
2 cups chopped tomatoes
1 tablespoon dried parsley flakes
1 teaspoon dried cilantro

1 teaspoon dried cumin
1/2 teaspoon dried oregano
1/2 teaspoon red pepper flakes
1/8 teaspoon black pepper
1 package (15 ounces)
  refrigerated pie crusts
1 egg white, beaten

In large skillet over medium-high heat, sauté turkey, garlic, onion and bell pepper in oil until turkey is no longer pink. Stir in tomato, parsley, cilantro, cumin, oregano, red pepper flakes and black pepper. Reduce heat to medium and cook for about 15 minutes or until most liquid is reduced, stirring occasionally.

Spray baking sheet with nonstick oil. Unfold one pie crust in center of baking sheet. Carefully spread half of turkey mixture to within 1 inch of edge of half of pie crust.

Brush pie crust edge with egg white. Encase meat by folding other half of pie crust over meat mixture. Using fork, press edges of crust together and pierce top of crust to make holes to allow steam to escape.

Repeat with remaining turkey mixture and pie crust.

Bake in preheated 400 degree oven for 20 to 25 minutes or until pastry is golden brown. To serve, cut each empanada into 4 wedges.

Makes 8 servings.

Per Serving (approx):
Calories 353
Carbohydrate 28 gm

Protein 13 gm
Sodium 374 mg

Fat 21 gm
Cholesterol 38 mg

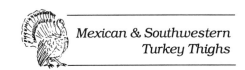

Turkey in Salsa

Delicious! May be served over pasta or rice, or on a bed of chopped lettuce.

6 pounds turkey thighs
  (approximately 4)
1 onion, coarsely chopped
2 stalks celery, coarsely
  chopped
1/2 cup loosely packed parsley
2 dried red chilies
1 whole clove
1 onion, finely chopped
3 cloves garlic, minced
3 tablespoons oil
2 tablespoons chili powder

1 cup very finely ground
  almonds
1/2 cup very finely ground
  peanuts
1 can (4 ounces) chopped
  green chilies
1/4 cup chopped cilantro
Sour cream, shredded Monterey jack or Cheddar cheese,
  green salsa and shredded
  warm tortillas, for garnish

Place turkey, coarsely chopped onion and celery, parsley, dried chilies and clove in large pot; cover with water. Bring to a boil; reduce heat and simmer for about 1 hour or until tender. Remove turkey from stock; let cool. Remove meat from bones; shred in bite-sized pieces. Discard skin. Strain stock; reduce to 1 quart.

Sauté finely chopped onion and minced garlic in oil until soft; stir in chili powder, ground nuts and chopped chilies. Sauté for 1 minute more. Stir in stock; simmer until smooth and thickened. Add turkey and cilantro.

Serve with sour cream, shredded cheese, salsa and shredded warm tortillas.   Makes 6 to 8 servings.

Per Serving (approx) excluding garnish:
Calories 985   *Protein 103 gm*   *Fat 48 gm*
Carbohydrate 28 gm   *Sodium 886 mg*   *Cholesterol 279 mg*

Enchiladas Santa Fe Style

2 tablespoons oil
1/2 to 3/4 cup chopped onion
1 to 1 1/4 pounds ground turkey
1 teaspoon chili powder
1/2 teaspoon ground cumin
1/2 teaspoon salt

2 cans (10 ounces each) enchila-
    da sauce (mild or hot to taste)
12 corn tortillas (6 inches)
1 cup shredded Monterey jack
    cheese
Sour cream or guacamole
    (optional)

In large skillet over medium heat, warm oil. Add onion and sauté for 5 minutes or until translucent. Add turkey, chili powder, cumin and salt; sauté for about 5 minutes or until meat is cooked through.

Transfer meat mixture to bowl and set aside. Into same skillet pour enchilada sauce; heat through.

Dip 4 tortillas in sauce to soften; place alongside eachother on lightly oiled or nonstick 12- x 14-inch jelly-roll pan and top evenly with half the turkey mixture. Dip 4 more tortillas into sauce and place on top of turkey; add another layer of turkey mixture. Dip remaining tortillas into sauce and place on top of turkey. Spoon a little sauce over each enchilada stack and sprinkle with cheese.

Bake enchiladas in preheated 375 degree oven for 20 minutes or until cheese is melted. To serve, top each enchilada stack with dollop of sour cream or guacamole, if desired.

Makes 4 to 6 servings.

*Per Serving (approx):
Calories 425
Carbohydrate 32 gm*

*Protein 27 gm
Sodium 800 mg*

*Fat 21 gm
Cholesterol 86 mg*

*Mexican & Southwestern
Ground Turkey*

Tex-Mex Potato Boats

This is one of those recipes that you can prepare a day or two in advance and pop in the oven for 15 minutes when you're ready to serve. It might be a good idea to double or triple this recipe and freeze the extras.

2 potatoes, baked
1/2 pound ground turkey
1/2 cup chopped onion
1 clove garlic, minced
1 can (8 ounces) stewed
   tomatoes

1 teaspoon chili powder
1/4 teaspoon dried oregano
1/4 teaspoon ground cumin
1/4 teaspoon red pepper flakes
1/4 teaspoon salt
1/2 cup grated reduced-fat
   Cheddar cheese

Slice potatoes in half lengthwise. Scoop out center of potato to within 1/4 inch of potato skin. Reserve potato for other use.

In medium skillet over medium-high heat, combine turkey, onion and garlic. Cook for 5 minutes or until turkey is no longer pink. Drain meat juices if necessary. Add tomatoes, chili powder, oregano, cumin, red pepper flakes and salt. Cook for 15 minutes or until most liquid has evaporated.

Spoon turkey mixture into potato shells and sprinkle with cheese. Arrange on 9- x 13- x 2-inch jelly-roll pan and bake in 375 degree oven for 15 minutes or until cheese melts.   **Makes 4 servings.**

Per Serving (approx):
Calories 209
Carbohydrate 20 gm

Protein 16 gm
Sodium 446 mg

Fat 7 gm
Cholesterol 51 mg

Mexican & Southwestern
Turkey Breast & Rolled Roasts

Turkey Molé

If you've never used chocolate with poultry before, you are in for a delightful surprise with this version of a traditional molé recipe.

1 turkey half breast (about 3 pounds)
3 quarts water
1 can (14 1/2 ounces) whole
 tomatoes
1/2 cup chopped onion
1/2 ounce unsweetened
 chocolate, melted
1/4 cup diced green chilies
1/4 cup cornmeal

1 tablespoon peanut butter
1 teaspoon chopped cilantro
1/2 teaspoon crushed red
 pepper flakes
1/4 teaspoon ground cinnamon
1/8 teaspoon ground cloves
1 clove garlic
Salt to taste
1/2 cup raisins

Poach turkey in water for 1 1/2 hours; drain and reserve 2 cups liquid. Blend remaining ingredients, except raisins, in blender for 30 seconds. Pour sauce over turkey; stir in raisins, cover and simmer for 20 minutes.

Makes 4 to 6 servings.

Per Serving (approx):
Calories 185
Carbohydrate 31 gm

Protein 5 gm
Sodium 339 mg

Fat 5 gm
Cholesterol 1 mg

It is quite reasonable to presume that the Mexican or southern turkey was the first introduced throughout Europe. Later, when the pilgrims settled here and found that the Indians were domesticating them and that they were numerous in the woods, they were no doubt used as a bird of feast, owing to their size and numbers. It was not until the Revolutionary War that the feast became national.

Spicy Lime and Cilantro Turkey Fajitas

The name of this recipe says it all!

1 tablespoon paprika
1/2 teaspoon onion salt
1/2 teaspoon garlic powder
1/2 teaspoon cayenne pepper
1/2 teaspoon fennel seeds
  1/2 teaspoon dried thyme

1/4 teaspoon white pepper
1 pound turkey breast tenderloins, butterflied
1 lime
4 pitas, cut in half, or 8 taco
  shells

In shallow, flat dish combine paprika, onion salt, garlic powder, cayenne pepper, fennel seeds, thyme and white pepper. Rub mixture over turkey; cover and refrigerate 1 hour. Prepare Sour Cream Sauce; refrigerate.

Prepare grill for direct-heat cooking. Grill turkey for 5 to 6 minutes or until meat thermometer registers 170 degrees in thickest part of tenderloin. Turn tenderloin after half of grilling time. Continue to grill. Remove to clean serving plate, and squeeze lime juice over tenderloins. Slice into 1/4-inch slices.

To serve, fill each pita half with turkey and top with Sour Cream Sauce. If desired, add shredded lettuce.   Makes 4 servings.

SOUR CREAM SAUCE:
In small bowl combine 1 cup fat-free sour cream, 1/4 thinly sliced green onion, 1/4 cup finely chopped cilantro, 1 can (4 ounces) green chilies, drained, 1 plum tomato, finely chopped, 1/2 teaspoon black pepper and 1/4 teaspoon cayenne pepper. Cover and refrigerate until ready to use.

Per Serving (approx):
Calories 371
Carbohydrate 46 gm

Protein 36 gm
Sodium 841 mg

Fat 3 gm
Cholesterol 59 mg

Tex-Mex Turkey Fillets

1 pound turkey breast
   fillets
1 tablespoon margarine
1/2 cup chopped green bell
   pepper
3/4 teaspoon chili powder

1 can (16 ounces) stewed
   tomatoes, chopped
1 can (4 ounces) sliced
   mushrooms, drained
3 green onions, thinly sliced
1 clove garlic, finely chopped

In large skillet over medium heat, cook turkey fillets in melted margarine for 8 to 11 minutes on each side or until turkey is no longer pink. Add remaining ingredients. Simmer, uncovered, for 5 to 7 minutes.

Makes 3 or 4 servings.

Per Serving (approx):
Calories 235
Carbohydrate 10 gm

Protein 26 gm
Sodium 376 mg

Fat 10 gm
Cholesterol 61 mg

Scientists recognize 5 subspecies within the United States. The Eastern Wild Turkey, *Meleagris gallipavos silvestris*, once extended from southern Maine and New Hampshire southward to northern Florida and westward to Eastern Texas and South Dakota.

Other subspecies include the Florida Turkey, the Rio Grande Turkey, Merrian's Turkey, and Gould's Turkey found only in the Southern tip of New Mexico. In addition, south of the border there are two other subspecies–Moore's Turkey and the Southern Mexican Turkey, *Meleagris gallopavo gallopavo*, the ancestor of our modern breeds.

Southwestern Turkey Hash

1 pound ground turkey
1 small onion, chopped
1 tablespoon oil
3 cups frozen potatoes O'Brien
Salt to taste

1/4 teaspoon black pepper
1 cup salsa
Sliced green onion (optional)
Sliced ripe olives (optional)

In large nonstick skillet over medium heat, sauté turkey and onion in oil for 5 to 6 minutes or until turkey is no longer pink.

Stir in potatoes, salt and pepper. Increase heat to medium-high and cook for 5 minutes, stirring occasionally. Stir in salsa. Continue cooking for 8 to 10 minutes or until potatoes are lightly browned, stirring occasionally. To serve, garnish with green onion and olives, if desired.

Makes 4 servings.

Per Serving (approx):
Calories 302
Carbohydrate 31 gm

Protein 24 gm
Sodium 467 mg

Fat 9 gm
Cholesterol 82 mg

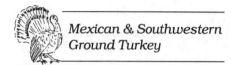

Turkey Picadillo #1

Usually pork or beef are used to make this dish, but we think you'll like our turkey version.

2 tablespoons oil
1 to 1 1/4 pounds ground turkey
1 large onion, diced
1 green bell pepper, diced
1 clove garlic, minced
1 can (16 ounces) tomatoes,
   undrained

1/4 cup raisins
1/4 teaspoon ground cinnamon
1/4 cup slivered almonds,
   toasted
1/4 cup sliced black olives

In large skillet over medium-high heat, warm oil. Add turkey, onion, bell pepper and garlic. Cook, stirring frequently, until turkey turns light brown. Drain off fat.

Add tomatoes and then juice, raisins and cinnamon; stir. Bring to a boil; reduce heat to medium-low, cover and simmer for 10 minutes. Stir in almonds and olives and heat through.   Makes 5 servings.

Per Serving (approx):
Calories 319	*Protein 23 gm*	*Fat 18 gm*
Carbohydrate 20 gm	*Sodium 724 mg*	*Cholesterol 65 mg*

Turkey meat is lowest in cholesterol of all red meats and poultry.

Turkey Picadillo #2

This version is quite different from Turkey Picadillo #1.

1 pound ground turkey
1/2 cup chopped onion
1/4 cup chopped green bell pepper
2 cloves garlic, minced
1 tablespoon oil
1 teaspoon sugar
1/2 teaspoon ground cinnamon
1/2 teaspoon ground cumin

1/4 teaspoon ground cloves
1 can (14 1/2 ounces) stewed
  tomatoes
1 cup chopped Granny Smith
  apple
1/4 cup raisins
2 tablespoons thinly sliced
  pimiento stuffed olives

In large skillet over medium-high heat, sauté turkey, onion, bell pepper and garlic in oil until turkey is no longer pink.

Stir in remaining ingredients. Bring to a boil. Reduce heat, cover and simmer for 15 to 20 minutes.

Serve over rice and top with toasted almonds, if desired.

Makes 4 servings.

Per Serving (approx):
Calories 280
Carbohydrate 23 gm

Protein 22 gm
Sodium 471 mg

Fat 12 gm
Cholesterol 76 mg

Mexico City Turkey Breast

2 tablespoons flour
1 package (1 1/2 ounces) taco
  seasoning mix
1 1/4 to 2 pounds turkey breast,
  boned and skinned
3 tablespoons oil
1 cup chopped onion
3/4 cup diced green bell pepper

1 can (16 ounces) tomatoes
1 can (15 1/2 ounces) dark red
  kidney beans, drained
1/4 pound mushrooms,
  sliced
1 cup red wine
1 teaspoon sugar

In plastic bag combine flour and half of taco seasoning. Place turkey in bag and shake to coat. Remove turkey from the bag. Save the flour mixture. In large skillet over medium-high heat, sauté coated turkey in 2 tablespoons of the oil until lightly browned on all sides. Transfer turkey to 2-quart casserole.

Add remaining oil to skillet and sauté onion and bell pepper for 5 minutes. Add remaining flour mixture and taco seasoning.

Fold in tomatoes, beans, mushrooms, wine and sugar. Bring to a boil. Pour mixture over turkey breast in casserole. Cover and bake in preheated 350 degree oven for 40 to 45 minutes. Slice turkey breast and serve with sauce.   Makes 8 servings.

Per Serving (approx):
Calories 223
Carbohydrate 20 gm

Protein 21 gm
Sodium 649 mg

Fat 7 gm
Cholesterol 41 mg

CASSEROLES & MEAT LOAVES

Turkey and Asparagus Terrine

This old English recipe originally called for boiled tongue. Substituting turkey makes it a truly elegant dish.

1 pound ground turkey, minced
1/2 pound ham thickly sliced
   and diced
2 green onions, thinly sliced
1/3 cup dry white wine
1 egg, beaten

4 tablespoons cottage cheese or
   Greek yogurt
Pinch of ground allspice
Salt and pepper to taste
1/2 pound thin asparagus

Mix together all ingredients except asparagus. Line base of 1 1/2-pint loaf pan with foil. Cut asparagus to fit bottom of pan. Layer half of asparagus neatly in alternate directions. Spoon half of turkey mixture on top. Cover with remaining asparagus, then with remainder of turkey mixture. Smooth top. Cover with foil and place in roasting pan half filled with boiling water.

Cook at 325 degrees for about 1 hour. Terrine is cooked when mixture shrinks from sides of pan. Let cool, then turn out terrine. Slice.

Makes 4 servings.

Per Serving (approx):
Calories 310
Carbohydrate 11 gm

Protein 33 gm
Sodium 723 mg

Fat 13 gm
Cholesterol 155 mg

Although turkeys are native to the Americas, they were not domesticated here. In 1498 explorers from the Old World took turkeys from America to Spain. The domestication process began here. From Spain the turkey spread across Europe and was introduced into England between 1524 and 1541.

Rice-n-Turkey Casserole

2 cups cooked long-grain white
   or brown rice
2 cups cubed cooked turkey
2 medium zucchini, cut into
   1/4-inch rounds
3/4 cup shredded Monterey
   jack cheese

1 can (4 ounces) chopped green
   chilies, drained
2 medium tomatoes, halved
   lengthwise, then sliced
   crosswise

Prepare topping. Spread rice in greased 2-quart baking dish. Layer turkey, zucchini, cheese, chilies and tomatoes over rice. Spread topping over casserole. Sprinkle with cheese and bake at 350 degrees for 30 minutes.   Makes 6 servings.

TOPPING:
Combine 1 cup sour cream, 1/3 cup chopped onion, 1/2 teaspoon salt, 1/4 teaspoon dried oregano and black pepper to taste.

Per Serving (approx):
Calories 523   *Protein 27 gm*   *Fat 20 gm*
Carbohydrate 59 gm   *Sodium 679 mg*   *Cholesterol 76 mg*

Meat Loaf Alaska

If you've ever had Baked Alaska (an ice cream loaf with a baked meringue frosting), you'll recognize this meat loaf with a mashed potato frosting as a similar concoction.

1 pound ground turkey
1 egg
1/2 cup seasoned bread crumbs
1/4 cup water
1 tablespoon dried onion
2 tablespoons catsup
1 tablespoon chopped green
  bell pepper

1/8 teaspoon black pepper
1 teaspoon prepared horseradish
1/2 teaspoon prepared mustard
4 servings instant mashed
  potatoes
1/2 cup grated cheese

Combine turkey, egg, bread crumbs, water, dried onion, catsup, bell pepper, black pepper, horseradish and mustard. Place in lightly greased 4 1/2- x 8 1/2- x 2 5/8-inch loaf pan, or shape in loaf form and place into lightly greased 1-inch baking dish.

Bake in preheated 350 degree oven for 45 to 60 minutes or until meat is no longer pink in center. Drain excess liquid. Prepare mashed potatoes and frost loaf with them. Sprinkle with cheese and return to oven. Bake for about 5 minutes or until cheese melts. Makes 4 servings.

Per Serving (approx):
Calories 237
Carbohydrate 13 gm

Protein 24 gm
Sodium 303 mg

Fat 10 gm
Cholesterol 136 mg

Turkey and White Bean Casserole

2 turkey drumsticks (about
   2 3/4 pounds total)
1 1/4 cups water
1 cup chopped onion
1 bay leaf
Salt to taste
1/2 teaspoon dried thyme

2 cans (16 ounces each) white
   beans
1/4 cup tomato paste
4 smoky link sausages
   (6 ounces total), preferably
   made from turkey, halved

Place turkey drumsticks in large kettle with water, onion, bay leaf, salt and thyme. Bring to a boil. Cover tightly, reduce heat to low and simmer until meat is tender, about 1 1/2 to 1 3/4 hours. Let cool sufficiently to handle, then remove skin and bones, pulling meat off in chunks. Cut meat into 2-inch pieces. Boil down remaining cooking liquid to 3/4 cup.

Drain 1 can of beans and discard 1/2 cup liquid. Combine with the second can of beans and remaining liquid, reduced turkey cooking liquid and tomato paste; mix well. Add turkey chunks and halved sausages. Turn into 2 1/2-quart baking dish. Cover and bake in 350 degree oven for 45 minutes, uncovering during last 15 minutes.

Makes 6 servings.

Per Serving (approx):
Calories 404
Carbohydrate 44 gm

Protein 37 gm
Sodium 436 mg

Fat 9 gm
Cholesterol 69 mg

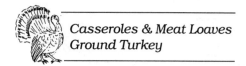

Mushroom-Stuffed Meat Loaf

1 pound ground turkey
1 egg
1/2 cup seasoned bread crumbs
1/4 cup water
1 tablespoon dried onion
2 tablespoons catsup

1 tablespoon chopped green bell
   pepper
1/8 teaspoon black pepper
1 teaspoon prepared horseradish
1/2 teaspoon prepared mustard

Prepare Mushroom Stuffing. Combine all meat loaf ingredients. Press half of meat mixture into lightly greased loaf pan. Top with 2 cups Mushroom Stuffing or your favorite vegetable stuffing, and spread remaining meat mixture over stuffing.

Bake in preheated 350 degree oven for 45 to 60 minutes or until meat is no longer pink in center. Makes 4 servings.

MUSHROOM STUFFING:
In small skillet melt 1 tablespoon margarine over medium heat. Add 1/4 cup chopped onion and 1/4 pound sliced mushrooms; sauté for 2 minutes. Toss in 2 slices whole wheat bread (torn into cubes), 1 teaspoon dried parsley flakes, 1/4 teaspoon dried thyme and dash of salt and pepper. Stir constantly; cook until bread is lightly browned.

Per Serving (approx):
Calories 313
Carbohydrate 22 gm

Protein 26 gm
Sodium 510 mg

Fat 14 gm
Cholesterol 137 mg

Turkey Noodle Dandy

You can make this casserole early in the day, then heat just before serving.

1 package (8 ounces) noodles
1 pound ground turkey
1 tablespoon butter
2 cans (8 ounces each) tomato sauce
1 cup cottage cheese

1/4 cup sour cream
1 package (8 ounces)
  cream cheese, softened
1/3 cup chopped green onion
2 tablespoons butter, melted

Cook noodles according to directions on package; drain. Meanwhile, sauté turkey in butter, stirring, until no longer pink. Stir in tomato sauce. Set aside.

In bowl combine cottage cheese, sour cream, cream cheese, and onion. In a lightly greased 2-quart casserole spread half the noodles; cover with cheese mixture, then with remaining noodles. Drizzle melted butter over all; top with turkey-tomato mixture. The casserole can be prepared ahead and refrigerated at this point.

If refrigerated, bake, uncovered, at 375 degrees for about 40 minutes. Or bake immediately after mixing at 375 degrees for 30 minutes.

Makes 6 servings.

Per Serving (approx):
Calories 378
Carbohydrate 8 gm

Protein 22 gm
Sodium 840 mg

Fat 28 gm
Cholesterol 121 mg

A Presidential Welcome

Q. Does the Federation do anything special to recognize Thanksgiving?

A. Since 1948 the National Turkey Federation has presented a live turkey and two dressed turkeys to the President of the United States.

Turkey Wings with Couscous Dressing

Inexpensive turkey wings served with couscous, the North African grain, results in an exotic dish worthy of becoming a favorite "new dish" in your home.

6 turkey wings
1 1/2 cups turkey or chicken
  broth
2 tablespoons butter
1 cup couscous
1/2 each red and green bell,
  pepper chopped

1/3 cup chopped onion
1 clove garlic, minced
2 tablespoons oil
1 egg, lightly beaten
Salt and pepper to taste
1/4 cup lemon juice
3 tablespoons honey

Fold turkey wings into triangles. Poach turkey wings in enough water to cover for 30 minutes. Drain the wings and reserve 1/2 cup liquid.

Bring broth and butter to a boil. Add couscous, cover and remove from heat; let stand for 5 minutes. Sauté bell peppers, onion and garlic in oil. Add to couscous with egg. Season to taste with salt and pepper.

Place turkey wings in baking dish; spoon couscous mixture into cavities. Mix lemon juice, honey and reserved poaching liquid; spoon over wings. Bake, covered, for 1 hour at 350 degrees, basting occasionally with pan juices. Uncover; bake for 15 minutes more. Makes 6 servings.

Per Serving (approx):
Calories 649
Carbohydrate 35 gm

Protein 55 gm
Sodium 593 mg

Fat 32 gm
Cholesterol 191 mg

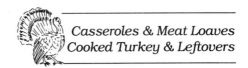

Turkey and Wild Rice Bake

This very simple recipe makes a very elegant dish. All you need is a can opener and an hour and twenty minutes. Or you may want to make it the previous day and warm it up before serving.

1 package (6 ounces) wild and
   white rice mix, uncooked
2 1/3 cups water
1 can (4 ounces) mushrooms,
   drained
1 can (14 ounces) whole
   artichoke hearts, quartered

1 jar (2 ounces) chopped
   pimiento, drained
2 cups cooked turkey, cubed
1 cup shredded Swiss cheese

In 2-quart casserole dish combine rice with seasoning packet, water, mushrooms, artichokes, pimiento and turkey. Cover and bake in pre-heated 350 degree oven for 1 hour and 15 minutes or until liquid is absorbed.

Top casserole with cheese and bake, uncovered, for 5 to 10 minutes or until cheese is melted and golden brown.   Makes 6 servings.

Per Serving (approx):
Calories 270
Carbohydrate 25 gm

Protein 24 gm
Sodium 572 mg

Fat 8 gm
Cholesterol 53 mg

Cashew-n-Cheese Cutlets

1/2 pound turkey breast cutlets
  or slices
1/8 teaspoon black pepper
2 ounces Swiss cheese, sliced
2 teaspoons seasoned bread
  crumbs

2 tablespoons white wine
  Worcestershire sauce
1 tablespoon coarsely
  chopped cashews

Lightly sprinkle cutlets with pepper. Place cheese slice on each cutlet. Roll up cutlet jelly-roll style to encase cheese. Carefully coat each cutlet roll in bread crumbs. In 14-ounce oval casserole dish, arrange cutlet rolls seam side down. Spoon Worcestershire sauce over cutlets. Bake in preheated 375 degree oven for 10 minutes.

Baste cutlets with pan drippings. Sprinkle cashews over top. Bake for 5 minutes or until turkey is no longer pink in center.   Makes 2 servings.

Per Serving (approx):
Calories 278
Carbohydrate 6 gm

Protein 36 gm
Sodium 343 mg

Fat 12 gm
Cholesterol 97 mg

Raising Turkeys

Modern turkey production methods have shortened the time it takes to bring turkeys to maturity. The hen usually takes 16 weeks and weighs 16—18 pounds when processed. This compares to the tom who takes 19 weeks to get to a market weight of 28—30 pounds.

Individual Turkey Loaves with Corn Bread Stuffing

1 pound ground turkey
1/2 cup quick-cooking oats
1/4 cup water
1 teaspoon dried Italian seasoning
1 package (1 1/2 ounces) dried
   vegetable soup mix

3/4 cup corn bread stuffing mix
1/4 cup plus 2 tablespoons
   boiling water
Nonstick vegetable cooking spray

In medium bowl combine turkey, oats, water, Italian seasoning and soup mix.

In small bowl combine stuffing mix and boiling water; cover and set aside.

Coat 4 custard cups (6 ounces each) with vegetable cooking spray. In bottom of each cup, press 1/3 cup turkey mixture. Top with 3 tablespoons stuffing mixture. Press another 1/3 cup turkey mixture over stuffing, sealing all edges.

Place custard cups on baking sheet and bake in 350 degree oven for 30 minutes or until turkey is no longer pink in center.

To serve, loosen edges of loaves with knife and invert custard cups onto serving plate. If desired, serve with cranberry/orange relish.

Makes 4 servings.

Per Serving (approx):
Calories 304
Carbohydrate 27 gm

Protein 25 gm
Sodium 1027 mg

Fat 10 gm
Cholesterol 83 mg

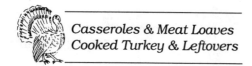

Creamy Creole Turkey Bake

2/3 cup chopped onion
2/3 cup chopped celery
1/4 cup chopped green onion
1/3 cup chopped green bell pepper
1 clove garlic, minced
1 tablespoon margarine
1/4 pound mushrooms, sliced
4 ounces light cream cheese,
  softened

1 can (8 ounces) reduced-
  sodium stewed tomatoes,
  drained
1 1/2 teaspoons creole
  seasoning
4 ounces fettuccine, cooked
2 cups cooked turkey cut in
  1/2-inch cubes
1/4 cup grated Parmesan cheese

In medium nonstick skillet over medium-high heat, sauté onion, celery, green onion, bell pepper and garlic in margarine for 4 to 5 minutes or until vegetables are tender-crisp. Add mushrooms and sauté for 2 minutes. Remove from heat.

In medium bowl blend cream cheese, tomatoes and creole seasoning. Fold in vegetable mixture, fettuccine and turkey.

Pour mixture into 9-inch-square pan sprayed with vegetable cooking spray. Sprinkle cheese over top and bake at 325 degrees for 30 minutes or until bubbly.   Makes 4 servings.

Per Serving (approx):
Calories 380
Carbohydrate 32 gm

Protein 32 gm
Sodium 691 mg

Fat 14 gm
Cholesterol 100 mg

Ribbon Turkey Loaf

The green of the vegetables, the cream color of the cheese, and the pink of the meat, when cut across the loaf, gives you a ribbon that makes this meatloaf into an elegant pâté.

1 pound ground turkey
1/2 cup uncooked instant rice
1 small onion, finely chopped
1 egg, lightly beaten
1 tablespoon instant beef bouillon
1 teaspoon dried thyme
1/2 teaspoon garlic powder

3 slices (1 ounce each) Swiss
    cheese
1 package (10 ounces) frozen
    chopped spinach or
    broccoli, thawed and
    well drained

Combine turkey, rice, onion, egg, bouillon and seasonings. Spoon half the mixture into lightly greased 9- x 5-inch loaf pan. Top with 1 slice of cheese, spinach, another slice of cheese and remaining turkey mixture. Bake in 350 degree oven for 40 minutes. Top with remaining slice of cheese. Bake 5 minutes more or until cheese melts.   Makes 6 servings.

Per Serving (approx):
Calories 270
Carbohydrate 19 gm

Protein 22 gm
Sodium 262 mg

Fat 11 gm
Cholesterol 103 mg

Sweet-n-Sour Barbecue Turkey Meatballs

1 pound ground turkey
1/2 cup unseasoned dry bread
  crumbs
2 tablespoons Worcestershire sauce
2 tablespoons oil

2/3 cup barbecue sauce
1/4 cup apricot jam
2 tablespoons each crushed
  pineapple and chopped green
  bell pepper

Combine turkey, bread crumbs and Worcestershire sauce. Shape into small meatballs, about 1 tablespoon of meat each. In large skillet heat oil. Cook meatballs, turning frequently, for 10 minutes. Combine remaining ingredients and pour over meatballs. Reduce heat to low and heat through.   Makes about 30 meatballs, 6 servings.

Per Serving (approx):
Calories 240
Carbohydrate 20 gm

Protein 15 gm
Sodium 367 mg

Fat 11 gm
Cholesterol 55 mg

Turkey Taco Bake

1 pound ground turkey
1/2 cup chopped onion
1 clove garlic, minced
1 tablespoon oil
1 package (1 1/2 ounces) taco
  seasoning mix

1 can (14 1/2 ounces) stewed
  tomatoes
1/3 cup skim milk
1 egg, beaten
1 package corn bread mix

In large skillet, sauté turkey, onion and garlic in oil until turkey is no longer pink. Stir in taco seasoning and tomatoes; reduce heat to low and cook until heated through. In medium bowl mix together milk and egg. Stir in corn bread mix until blended. Pour meat mixture into lightly greased 8-inch-square baking dish. Top with corn bread mixture. Bake in preheated 400 degree oven for 25 to 30 minutes or until corn bread is golden brown and toothpick comes out clean when inserted in center.

Makes 6 servings.

Per Serving (approx):
Calories 330
Carbohydrate 38 gm

Protein 20 gm
Sodium 1098 mg

Fat 11 gm
Cholesterol 97 mg

Swedish Turkey Meat Loaf

1 to 1 1/4 pounds ground turkey
1 cup pumpernickel bread crumbs
1 1/4 cups sour cream
1/2 cup chopped onion

1 tablespoon plus 1 teaspoon
  Worcestershire sauce
1/2 teaspoon salt
1/4 teaspoon black pepper
1/4 teaspoon ground allspice

In large bowl combine turkey with bread crumbs, 1 cup of the sour cream, the chopped onion, 1 tablespoon of the Worcestershire sauce, the salt, pepper and allspice. Pat mixture evenly into 9- x 5-inch loaf pan. Cover with foil and bake in preheated 350 degree oven 35 to 40 minutes or until loaf springs back to the touch and juices run clear when loaf is pierced. In small bowl combine remaining sour cream and Worcestershire sauce. Top meat loaf with mixture and place under broiler 6 to 8 inches from heat; broil for 1 to 4 minutes or until golden brown.

Makes 4 servings.

Per Serving (approx):
Calories 439
Carbohydrate 20 gm

Protein 30 gm
Sodium 615 mg

Fat 26 gm
Cholesterol 132 mg

Family Meat Loaf

1 pound ground turkey
1 egg
1/2 cup seasoned bread crumbs
1/4 cup water
1 tablespoon dried onion or
  1 medium onion, chopped

2 tablespoons catsup
1 tablespoon chopped green
  chopped green bell pepper
1/8 teaspoon black pepper
1 teaspoon prepared horseradish
1/2 teaspoon prepared mustard

Combine all ingredients; place in lightly greased 9- x 5- x 3-inch loaf pan, or shape in loaf form and place in lightly greased 1-quart baking dish. Bake in preheated 350 degree oven for 55 to 60 minutes or until meat is no longer pink in center of loaf. Unmold on platter; top with sliced tomatoes and garnish with parsley, if desired. Makes 4 servings.

Per Serving (approx):
Calories 263
Carbohydrate 14 gm

Protein 24 gm
Sodium 603 mg

Fat 12 gm
Cholesterol 141 mg

Spicy Turkey Meat Loaf

1 pound ground turkey
1 egg, lightly beaten
1 can (8 ounces) tomato sauce
1 small onion, chopped
1/2 cup crushed tortilla chips

1 package (1 1/2 ounces) taco
  seasoning mix
1 1/2 cups shredded lettuce
3/4 cup chopped tomato
3 tablespoons sour cream
2 tablespoons salsa

In medium bowl combine turkey, egg, tomato sauce, onion, tortilla chips and taco seasoning mix. Press turkey mixture into 9- x 5- x 3-inch loaf pan. Bake at 350 degrees for 50 minutes or until meat thermometer reaches 160 to 165 degrees and meat juices are no longer pink.

To serve, cut loaf into 6 equal slices and top each serving with lettuce, tomato, sour cream and salsa.   Makes 6 servings.

Per Serving (approx):
Calories 198
Carbohydrate 12 gm

Protein 16 gm
Sodium 748 mg

Fat 10 gm
Cholesterol 93 mg

Great Meatballs

1 pound ground turkey
1 egg
1/2 cup seasoned bread crumbs
1/4 cup water
1 tablespoon dried onion

1 tablespoon chopped green
  bell pepper
1/8 teaspoon black pepper
2 tablespoons catsup

Combine all ingredients and mix thoroughly. Form about 1 tablespoon of mixture into each meatball. Arrange on lightly greased 10- x 15- x 1-inch baking pan. Bake in preheated 400 degree oven for 15 to 20 minutes or until meatballs are no longer pink in center.   Makes 6 servings.

Per Serving (approx):
Calories 180
Carbohydrate 9 gm

Protein 16 gm
Sodium 406 mg

Fat 9 gm
Cholesterol 99 mg

California Meat Loaf

1 to 1 1/4 pounds ground turkey
1/2 cup bread crumbs
1/2 teaspoon salt
1/2 teaspoon dried oregano
1/2 teaspoon dried basil
1/2 teaspoon black pepper
1 can (8 ounces) tomato sauce

6 slices onion
6 slices bacon, cooked crisp
6 slices tomato
1/2 cup sliced California black olives
1 cup shredded Monterey jack cheese

In large bowl combine turkey, bread crumbs, salt, oregano, basil, pepper and 3/4 cup of the tomato sauce.

Divide meat mixture into thirds; pat one-third into bottom of 8 1/2- x 4 1/2-inch loaf pan. Arrange 3 slices each of the onion, bacon and tomato over meat mixture; sprinkle with 1/4 cup of the olives and 1/3 cup of the cheese, then top with another one-third of meat mixture. Repeat layering, ending with meat. Spread with remaining tomato sauce and top with remaining 1/3 cup cheese.

Bake in preheated 375 degree oven for 45 to 50 minutes. Meat loaf is cooked through when it springs back to the touch and meat thermometer inserted in loaf registers 165 degrees.   Makes 4 to 6 servings.

Per Serving (approx):
Calories 395
Carbohydrate 33 gm

Protein 26 gm
Sodium 907 mg

Fat 18 gm
Cholesterol 79 mg

Top Producing Turkey States*			
1. North Carolina	61.0	6. Missouri	19.5
2. Minnesota	42.5	7. Indiana	14.8
3. Arkansas	23.0	8. Pennsylvania	8.6
4. California	23.0	9. Iowa	8.6
5. Virginia	21.0	10. South Carolina	6.1

In millions of turkeys
Based on estimated production in 1993

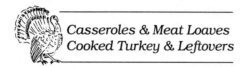

Turkey Pumpernickel Strata

Like the Turkey Pastrami and Cheese Strata on the next page, this dish is one to prepare a day or two in advance.

4 slices pumpernickel bread,
   cut into 1/2-inch cubes
1 cup cooked turkey cut into
   1/2-inch cubes
1 can (4 ounces) sliced
   mushrooms, drained
1 jar (2 ounces) chopped
   pimiento, drained

1 tablespoon dried onion
1 tablespoon dried chives
1 teaspoon garlic powder
1/4 teaspoon black pepper
1 cup grated reduced-fat
   Cheddar cheese
1 1/2 cups skim milk
4 eggs, lightly beaten

Reserve 1/2 cup bread cubes for topping. On ungreased 10- x 15- x 1-inch jelly-roll pan, bake remaining bread cubes at 400 degrees for 5 to 10 minutes or until bread is dry. Arrange cubes in bottom of 9-inch-square baking dish.

In medium bowl combine turkey, mushrooms, pimiento, onion, chives, garlic powder and black pepper. Spread turkey mixture over bread cube layer and top with cheese. Sprinkle reserved bread cubes over cheese.

In same bowl combine milk and eggs; pour over bread layer. Cover dish and refrigerate overnight. In preheated 325 degree oven, bake strata for 50 to 60 minutes or until knife inserted in center comes out clean. Allow strata to stand for 10 to 15 minutes before serving.   Makes 4 servings.

Per Serving (approx):
Calories 347
Carbohydrate 25 gm

Protein 31 gm
Sodium 862 mg

Fat 13 gm
Cholesterol 262 mg

Turkey Pastrami and Cheese Strata

This is a wonderful dish for a crowd. You can assemble it the night before and bake it in the morning.

6 slices light rye bread,
  trimmed of all crusts*
1/2 pound turkey pastrami, cut in
  1/4-inch strips
6 slices white bread, trimmed
  of all crusts
6 eggs

3 cups milk
1 1/2 cups (about 6 ounces)
  grated Swiss cheese
1/8 teaspoon black pepper
1 teaspoon caraway seeds
  (optional)
1 teaspoon dry mustard

Generously grease 9- x 13-inch glass baking dish. Arrange rye bread slices on the bottom of the dish. Distribute turkey pastrami over bread slices. Top with white bread slices to make "sandwiches."

Beat eggs in large bowl. Add milk, cheese, pepper, caraway (if used) and dry mustard. Pour over sandwiches. Cover and refrigerate as long as overnight, as little as 1 hour. Bake, uncovered, in a 325 degree oven until puffed and golden, about 50 to 55 minutes.   Makes 6 servings.

*Note: If desired, 12 slices rye bread may be used instead of half rye and half white.

Per Serving (approx):
Calories 470
Carbohydrate 39 gm

Protein 31 gm
Sodium 914 mg

Fat 21 gm
Cholesterol 277 mg

Turkey and Broccoli Skillet Soufflé

This dish takes a little extra effort but is well worth it.

4 eggs, separated
1/4 cup water
1/2 teaspoon cream of tartar
1 cup shredded Swiss cheese
1 tablespoon butter or margarine

1 cup finely chopped cooked
  broccoli
1 cup chopped cooked turkey
2 tablespoons chopped green
  onion
1 clove garlic, chopped

In large bowl with electric mixer at high speed, beat egg whites with water and cream of tartar until stiff peaks form. In small bowl with mixer at high speed, beat egg yolks until thick and lemon colored. Gently fold yolks into whites. Fold in 1/4 cup of the cheese.

In 10-inch ovenproof skillet over medium-high heat, melt butter. Stir in broccoli, turkey, green onion and garlic. Gently pour egg mixture into skillet; smooth top. Reduce heat to medium and cook for 5 minutes or until soufflé is lightly browned on bottom. Place skillet in preheated 350 degree oven and bake for 10 to 12 minutes or until puffed and golden. Sprinkle remaining cheese over soufflé and serve immediately.

Makes 4 servings.

Per Serving (approx):
Calories 272
Carbohydrate 3 gm

Protein 25 gm
Sodium 230 mg

Fat 17 gm
Cholesterol 265 mg

Turkey eggs, slightly larger than jumbo chicken eggs, occasionally may be purchased at health food stores or at farm markets. They are not a common retail item. Even though excellent for cooking and nutritious, they are expensive, costing abaout 75 cents per egg. The majority of turkey eggs are used to support turkey production.

Pumpkin Turkey Bake

This recipe solves the problem of what to do with Thanksgiving pumpkins. You can stuff them and eat them.

1 pumpkin (4 1/2 to 5 pounds)
1 pound turkey thighs skinned, boned and cut into 1/2-inch cubes
1 tablespoon vegetable oil
1 cup coarsely chopped onion
3/4 cup thinly sliced celery
1/2 cup coarsely chopped green bell pepper

1 clove garlic, minced
1 package (8 ounces) frozen sugar snap peas, thawed
2 tablespoons brown sugar
1/8 teaspoon red pepper flakes
1/8 teaspoon ground cinnamon
1/4 cup turkey or chicken broth

Cut top from pumpkin; remove and set aside. With spoon scoop out seeds and discard.

Replace pumpkin top and place pumpkin in 8-inch-square baking pan. Bake in preheated 350 degree oven for for 50 to 60 minutes or until pumpkin feels slightly tender when squeezed (pumpkin should not be completely done at this point).

In large skillet over medium-high heat, sauté turkey in oil for 5 to 6 minutes or until lightly browned; remove from skillet and set aside. Add onion, celery, bell pepper and garlic to skillet; sauté for 2 minutes. Add peas and sauté mixture 1 additional minute. Stir in brown sugar, red pepper flakes, cinnamon and browned turkey.

Spoon turkey mixture into pumpkin; sprinkle with turkey broth. Replace pumpkin top and return to baking pan. Bake for 35 to 45 minutes or until pumpkin is tender and turkey cubes are done.

To serve, scoop out some of the pumpkin with turkey/vegetable mixture.
                                        Makes 4 servings.

Per Serving (approx):
Calories 350   *Protein 29 gm*   *Fat 9 gm*
Carbohydrate 43 gm   *Sodium 122 mg*   *Cholesterol 85 mg*

Barbecue Meat Loaf

You can stay indoors and still have your barbecue with this dish.

6 tablespoons barbecue sauce
2 tablespoons water
2/3 cup rolled oats
   (old-fashioned or quick cooking)
1 large egg, lightly beaten
2 teaspoons chili powder, or to taste
2 teaspoons Worcestershire
   sauce
Salt to taste

1 to 1 1/4 pounds ground turkey
1/3 cup chopped red and/or
   green bell pepper
1/4 cup finely chopped onion
1/2 cup fresh or thawed frozen
   corn kernels
2 tablespoons drained canned
   chopped green chilies
Additional barbecue sauce or
   catsup (optional)

In large bowl combine 3 tablespoons of the barbecue sauce and the water. Add oats, egg, chili powder, Worcestershire sauce and salt; mix well. Add turkey, bell pepper, onion, corn and chilies; mix well. Pat into 9- x 5-inch loaf pan.

Bake in preheated 375 degree oven for 45 to 50 minutes; spread top of loaf with remaining 3 tablespoons barbecue sauce during last 10 minutes of cooking. Meat loaf is cooked through when it springs back to the touch and meat thermometer inserted in loaf registers 165 degrees.

Serve warm or cold, with additional barbecue sauce, if desired.

Makes 4 to 6 servings.

Per Serving (approx):
Calories 186
Carbohydrate 13 gm

Protein 17 gm
Sodium 253 mg

Fat 7 gm
Cholesterol 90 mg

POT PIES &
PASTRIES

Turkey En Croute #1

Elegance is yours with this turkey tenderloin encased in a puff pastry with an oh-so-subtle sauce.

1 pound turkey breast
   tenderloins (2 pieces)
1 tablespoon butter

1 package (17 1/2 ounces)
   frozen puff pastry, thawed

Cook turkey in butter in skillet over medium-high heat for 5 minutes, turning to brown. Remove turkey and allow to cool slightly. Cut pastry in half; wrap each half around a tenderloin, gently stretching pastry to cover turkey.

Pinch edges of pastry together to seal. Decorate with additional pastry. Place seam side down on ungreased baking sheet. Bake in 375 degree oven for 25 to 30 minutes or until golden brown. Serve with sauce.

Makes 2 to 4 servings.

SAUCE:
In skillet used to brown turkey, combine 1 1/4 cups half-and-half, 1 tablespoon cornstarch, 1/2 teaspoon chopped dill weed, 1/8 teaspoon dried basil, 1/8 teaspoon black pepper and 1/8 teaspoon onion powder. Cook over medium heat, stirring constantly until thickened.

Per Serving (approx):
Calories 816
Carbohydrate 50 gm

Protein 35 gm
Sodium 699 mg

Fat 53 gm
Cholesterol 97 mg

Q. What breed of turkeys is most used by the industry?

A. All commercial turkeys produced today are the white broad breasted turkey breed. This breed was first used for commercial turkey production in the late 1950s. By the late 1960s, the majority of the industry used this turkey breed.

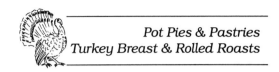

Turkey En Croute #2

So simple to make—so impressive to serve.

5 pound boneless turkey or
   boneless turkey breast
1 pound mushrooms, chopped
1/2 cup sliced green onion
2 cloves garlic, minced

1/4 cup butter, melted
2 tablespoons dry sherry
1/4 cup seasoned bread crumbs
2 eggs
Half of 17 1/4-ounce package
   frozen puff pastry, thawed

Roast turkey in preheated 350 degree oven until internal temperature registers 165 degrees, about 1 hour. Let cool slightly; remove netting.

Sauté mushrooms, onion and garlic in butter until soft. Stir in sherry, bread crumbs and 1 lightly beaten egg.

Cut turkey on diagonal into slices 1 inch thick, cutting only three-quarters of the way through meat. Fill space between slices with mushroom mixture.

Roll out pastry according to package directions. Place turkey cut side down in center of pastry; wrap pastry around turkey to cover completely, sealing edges with water. Place seam side down on baking sheet; brush remaining beaten egg over pastry. Prick surface with fork. Bake at 350 degrees until golden brown, about 1 hour. Let stand for 10 minutes. Slice to serve. Makes 10 to 12 servings.

Per Serving (approx):
Calories 495
Carbohydrate 12 gm

Protein 53 gm
Sodium 293 mg

Fat 26 gm
Cholesterol 178 mg

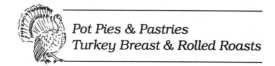

Turkey Pot Pies

You really should double this recipe and put the extra in your freezer. You may want to substitute prepared pie crust for pastry dough.

1 turkey quarter breast, (about 1 1/2 pounds)	1/4 teaspoon finely crumbled dried tarragon
1 teaspoon salt	1/8 teaspoon black pepper
1 cup sour cream	1 1/4 cups finely diced raw potato (2 small)
1 cup shredded sharp Cheddar cheese	1/3 cup chopped onion

Prepare pastry. To make 5 pies, divide dough in 10 wedges; shape each into small ball. Roll each out on lightly floured board to 6-inch circle. Fit 5 of the circles into 5 individual pie pans (5 inches diameter, 1 inch deep).

Remove bones and skin from turkey breast and cut turkey into 3/4-inch chunks. Sprinkle with 1/2 teaspoon of the salt. Place about 1/2 cup of chunks in each pan. In large bowl combine sour cream, cheese, tarragon and pepper. Mix in potato and onion. Spoon about 1/2 cup of this mixture over turkey in each pan. Moisten top edge of pastry and fit top pastries over pies. Fold edges under and press firmly together with fork; cut slits in top to allow steam to escape (decorative cutter may be used, if desired).

Bake in 350 degree oven for 1 hour or until pastry is nicely browned. Serve warm or cold.   Makes 5 servings.

PASTRY:
Mix 1/2 teaspoon salt with 3 cups sifted flour. Cut in 1 cup shortening until particles are size of peas. Sprinkle with about 1/2 cup cold milk; use just enough to make stiff dough. Shape into ball.

Per Serving (approx):
Calories 280
Carbohydrate 18 gm

Protein 12 gm
Sodium 298 mg

Fat 18 gm
Cholesterol 30 mg

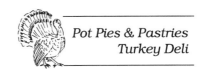

Torta Rustica

You see them often in gourmet delis—golden loaves of pastry stuffed with a savory filling. They're called "torta rustica," and with this recipe you can make them yourself.

2 loaves (1 pound each) frozen
  bread dough, thawed
2 each red and yellow bell peppers,
  halved and seeded
1 medium red onion, coarsely chopped
2 tablespoons olive oil
2 tablespoons drained capers
1/4 cup pitted and chopped
  oil-cured black olives
3 eggs, lightly beaten

4 tablespoons tomato paste
3 tablespoons chopped fresh
  basil or 1 tablespoon dried
1 teaspoon each dried thyme,
  sage and rosemary
8 ounces turkey salami slices
8 ounces turkey ham slices
1/2 pound fontina or
  mozzarella cheese, shredded
Additional oil, for brushing
  dough

Combine loaves of dough; let rise according to package directions until doubled.

Broil peppers, skin side up, until charred. Place in a plastic bag and seal for 5 minutes; peel off and discard skin; chop pepper.

In medium skillet sauté onion in oil until soft; add chopped peppers, capers and olives. Combine eggs, tomato paste and basil; stir into vegetable mixture.

To assemble torta, roll dough on floured surface into approximately 20-inch circle; sprinkle with thyme, sage and rosemary while rolling. Place in greased 10-inch-round pan, letting excess dough drape over sides. Layer half turkey salami and turkey ham slices on bottom and sides of dough; fill with egg mixture. Top with cheese and remaining turkey slices. Bring excess dough together in middle, leaving small vent for steam. Brush with additional oil and bake at 375 degrees for 50 to 55 minutes. Cut into wedges and serve warm or at room temperature.

Makes 10 to 12 servings.

Per Serving (approx):
Calories 191
Carbohydrate 8 gm

Protein 13 gm
Sodium 539 mg

Fat 12 gm
Cholesterol 94 mg

Savory Stuffing Pie

2 to 3 cups cooked bread stuffing
2 cups diced cooked turkey
2 cups cooked or canned
   corn kernels
2 cups shredded Cheddar cheese
1 cup whipping cream
1/2 cup thinly sliced green onion

1/2 cup diced red bell pepper
3 eggs, beaten
2 tablespoons flour
1 teaspoon salt
1/4 teaspoon black pepper
1/4 teaspoon hot pepper sauce

Lightly grease deep 9 1/2-inch pie plate. Press stuffing into bottom and up sides of pie plate to form shell. In medium bowl, combine remaining ingredients; mix well. Pour mixture into shell and bake in preheated 375 degree oven for 25 to 30 minutes or until heated through and golden.

Makes 6 servings.

Per Serving (approx):
Calories 530
Carbohydrate 28 gm

Protein 31 gm
Sodium 875 mg

Fat 33 gm
Cholesterol 236 mg

Mini Turkey Ham Quiche

1/3 cup diced turkey ham
1/4 cup reduced-calorie
   Cheddar cheese, shredded

1 frozen pie shell (6 inches)
1 egg, beaten
1/4 cup skim milk

Prepare pie shell according to package directions. Sprinkle ham and cheese over pie shell. In small bowl combine egg and milk; pour evenly into pie shell. Place on baking sheet and bake in preheated 350 degree oven for 20 to 25 minutes or until knife inserted in center comes out clean.

Makes 2 servings.

Per Serving (approx):
Calories 314
Carbohydrate 22 gm

Protein 14 gm
Sodium 575 mg

Fat 19 gm
Cholesterol 142 mg

California Turkey Puff

2 1/2 pounds turkey drumsticks
2/3 cup water
7 tablespoons butter
1/4 teaspoon each salt, dried thyme
   and dried dill weed
2/3 cup flour
3 eggs

2 carrots, thinly sliced
1 zucchini, sliced
1 green bell pepper, sliced
1 onion, sliced
1 cup sour cream
2 tablespoons Dijon-style
   mustard

Poach turkey drumsticks until tender, about 1 1/2 to 2 hours; let cool. Remove meat from bones and chop. Discard skin and bones.

Combine water, 5 tablespoons of the butter and the seasonings in 2-quart saucepan. Bring to a boil; add flour all at once. Remove from heat; beat with whisk until smooth. Beat in eggs one at a time until mixture is smooth and glossy. Spread in greased 9-inch pie plate. Bake at 400 degrees for 40 minutes. Turn off oven; leave popover in oven for 10 minutes, then remove.

Sauté vegetables in remaining 2 tablespoons butter; mix with turkey, sour cream and mustard. Spoon into popover. Bake at 350 degrees for 10 minutes or until heated through. Cut in wedges and serve.

Makes 6 servings.

Per Serving (approx):
Calories 597
Carbohydrate 20 gm

Protein 44 gm
Sodium 521 mg

Fat 38 gm
Cholesterol 270 mg

It was not only Californians who herded turkeys. In the 1700's turkeys raised near Suffolk were herded the 50 miles into London. Due to the severe weather, the turkeys were shod. That is, their feet were tied in cloth and covered with leather boots.

Cajun Skillet Pot Pie

World-famous Cajun cuisine traveled with French immigrants first to Acadia (now Nova Scotia) and then to Louisiana. Along the way, regional ingredients such as peppers and corn helped make these dishes unique.

2 cans (14 ounces) beef broth
2 turkey thighs (approximately
  2 pounds)
Worcestershire sauce to taste
Hot pepper sauce to taste
3 tablespoons oil
5 tablespoons flour

2/3 cup chopped onion
1/2 cup chopped green bell
  pepper
1 package (10 ounces) frozen
  succotash, thawed
10 ready-to-bake refrigerated
  biscuits

In large saucepan over medium heat, bring beef broth to a boil. Add thighs, 1 tablespoon Worcestershire sauce and 1/2 teaspoon hot pepper sauce. Reduce heat to low; simmer thighs, uncovered, in broth mixture for 1 1/2 hours. Skim and discard foam.

Remove thighs to cutting board; discard skin and bones. Cut meat into pieces; reserve. Over high heat boil broth in saucepan until reduced to about 3 cups; reserve.

In 10-inch ovenproof skillet over medium heat, combine oil and flour. Cook for 5 to 6 minutes or until flour turns a deep reddish brown, stirring constantly. Stir in onion, bell pepper and succotash; gradually add broth and cook for 1 to 2 minutes or until sauce thickens, stirring constantly. Stir in turkey, adding Worcestershire and hot pepper sauce to taste.

Arrange biscuits on top of turkey mixture. Bake in preheated 400 degree oven for 10 minutes; reduce heat to 350 degrees and bake for 20 minutes longer or until biscuit topping is browned and filling is bubbly.

Makes 4 to 6 servings.

Per Serving (approx):
Calories 855
Carbohydrate 40 gm

Protein 90 gm
Sodium 1092 mg

Fat 37 gm
Cholesterol 257 mg

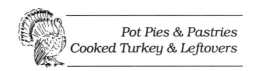

Mexican Shepherd's Pie

We have no idea where the title for this recipe came from, but we doubt that a shepherd made it. It is a delicious dish.

1/4 cup olive oil
3 tablespoons flour
1 cup chopped onions
1/2 cup chopped green or red
   bell pepper
1 garlic clove, minced
1 cup chicken broth
2 teaspoons chili powder
Salt to taste
1/2 teaspoon ground cumin
3 cups diced cooked turkey
2 cups shredded Monterey
   jack cheese

2 cups peeled, seeded and
   diced tomatoes
2 cups fresh corn kernels or
   1 package (10 ounces) frozen
   corn kernels, thawed
1 can (4 ounces) chopped mild
   green chilies
2 cups seasoned mashed
   potatoes
1 small pickled jalapeño
   pepper, chopped

In large skillet over medium-high heat, combine oil and flour. Cook for 5 to 6 minutes or until thickened and deep brown, stirring constantly. Add onion, bell pepper and garlic; sauté for 1 to 2 minutes. Gradually stir in broth. Continue cooking for 3 to 5 minutes or until sauce has thickened. Season with 1 1/2 teaspoons of the chili powder, the salt and cumin. Stir in diced turkey, cheese, tomatoes, corn and chilies.

In small bowl combine mashed potatoes with remaining 1/2 teaspoon chili powder and jalapeño. Transfer turkey mixture to 2-quart baking dish; spoon or pipe potato mixture on top. Bake in preheated 375 degree oven for 25 to 30 minutes or until golden and bubbly. Makes 6 servings.

Per Serving (approx):
Calories 517
Carbohydrate 37 gm

Protein 35 gm
Sodium 712 mg

Fat 25 gm
Cholesterol 88 mg

Sausage and Broccoli Quiche

2 tablespoons oil
1 pound turkey breakfast sausage
  patties
6 eggs
2 cups half-and-half
1/4 teaspoon salt
1/2 teaspoon black pepper

1/4 teaspoon ground nutmeg
2 unbaked 9-inch pie shells
2 cups shredded Swiss or
  Gruyère cheese
1 1/2 cups broccoli florets,
  cooked tender-crisp

In large skillet over medium-high heat, warm oil. Add sausage; cook for about 5 minutes or until firm and lightly browned, turning occasionally. Drain on paper towels and set aside.

In medium bowl combine eggs, half-and-half, salt, pepper and nutmeg; beat until well mixed.

Arrange sausage patties on bottom of pie shells. Equally divide cheese and broccoli between pie shells; divide egg mixture evenly over top. Bake in preheated 375 degree oven for 35 to 45 minutes or until set. Serve warm or at room temperature, cut into wedges. Makes 8 to 10 servings.

Recipe may be cut in half. If you're freezing extra quiche, thaw completely before use. To serve, cover loosely with foil and reheat in 350 degree oven for 15 minutes.

Per Serving (approx):
Calories 466
Carbohydrate 20 gm

Protein 21 gm
Sodium 610 mg

Fat 34 gm
Cholesterol 190 mg

The incubation period to hatch a turkey egg is 28 days.

Sausage-Spinach Turnovers

For a special luncheon, these turnovers are ideal.

2 tablespoons olive oil
10 ounces turkey breakfast
  sausage links
1 tablespoon butter or
  margarine
1/4 cup chopped onion
1 package (10 ounces) frozen
  chopped spinach, thawed and
  well drained
1/2 teaspoon dried oregano

Salt to taste
Cayenne pepper to taste
1/3 cup shredded Swiss cheese
1/3 cup ricotta cheese
2 sheets frozen puff pastry,
  thawed, or pie pastry
  for 2-crust pie
1 egg
1 tablespoon water

In large skillet over medium-high heat, warm oil. Add sausage; cook for about 5 minutes or until firm and browned, turning occasionally. Remove from skillet; drain on paper towels and set aside.

Add butter and onion to skillet; sauté for 5 minutes or until onion is translucent. Stir in spinach, oregano, salt and cayenne. Remove from heat and let cool. Stir in Swiss cheese and ricotta until thoroughly combined.

On lightly floured surface with rolling pin, roll out each sheet of pastry to 10-inch square. Cut each sheet into 4 equal squares. On large baking sheet, place 6 squares. Top each with 2 sausage links; divide spinach mixture evenly over sausage. Fold opposite corners of pastry together to form triangles, crimping edges with fork.

In small bowl beat together egg and water; brush pastries with egg wash. Cut decorative shapes out of remaining 2 pastry squares and place on turnovers; brush decorations with egg wash. Bake in preheated 400 degree oven for 20 minutes or until golden brown. Serve warm.

Makes 6 servings.

Per Serving (approx):
Calories 213
Carbohydrate 6 gm

Protein 13 gm
Sodium 337 mg

Fat 15 gm
Cholesterol 72 mg

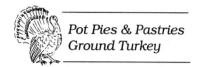

Italian Turkey Crust Pie

1 pound ground turkey or
  ground turkey breast
1/4 cup seasoned dry bread
  crumbs
1/4 cup milk
1 teaspoon garlic salt
1/2 teaspoon crushed dried
  oregano

1/4 teaspoon black pepper
1/2 cup tomato paste
1/2 cup sliced mushrooms
1/2 cup grated mozzarella
  cheese
2 tablespoons chopped green
  bell pepper
2 tablespoons sliced olives

In 9-inch pie plate, combine turkey, bread crumbs, milk, garlic salt, oregano and black pepper. Mix well.

Press mixture evenly over bottom and up sides of pie plate. Spread tomato paste evenly over turkey "crust." Top with mushrooms. Bake in preheated 350 degree oven for 25 minutes or until turkey is no longer pink. Sprinkle with cheese, bell pepper and olives. Bake an additional 10 minutes or until cheese is melted. Let cool for 5 minutes, then cut into wedges. Makes 6 servings.

Per Serving (approx):
Calories 181
Carbohydrate 8 gm

Protein 17 gm
Sodium 191 mg

Fat 9 gm
Cholesterol 64 mg

Super Turkey Burger Pie

Actually, this is a pie in which the turkey is the top and bottom crust, and the stuffing is the filling. It's perfect for an after-the-game meal. Prepare it a day or two ahead and refrigerate, then warm it up just before serving.

2 pounds ground turkey
2 eggs or 1/2 cup egg substitute
1/4 cup skim milk
1/4 cup bread crumbs

3 tablespoons chopped parsley
2 tablespoons chili sauce
Salt to taste
Dash of black pepper

In large bowl combine turkey, eggs, milk, bread crumbs, parsley, chili sauce, salt and pepper. On 2- x 10- x 15-inch jelly-roll pan, shape half of turkey mixture into 7-inch-diameter patty. On 10- by 11-inch piece of waxed paper, shape remaining turkey mixture into 8-inch-diameter patty.

Prepare stuffing and glaze. Spoon stuffing over 7-inch circle of turkey mixture to within 1/2 inch of edge. Carefully lift waxed paper and place 8-inch turkey patty over stuffing. Remove waxed paper. Press turkey mixture edges together to seal. Bake at 350 degrees for 60 to 70 minutes or until 165 degrees is reached on meat thermometer. Spread glaze over burger during last 10 minutes of baking.   Makes 8 servings.

VEGETABLE AND BREAD STUFFING:
In 10-inch skillet over medium-high heat, sauté 1 cup shredded potato, 1/2 cup shredded carrot, 1/2 cup zucchini and 1/4 cup chopped onion in 2 tablespoons margarine for 4 to 5 minutes or until vegetables are tender. In medium bowl combine vegetable mixture, 1 egg or 1/4 cup egg substitute, 1 tablespoon bread crumbs and 1/2 cup shredded mozzarella cheese.

GLAZE:
In small bowl combine 1/4 cup catsup, 2 tablespoons brown sugar and 1 teaspoon dry mustard.

Per Serving (approx):
Calories 295
Carbohydrate 14 gm

Protein 26 gm
Sodium 310 mg

Fat 15 gm
Cholesterol 168 mg

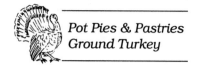

Spicy Spanakopita

We've added ground turkey to the traditional Greek cheese and spinach pie, to bring a whole new dimension to turkey and to your home with this recipe.

1 1/2 pounds ground turkey
2 tablespoons butter
2 pounds fresh spinach, steamed and drained, or 2 packages (10 ounces each) frozen spinach, thawed and well drained
4 ounces feta cheese, crumbled

1/2 cup chopped walnuts
1/2 teaspoon each black pepper and ground allspice
1 egg
8 to 10 phyllo leaves, folded lengthwise
1/2 cup butter, melted

Brown turkey in the 2 tablespoons butter; combine with spinach, cheese, walnuts, seasonings and egg.

In greased 10-inch pie plate, lay first folded phyllo leaf across plate so both ends extend over edge. Brush with melted butter. Working quickly, fan remaining leaves around plate, brushing each with melted butter, so entire bottom of plate is covered. Keep unused leaves covered. Spoon filling onto phyllo leaves in pan. Fold edges over and add more leaves to cover top. Brush with butter. Bake at 350 degrees for 40 to 45 minutes or until golden brown.   Makes 8 servings.

Per Serving (approx):
Calories 431
Carbohydrate 19 gm

Protein 23 gm
Sodium 547 mg

Fat 29 gm
Cholesterol 140 mg

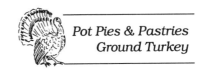

Turkey Lurky Pie

This very, very British dish was made for centuries with beef. This is one of their recipes which they converted to turkey.

4 tablespoons margarine or
   butter
1 tablespoon oil
1 onion, chopped
1 pound ground turkey
1/2 pound carrots,
   coarsely chopped

2 teaspoons tomato puree
1 teaspoon flour
2 tablespoons water
Pinch of dried thyme (optional)
Salt and pepper to taste
2 pounds potatoes, peeled and
   cut into 1/8-inch slices

Heat 1 tablespoon of the margarine and the oil in a pan. Lightly brown onion and turkey.

Add carrots and tomato puree. Sprinkle in flour and mix well. Add water, thyme and seasoning. Remove from heat and spoon into casserole (gratin) dish. Layer potatoes over top, overlapping. Sprinkle with salt and additional pepper, and dot with remaining margarine. Cover with foil.

Bake at 375 degrees for 45 to 50 minutes or until potatoes are almost cooked. Remove foil. Increase heat to 450 degrees and bake for 15 minutes more or until potatoes are golden brown and crisp on surface. Serve with green vegetable or salad. Makes 4 servings.

Per Serving (approx):
Calories 587
Carbohydrate 66 gm

Protein 27 gm
Sodium 371 mg

Fat 24 gm
Cholesterol 82 mg

The largest turkey ever raised was in Petersborough, England by Leacraft Turkeys, Ltd. He weighed in at 86 pounds!

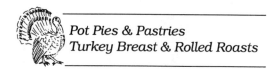

Lattice-Crust Turkey Pot Pies

2 cans (13 3/4 ounces each)
  reduced-sodium chicken broth
1 cup water
1 skinless, boneless turkey breast
  (about 1 1/2 pounds)
5 tablespoons light margarine
1 package (10 ounces) frozen pearl
  onions, thawed
1/2 teaspoon sugar
1/4 cup flour
2 1/2 cups low-fat milk

1/2 teaspoon dried marjoram
Salt and pepper to taste
10 ounces frozen petite peas,
  thawed
2 cups carrots in matchstick
  pieces
1 prepared pie crust pastry or
  1 frozen unbaked pie crust,
  thawed
1 egg beaten with 1 tablespoon
  water

In Dutch oven over high heat, bring chicken broth and water to a boil. Add turkey and more water to cover, if necessary. Reduce heat to low; simmer, uncovered, for about 25 minutes per pound or until turkey is cooked through. If time allows, refrigerate turkey to cool in broth.

Remove turkey from broth and cut into cubes; set aside. Skim and discard fat from broth. Strain broth, reserving 1 cup for sauce; reserve remainder for another use.

In large saucepan over medium-high heat, melt 1 tablespoon of the margarine. Add onions and sugar; reduce heat to medium and sauté for 5 minutes. Remove onions; stir remaining margarine and flour into saucepan. Cook for 1 to 2 minutes or until mixture is bubbling and slightly golden, stirring constantly.

Whisk in milk and reserved 1 cup chicken broth; cook until thickened, stirring constantly. Season with marjoram, salt and pepper. Stir in cubed turkey, cooked onions, peas and carrots; remove from heat.

Divide turkey mixture among six 2-cup baking dishes or ramekins. With pastry wheel or knife, cut pie pastry into strips. Brush rim of each ramekin lightly with egg wash.

Arrange pastry strips decoratively on top of turkey mixture, pressing onto rim of dish. Bake pies in preheated 400 degree oven for 10 minutes. Reduce temperature to 350 degrees and bake for 25 minutes longer or until crusts are golden and turkey mixture is bubbly. Makes 6 servings.

Per Serving (approx):
Calories 446
Carbohydrate 39 gm

Protein 36 gm
Sodium 808 mg

Fat 16 gm
Cholesterol 113 mg

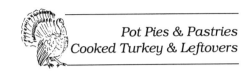

Country-Style Turkey Pie

A classic!

1/4 cup butter or margarine
1/3 cup sifted flour
3 cups milk
1 tablespoon chicken seasoned
   stock base
Salt to taste
1/2 teaspoon Worcestershire
   sauce
2 tablespoons dry sherry
3 drops hot pepper sauce

2 cups diced cooked turkey
   meat
1 1/2 cups sliced mushrooms
1 cup cooked chopped carrot
1 can (8 ounces) small whole
   onions, drained
1 tablespoon melted butter,
   for pastry
1 tablespoon grated Parmesan
   cheese

Prepare Herb Pastry. Melt butter in saucepan; blend in flour. Stir in milk slowly; add chicken base, salt and Worcestershire sauce. Cook, stirring, until sauce boils and thickens. Stir in sherry and hot pepper sauce. Add turkey, mushrooms, carrot, and drained onions; heat through.

Turn into 1 1/2-quart baking dish. Place Herb Pastry over dish, fluting edge of pastry against rim. Bake in 400 degree oven for about 20 minutes or until pastry is almost done. Brush top with melted butter and sprinkle with cheese. Bake for 10 minutes longer or until nicely browned.

Makes 6 servings.

HERB PASTRY:
Combine 1 1/2 cups sifted flour, 3/4 teaspoon salt and 1/4 teaspoon dried poultry seasoning. Cut in 1/2 cup shortening until particles are about size of peas. Sprinkle with about 1/3 cup cold milk, using just enough to make dough hold together. Roll pastry to fit top of baking dish. Cut out steam vents in pie crust.

Per Serving (approx):
Calories 593
Carbohydrate 42 gm

Protein 24 gm
Sodium 535 mg

Fat 36 gm
Cholesterol 81 mg

Pot Pies & Pastries
Turkey Deli

Bacon and Vegetable Bread

1/2 cup margarine, melted
1/3 cup grated Parmesan cheese
3 packages (10 ounces each) flaky
   refrigerated biscuits,
   quartered
Nonstick vegetable cooking spray

12 ounces turkey bacon,
   cooked and crumbled
1/2 cup chopped green bell
   pepper
1/2 cup chopped onion

In small bowl combine margarine and cheese. Roll biscuit quarters in mixture. In bottom of bundt pan sprayed with vegetable cooking spray, layer one-third of the biscuits. Sprinkle with half the bacon, bell pepper and onion. Repeat layers, ending with layer of biscuits.

Bake at 350 degrees for 25 to 30 minutes or until bread is golden brown. Makes 20 slices.

Per Slice (approx):
Calories 238
Carbohydrate 20 gm

Protein 7 gm
Sodium 872 mg

Fat 15 gm
Cholesterol 19 mg

Talking Back

Q Are turkeys really dumb?

A Turkeys are not dumb. Ask any hunter who has gone after wild turkey! However, the domesticated bird is far less cunning and more docile, probably because food, water, and shelter are provided.

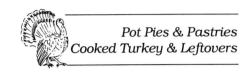

Turkey Quiche in Potato Shells

4 large potatoes, baked and cooled
1/4 cup margarine, melted
1 pound cooked turkey breast,
   cut into 1/2-inch cubes
5 large eggs, beaten
2 ounces cream cheese, softened
1/4 cup finely chopped
   green onion

1/4 cup finely chopped
   red bell pepper
Salt and pepper to taste
1/2 cup sour cream (optional)
1 cup shredded Cheddar
   cheese, (optional)

Slice potatoes in half lengthwise. With spoon remove center of potato to within 1/4 inch of potato skin. Save removed potato for another use. Place potato shells on 2- x 10- x 15-inch jelly-roll pan. Brush inside of each potato shell with margarine.

In large bowl combine turkey, eggs, cream cheese, onion, bell pepper, salt and pepper. Divide turkey mixture evenly among potato shells. Bake at 400 degrees for 15 to 20 minutes or until mixture is puffed and knife inserted in center of mixture comes out clean. Serve with sour cream and cheese, if desired.   Makes 8 servings.

Per Serving (approx):
Calories 325
Carbohydrate 25 gm

Protein 24 gm
Sodium 224 mg

Fat 14 gm
Cholesterol 184 mg

Pot Pies & Pastries
Turkey Sausage

Italian Turkey Sausage Roll

1 pound turkey sausage,
  crumbled
2 cloves garlic, minced
1/2 green or red bell pepper,
  chopped
1/2 red onion, chopped
Olive oil, as needed
1 can (14 1/2 ounces) stewed
  tomatoes, drained

1 cup grated Monterey jack
  cheese
1/4 cup chopped fresh basil
  or 1 tablespoon dried
1 teaspoon dried Italian
  seasoning
2 tablespoons grated
Parmesan
  cheese

Sauté sausage, garlic, bell pepper and onion in oil until sausage is browned. Add tomatoes. Add chopped zucchini or mushrooms, if desired. Simmer for 10 minutes. Let cool.

On lightly floured surface, roll out dough to 14- by 18-inch rectangle. Top with sausage filling and sprinkle with jack cheese, herbs and Parmesan. With long side of rectangle nearest you, carefully roll up into log. Pinch seams. Place on greased baking sheet. Brush with olive oil. Bake in preheated 400 degree oven for 30 to 35 minutes. Let cool for at least 15 minutes before slicing.   Makes 18 to 20 slices.

YEASTED DOUGH:
Dissolve 1 package dry yeast in 1/2 cup warm water (105 to 115 degrees). Add 2 tablespoons olive oil, 1 cup warm water, 4 cups flour and 1 teaspoon salt. Stir and mix with fork. Knead on lightly floured surface until smooth and elastic, about 5 minutes. Form into ball. Put into oiled bowl, turning to coat all surfaces with oil. Cover and let rise in warm place until doubled, about 45 minutes.

Per Slice (approx):
Calories 168
Carbohydrate 21 gm

Protein 8 gm
Sodium 316 mg

Fat 6 gm
Cholesterol 18 mg

SAUTÉ & STIR-FRY

Turkey Framboise

This sample of nouvelle cuisine takes just minutes to prepare, and its elegant flavor is impressive. Keep this recipe in mind for a special meal when you have little time to cook and are ready for a culinary triumph.

4 turkey fillets	1/2 cup whipping cream
(about 1 1/4 pounds)	1 tablespoon raspberry jam
Salt and pepper to taste	1/3 cup fresh or frozen
3 tablespoons butter	raspberries
2 tablespoons raspberry liqueur	

Season turkey with salt and pepper to taste. Heat butter in skillet and sauté turkey for 4 minutes per side. Add raspberry liqueur; cook for 2 minutes more. Remove turkey and keep warm. Add cream and jam to skillet; cook until thickened, about 5 minutes. Add raspberries and heat through. Pour over turkey fillets and serve immediately.

Makes 4 servings.

Per Serving (approx):
Calories 197

Protein 1 gm

Fat 16 gm

Carbohydrate 9 gm

Sodium 197 mg

Cholesterol 50 mg

Poached Turkey Normande

2 turkey breast tenderloins
1/2 cup chopped onion
1/2 cup sliced celery
3 peppercorns
1/2 teaspoon salt

2/3 cup diced apple
1/3 cup orange juice
3 tablespoons jellied
   cranberry sauce
4 teaspoons orange marmalade

Place tenderloins, onion, celery, peppercorns and salt in large skillet. Pour in enough boiling water to cover turkey. Place lid on skillet and poach tenderloins over low heat for about 30 minutes or until done. Remove tenderloins from liquid.

In small saucepan over medium heat, combine apple, orange juice, cranberry sauce and orange marmalade. Cook until sauce is hot and apple pieces are tender but hold their shape. Spoon over tenderloins.

Makes 4 servings.

Per Serving (approx):
Calories 198
Carbohydrate 17 gm

Protein 27 gm
Sodium 364 mg

Fat 2 gm
Cholesterol 70 mg

Glazed Turkey Steaks
with Apricot Nut Pilaf

No, this is not a California recipe. It came to us from England, where nouvelle cuisine has become widespread.

2 tablespoons olive oil
1 onion, chopped
1/2 cup chopped dried apricots
3 tablespoons pine nuts
1/4 teaspoon ground turmeric
1/2 pound long-grain rice
2 cups vegetable stock
Salt and pepper to taste
2 teaspoons chopped fresh rosemary

1 clove garlic, crushed
4 turkey breast steaks
   (approximately 4 ounces each)
Grated zest and juice of
   1 large orange
1 teaspoon honey
2 teaspoons cornmeal
2 tablespoons water

Heat 1 tablespoon of the oil in saucepan. Stir in onion, apricots, pine nuts, turmeric and rice. Cook quickly for 1 to 2 minutes. Pour in vegetable stock, salt and pepper. Bring to a boil, stirring occasionally. Cover and cook gently for 20 minutes or until all stock has been absorbed.

Meanwhile, put remaining oil in frying pan. Add rosemary, garlic and turkey steaks. Fry quickly to brown on all sides. Add orange zest, juice and honey. Cover and cook for 5 minutes.

Blend cornmeal with water. Stir into liquid in frying pan. Bring to a boil and cook for 1 minute. Serve with pilaf, garnished with orange segments and fresh rosemary, if desired.   Makes 4 servings.

Per Serving (approx):
Calories 570
Carbohydrate 86 gm

Protein 14 gm
Sodium 1047 mg

Fat 19 gm
Cholesterol 12 mg

Sauté & Stir-Fry
Turkey Wings

Turkey Fricassee with Dumplings

This dish combines a time-honored cooking method with all of the flavor reminiscent of American Sunday dinners on a farm—nourishing, delicious, comforting and warming.

2 pounds turkey wings, each
    cut into 2 or 3 pieces
2 tablespoons butter or
    margarine
2 tablespoons oil
1/3 cup finely chopped onion
8 medium mushrooms, sliced
1 can (10 3/4 ounces) cream of
    chicken soup

1/2 cup dry white wine
1/2 teaspoon dried thyme
1/4 cup whipping cream
2 cups buttermilk baking mix
2 teaspoons dried parsley
    flakes
2/3 cup milk

In a Dutch oven melt butter with oil. Sauté wings until browned; remove. In the same pan sauté onion and mushrooms until onion is soft and transparent Stir in soup, wine and thyme.

Return wings to pot. Cover and cook over low heat for 1 1/2 hours or until wings are tender. Stir in cream. Mix together baking mix, parsley flakes and milk with fork. Drop by spoonfuls onto turkey mixture that is at a slow boil. Cook for 10 minutes. Cover; cook for an additional 10 minutes.   Makes 4 to 6 servings.

Per Serving (approx):
Calories 721   *Protein 42 gm*   *Fat 41 gm*
Carbohydrate 42 gm   *Sodium 1251 mg*   *Cholesterol 141 mg*

191

French Turkey Fillets

Yes, you can have elegant entrees that are low in calories, fat and cholesterol.

1 pound skinless, boneless turkey breast fillets	2 tablespoons light margarine
Salt and pepper to taste	3 tablespoons minced shallot or green onion
1 tablespoon oil	1 cup white wine

Season fillets with salt and pepper. In a large nonstick skillet over medium-high heat, warm oil. Add fillets and cook for 2 minutes on each side or until lightly browned. Reduce heat to medium-low; cook for 2 to 3 minutes longer on each side or until cooked through. Remove fillets and set aside; keep warm.

Heat 1 tablespoon of the margarine in skillet until melted. Add shallots and sauté for 1 minute. Stir in wine. Increase heat to medium-high; boil wine for 1 to 2 minutes or until it reduces to thick, syrupy sauce. Remove skillet from heat and swirl in remaining margarine. To serve, pour sauce over turkey fillets.   Makes 4 servings.

Per Serving (approx):
Calories 214
Carbohydrate 2 gm

Protein 28 gm
Sodium 126 mg

Fat 7 gm
Cholesterol 70 mg

Spicy Breakfast Sausage

1 pound ground turkey
1 egg or 2 egg whites,
   lightly beaten
1/3 cup dry bread crumbs
2 green onions, minced
1 clove garlic, minced

1/2 teaspoon crushed fennel seed
1/2 teaspoon each dried thyme
   and ground cumin
1 pinch each red pepper flakes,
   salt and ground nutmeg
1 tablespoon oil

Mix together all ingredients except oil. Form into 8 patties. Brown patties in hot oil for 4 to 5 minutes on each side.   Makes 8 servings.

Per Serving (approx):
Calories 122   *Protein 12 gm*   *Fat 7 gm*
Carbohydrate 4 gm   *Sodium 137 mg*   *Cholesterol 68 mg*

Spicy Cajun Hash

2 tablespoons oil
1 to 1 1/4 pounds ground turkey
2 tablespoons butter or
   margarine
2 tablespoons flour
1 cup chopped onion
1/2 cup chopped bell pepper
1 cup chicken broth

1 1/2 tablespoons
   Worcestershire sauce
1 package (10 ounces) frozen
   corn kernels, thawed
2 cups diced cooked potato
Salt and pepper to taste
Hot pepper sauce to taste
Hot biscuits (optional)

In large skillet over medium heat, warm oil. Add turkey; sauté for 10 minutes, stirring frequently, until cooked through. Remove turkey and set aside. Add butter and flour to skillet. Cook for 4 to 5 minutes or until mixture is browned, stirring constantly. Add onion and bell pepper. Cook for 5 minutes or until vegetables are tender, stirring often. Stir in chicken broth and Worcestershire sauce; cook until thickened, stirring constantly. Add cooked turkey, corn and potato; cook for 2 to 3 minutes longer or until heated through. Season with salt, pepper and hot pepper sauce. Serve over biscuits, if desired.   Makes 4 to 6 servings.

Per Serving (approx):
Calories 330   *Protein 20 gm*   *Fat 16 gm*
Carbohydrate 26 gm   *Sodium 444 mg*   *Cholesterol 79 mg*

Homemade Turkey Sausage

1 pound ground turkey
1/2 teaspoon fennel seed
1 teaspoon Italian seasoning

1 1/2 teaspoons onion powder
1/4 teaspoon ground or rubbed
   sage

Combine all ingredients well to blend flavors. Shape into 6 patties and fry in nonstick skillet coated with nonstick vegetable cooking spray until lightly browned and cooked through, 5 to 6 minutes per side.

Makes 6 servings.

Per Serving (approx):
Calories 126
Carbohydrate .5 gm

Protein 14 gm
Sodium 63 mg

Fat 7 gm
Cholesterol 46 mg

Morning Sausage and Apples

Granny Smith apples are particularly good in this dish.

1 pound turkey breakfast sausage
1/2 cup firmly packed brown sugar
1/2 cup whipping cream

1/2 teaspoon ground cinnamon
2 apples, cut into wedges
4 frozen waffles, toasted

Cut turkey into 8 patties. Place in nonstick skillet and cook over medium heat for 10 minutes, turning occasionally. Add sugar, cream, cinnamon and apples.

Cook for 5 minutes more, stirring constantly until thickened. Serve over hot waffles.   Makes 4 servings.

Per Serving (approx):
Calories 452
Carbohydrate 44 gm

Protein 20 gm
Sodium 708 mg

Fat 22 gm
Cholesterol 92 mg

Turkey Mornay

1 pound turkey breast slices
  (approximately 8 slices)
2 eggs, beaten
2/3 cup fine dry bread crumbs
4 tablespoons oil

2 packages (3 ounces each)
  cream cheese
4 slices (3/4 ounce each)
  processed Swiss cheese
1/3 cup milk
2 tablespoons dry white wine

Dip turkey in egg; coat with bread crumbs. Heat 2 tablespoons of the oil in skillet over medium-high heat. Add half the turkey. Cook for 3 minutes; turn and cook for 2 minutes more. Place turkey on platter; cover to keep warm. Repeat with remaining oil and turkey.

Meanwhile, combine cheeses and milk in saucepan. Warm over low heat, stirring until cheeses melt and mixture is smooth. Stir in wine. Serve over turkey.   Makes 4 servings.

Per Serving (approx):
Calories 597
Carbohydrate 15 gm

Protein 41 gm
Sodium 641 mg

Fat 41 gm
Cholesterol 237 mg

Turkey Slices with Green Peppercorn Sauce

1 1/4 pounds thin slices of
  turkey breast
Salt and pepper to taste
2 tablespoons each oil and butter

1 cup dry white wine
3 green onions, minced
1 tablespoon Dijon-style mustard
1 tablespoon green peppercorns

Season turkey slices and sauté in hot oil and butter for 2 minutes on each side; remove and keep warm. Add white wine, onions, mustard and peppercorns to pan and simmer for 5 minutes. Serve over turkey slices.
Makes 6 servings.

Per Serving (approx):
Calories 239
Carbohydrate 1 gm

Protein 21 gm
Sodium 210 mg

Fat 14 gm
Cholesterol 61 mg

Turkey Steaks Kiev

This delicious entree comes from Kiev, where this classic recipe was born. Now it is world famous. We have adapted it using turkey, with wonderful results. See for yourself.

1/2 stick (1/4 cup) butter or
   margarine, chilled
8 turkey breast steaks or slices
   (about 1 pound total)
1/4 cup finely chopped parsley

1 egg
1 teaspoon salt
1/8 teaspoon black pepper
3/4 cup fine dry bread crumbs
Oil, for frying

Cut stick of butter into 8 pieces; chill in freezer. Meanwhile, place each turkey steak between 2 sheets of waxed paper and pound to about 1/8 inch thickness.

Place 1 piece of butter and 1 teaspoon parsley on each pounded steak. Fold sides to seal in butter, then roll up, securing each roll with wooden pick. Beat egg slightly. Mix together salt, pepper and bread crumbs.

One at a time, dip rolled turkey steaks in egg, then in crumb mixture to coat well. Place steaks in refrigerator for at least 1 hour or until thoroughly chilled.

When ready to cook, heat 1/2 inch oil in skillet to 350 degrees. Fry rolled turkey steaks for 5 to 7 minutes or until tender and golden brown, turning once. Drain well and serve hot.   Makes 4 servings.

Per Serving (approx):
Calories 442
Carbohydrate 14 gm

Protein 4 gm
Sodium 860 mg

Fat 41 gm
Cholesterol 85 mg

Turkey Veronique

We have enjoyed Chicken Veronique, Veal Veronique and now Turkey Veronique (with cream sauce)—a very special entree.

1 1/2 tablespoons cornstarch	1/3 cup finely chopped shallot
Salt and pepper to taste	1/2 cup white wine
1 pound turkey breast tenderloins	1 1/2 cups seedless green
2 to 3 tablespoons butter or	and/or red grapes
margarine	1/2 cup half-and-half

On waxed paper, combine 1 tablespoon of the cornstarch, the salt and pepper. Dust tenderloins with mixture.

In large skillet over medium heat, melt 2 tablespoons of the butter. Sauté tenderloins for about 4 minutes on each side or until golden brown. Remove tenderloins from skillet; cover to keep warm.

In same skillet cook shallot in drippings for 2 to 3 minutes or until soft, adding remaining butter if needed. Stir in wine, scraping up browned bits; bring to a boil. Add tenderloins; reduce heat to low, cover and simmer for 10 to 15 minutes. Add grapes; cook for 1 minute or until heated through.

In cup stir remaining cornstarch into half-and-half until well blended. Increase heat to medium; stir cornstarch mixture into liquid in skillet and cook until thickened, stirring constantly. Serve sauce over tenderloins. Makes 4 servings.

Per Serving (approx):
Calories 297 *Protein 28 gm* *Fat 13 gm*
Carbohydrate 17 gm *Sodium 166 mg* *Cholesterol 101 mg*

Champagne-Sauced Turkey

This sophisticated dish is best for a small dinner party because it needs some last-minute attention.

4 turkey breast tenderloins (approximately 1 1/4 pounds total)
2 shallots, chopped
1 1/2 cups sliced mushrooms
1/4 cup butter

2 cups Champagne
2 cups whipping cream
Salt and pepper to taste
8 ounces angel hair pasta, cooked and drained

Sauté turkey, shallots and mushrooms in butter until turkey is browned. Add Champagne; cover and simmer until turkey is cooked through, about 10 minutes. Remove turkey to plate; cover and keep warm. With slotted spoon, remove mushrooms and shallots to another plate.

In the same pan over high heat simmer Champagne until reduced by about half. Stir in cream and simmer until slightly thickened, about 10 to 15 minutes. Return mushrooms to pan and stir. Season with salt and pepper.

Slice turkey neatly against grain. Serve over pasta with Champagne sauce.
Makes 4 to 6 servings.

Per Serving (approx):
Calories 595
Carbohydrate 25 gm

Protein 30 gm
Sodium 251 mg

Fat 41 gm
Cholesterol 215 mg

To meet market demand for turkeys during the holiday season, the industry "sets" more eggs during April, May and June.

Turkey Steak Diane

4 tablespoons margarine
1 pound turkey breast steaks
3 tablespoons chopped green
   onion
2 tablespoons dry sherry

2 tablespoons Worcestershire
   sauce
2 teaspoons finely chopped
   parsley

Melt 1 tablespoon of the margarine in skillet over medium heat. When margarine begins to bubble, add turkey. Cook for 3 minutes; turn. Reduce heat to medium low. Cover; cook for 5 minutes more or until juices run clear.

Meanwhile, melt another tablespoon margarine in small saucepan over medium heat. Add green onion; cook and stir for 2 to 3 minutes. Add sherry and Worcestershire sauce; cook for 2 minutes more to reduce sauce. Stir in remaining 2 tablespoons margarine. Serve sauce immediately over turkey steaks. Sprinkle with parsley.   Makes 4 servings.

Per Serving (approx):
Calories 268
Carbohydrate 1 gm

Protein 25 gm
Sodium 202 mg

Fat 18 gm
Cholesterol 61 mg

Basic Turkey Schnitzel

Our personal favorite variation is Champignon Schnitzel.

6 turkey breast cutlets
Salt and pepper to taste
1/2 cup flour
2 tablespoons each butter and
  oil

1/4 cup butter
1/4 cup lemon juice
2 tablespoons chopped parsley

Flatten turkey cutlets to 1/4 inch thickness by pounding between 2 sheets of plastic wrap. Salt and pepper cutlets. Dip one side in flour.

Meanwhile, heat the 2 tablespoons butter and 2 tablespoons oil in skillet. Sauté cutlets for 3 minutes on each side. Remove to warmed platter.

Add the 1/4 cup butter, lemon juice and parsley to skillet. Bring to a boil. Cook to reduce slightly, then pour over cutlets.   Makes 6 servings.

SCHNITZEL A LA HOLSTEIN: Garnish basic schnitzel with egg fried in butter and topped with crisscrossed flat anchovies. Serve with capers and chopped onion.

CHAMPIGNON SCHNITZEL: Sauté sliced mushrooms in butter; add whipping cream to make sauce and serve basic schnitzel smothered in this rich sauce.

Per Serving (approx) for basic schnitzel:
Calories 211
Carbohydrate 5 gm

Protein 6 gm
Sodium 194 mg

Fat 17 gm
Cholesterol 43 mg

California Turkey Schnitzel

When you start with turkey cutlets and use your imagination, a whole new world of "veal" cookery is open to you—at a very small price!

6 turkey breast cutlets
2 eggs, lightly beaten
1 cup dry bread crumbs or
   1/2 cup crumbs and
1/2 cup grated Parmesan cheese*

2 tablespoons each butter and
   oil
1/4 cup butter
1/4 cup lemon juice
2 tablespoons chopped parsley

Flatten turkey cutlets to 1/4 inch thickness by pounding between 2 sheets of plastic wrap. Dip in egg, then in bread crumbs. Refrigerate for 15 minutes.

Heat the butter and oil; sauté cutlets for 3 minutes on each side; remove to warmed platter. Add the 1/4 cup butter, lemon juice, and parsley to skillet; bring to a boil. Cook to reduce slightly; pour over cutlets. Serve with noodles or spaetzle. Makes 6 servings.

*Note: Salt and pepper may be needed if cheese is omitted.

Per Serving (approx):
Calories 263
Carbohydrate 13 gm

Protein 9 gm
Sodium 272 mg

Fat 19 gm
Cholesterol 114 mg

Turkey Drives

In the late 1800s, there was a concentration of turkey growers in the area known as Round Valley near Covelo (parallel with Legget and Orland in Northern California). The flocks ranged in size from 100—500 birds. When the poults were big enough to forage well, the owners brought the broods together. The journey involved traversing Ham's Pass, going through Stony Creek Valley, and ended in West Sacramento. Those in charge of the drive were usually a few adult males; they were accompanied by some boys, dogs, and a supply wagon. It took the group 75—100 days to make the 250 mile trip. Once at West Sacramento, the turkeys were either sold to customers in the capital city or placed on river boats and sent to San Francisco.

Schnitzel Florentine

6 turkey breast cutlets
1/2 cup flour
Salt and pepper to taste
2 tablespoons each butter and
  oil

1 1/2 pounds spinach, cooked
  and well drained
2 tablespoons grated Parmesan
  cheese

Flatten turkey cutlets to 1/4 inch thickness by pounding between 2 sheets of plastic wrap. Dip in flour. Salt and pepper each side.

Heat butter and oil in skillet. Sauté turkey for 3 minutes on each side. Prepare Hollandaise Sauce.

Arrange schnitzel on mound of freshly boiled and drained spinach. Top with Hollandaise Sauce. Sprinkle with Parmesan cheese and heat in oven to brown slightly. Serve with noodles, if desired.

Makes 6 servings.

HOLLANDAISE SAUCE:
Melt 1/2 cup butter over hot water in top of double broiler. Remove from heat and let cool. Blend 4 beaten egg yolks into butter. Add 1/3 cup boiling water slowly, stirring constantly. Cook over hot water, stirring constantly until thickened. Remove from heat. Stir in 3 tablespoons lemon juice, 1/4 teaspoon salt and dash of cayenne.   Makes about 1 cup.

Per Serving (approx):
Calories 359
Carbohydrate 13 gm

Protein 12 gm
Sodium 502 mg

Fat 29 gm
Cholesterol 202 mg

Peppered Turkey Medallions with Chutney Sauce

1/2 to 1 tablespoon mixed
  peppercorns
1 pound turkey breast tenderloins,
  cut into 3/4-inch medallions
1 teaspoon margarine
2 teaspoons olive oil

2 tablespoons minced green
  onion
1/4 cup reduced-sodium
  chicken bouillon
2 tablespoons brandy
1/4 cup chutney

Crush peppercorns in spice grinder, food processor or mortar with pestle. Pat peppercorns on both sides of turkey medallions. Refrigerate for 30 minutes.

In large nonstick skillet over medium heat, sauté medallions in margarine and 1 teaspoon of the oil for 4 to 5 minutes per side or until no longer pink in center. Remove medallions from pan and keep warm.

Add remaining teaspoon of oil to skillet and sauté onion for 30 seconds. Add bouillon and cook for 45 seconds to reduce liquid. Stir in brandy and cook for 1 to 2 minutes. Reduce heat to low and blend in chutney.

To serve, pour chutney sauce over medallions.   Makes 4 servings.

Per Serving (approx):
Calories 218
Carbohydrate 11 gm

Protein 28 gm
Sodium 142 mg

Fat 4 gm
Cholesterol 70 mg

Turkey Viennese

1 teaspoon paprika
1/8 teaspoon white pepper
1 1/2 pounds turkey thighs,
  skinned, boned and
  cut into 1/4-inch strips
2 tablespoons margarine
1 1/2 cups finely chopped onion

1 clove garlic, minced
1 bay leaf
1/3 cup reduced-sodium
  chicken bouillon
1/4 cup tomato sauce
1/4 cup imitation sour cream
1/2 teaspoon sugar

In small bowl mix paprika and pepper; sprinkle over turkey strips to coat.

In 3-quart saucepan over medium-high heat, sauté turkey strips in 1 tablespoon of the margarine until lightly browned; remove from pan and set aside.

In same saucepan sauté onion and garlic in remaining margarine. Cook and stir until onion begins to brown. Add bay leaf, bouillon and tomato sauce; bring to a boil. Reduce heat to medium and simmer for about 5 minutes; stir to prevent mixture from sticking to pan.

Add turkey to sauce, cover and reduce heat to low. Simmer 12 minutes or until turkey is tender. Fold sour cream and sugar into mixture; heat through. Serve with egg noodles, if desired.   Make 4 servings.

Per Serving (approx):
Calories 254
Carbohydrate 8 gm

Protein 24 gm
Sodium 271 mg

Fat 14 gm
Cholesterol 85 mg

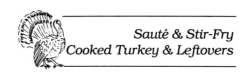

Spicy Orange Turkey

12 ounces cooked turkey breast
1/2 cup water
3 tablespoons orange juice
 concentrate
1 tablespoon lemon juice
1 teaspoon chili powder

1/2 teaspoon onion powder
4 teaspoons cornstarch
1 medium green bell pepper, cut
 into 1-inch chunks
1 large orange, peeled and
 sliced crosswise

Cut turkey into 1/8-inch slices; set aside. Combine water, orange juice concentrate, lemon juice, seasonings and cornstarch in skillet. Cook over medium heat, stirring constantly until thickened.

Layer turkey, bell pepper and orange slices in skillet. Bring to a boil; reduce heat, cover and simmer for 6 to 8 minutes.

To serve, place orange slices and bell pepper around edge of platter; place turkey in center. Stir sauce; pour small amount over turkey. Pass remaining sauce.   Makes 4 servings.

Per Serving (approx):
Calories 148
Carbohydrate 13 gm

Protein 19 gm
Sodium 43 mg

Fat 5 gm
Cholesterol 46 mg

Turkey Medallions with Cumberland Sauce

Cumberland sauce, of English origin, is customarily served with baked ham, but we think you'll like it with turkey as much as we do.

1/2 cup red or black currant
   jelly
3 tablespoons port wine
1 1/2 teaspoons Dijon mustard
4 teaspoons lemon juice
Dash of cayenne pepper
2 teaspoons margarine

2 teaspoons cornstarch
4 teaspoons cold water
2 turkey breast tenderloins
Salt and pepper to taste
2 tablespoons olive oil
1 tablespoon margarine

In small saucepan over medium-high heat, combine jelly, port wine, mustard, lemon juice, cayenne pepper and the 2 teaspoons margarine until jelly is melted.

In small bowl combine cornstarch and water. Stir into jelly mixture. Bring sauce to a boil and cook until thickened. Reduce heat and keep warm.

Cut tenderloins into medallion-shaped slices (about 3/4 inch thick). Season to taste with salt and pepper. In large skillet over medium-high heat, sauté medallions in the olive oil and 1 tablespoon margarine for about 2 1/2 minutes per side or until no longer pink in thickest part.

Spoon thin layer of sauce on each plate; arrange medallions over sauce. Garnish with sour cream, if desired. **Makes 4 servings.**

Per Serving (approx):
Calories 347
Carbohydrate 29 gm

Protein 27 gm
Sodium 144 mg

Fat 13 gm
Cholesterol 70 mg

Turkey Lemon Cutlets

This is a personal favorite of one of the editors of this cookbook. Besides the great taste, it is low in fat, calories and sodium. We serve it with steamed rice and slices of fruit, such as mango and pineapple.

2 tablespoons flour
1/4 teaspoon salt
1/4 teaspoon black pepper
8 turkey breast cutlets
2 tablespoons margarine

1/2 cup white wine
6 thin slices lemon
1/4 cup chopped parsley
1/4 cup chopped fresh basil

In shallow plate combine flour, salt and pepper. Dip turkey cutlets lightly in flour mixture to coat each side.

In large nonstick skillet over medium-high heat, sauté turkey in margarine for 1 to 2 minutes per side or until turkey is no longer pink in center. Remove turkey from skillet and keep warm.

In same skillet add wine, lemon slices, parsley and basil. On medium-high heat cook for 3 to 4 minutes or until sauce is slightly thickened, stirring occasionally. Return turkey to skillet; reduce heat, cover and heat for 1 to 2 minutes. Makes 8 servings.

Per Serving (approx):
Calories 64
Carbohydrate 6 gm

Protein 1 gm
Sodium 109 mg

Fat 3 gm
Cholesterol 90 mg

Gypsy Cutlets

This started out as a Magyar (Hungarian) gypsy dish made with chicken. We made a few changes that we think you'll like.

1 pound skinless turkey breast
   cutlets, thinly sliced
2 teaspoons paprika
Salt and pepper to taste
1 1/2 tablespoons oil
1/2 cup thinly sliced onion

1 can (14 1/2 ounces) Cajun-
   or Mexican-style stewed
   tomatoes, including juice
1/4 cup sour cream substitute
   or low-fat sour cream

Season cutlets on both sides with paprika, salt and pepper. In large non-stick skillet over medium-high heat, warm oil. Add cutlets and brown for 1 minute on each side. Remove and set aside.

To same skillet add onion and sauté for 1 minute or until slightly softened. Add tomatoes and their liquid. Cook for 5 minutes or until sauce thickens, stirring often. Stir in sour cream substitute until well mixed.

Reduce heat to medium-low. Return cutlets and any juices to skillet and simmer for 1 to 2 minutes or until turkey is just cooked through. To serve, spoon sauce over turkey. Makes 4 servings.

Per Serving (approx):
Calories 207
Carbohydrate 7 gm

Protein 30 gm
Sodium 479 mg

Fat 6 gm
Cholesterol 70 mg

Turkey Fillets in Mustard Cream Sauce

This is one of four recipes in this book that came to us from the British Turkey Federation. We think you'll like it as much as we do.

2 tablespoons butter
1 tablespoon olive oil
4 skinless turkey fillets
   (approximately 4 ounces each)
1 small onion, finely
   chopped

1 cup dry white wine
1/3 cup light stock
1/3 cup half-and-half
2 tablespoons Dijon mustard
Salt and pepper to taste

Heat butter and oil in large, deep frying pan. Add turkey fillets and cook on both sides until light brown. Add onion and cook for 2 more minutes. Pour wine and stock over fillets; cover and simmer for 15 to 20 minutes or until tender.

Remove turkey fillets from pan and keep warm. Boil liquid until reduced by half. Remove from heat, stir in half-and-half and mustard, then heat gently without boiling. Season to taste.

Strain sauce and pour over turkey. Serve with fresh vegetables, if desired. Makes 4 servings.

Per Serving (approx):
Calories 357
Carbohydrate 3 gm

Protein 29 gm
Sodium 429 mg

Fat 22 gm
Cholesterol 109 mg

Skillet-Simmered Turkey Thighs

3 turkey thighs
(about 1 1/2 pounds each)
2 tablespoons oil
1 tablespoon margarine
1 can (10 3/4 ounces)
condensed chicken broth
1 cup chopped fresh
mushrooms
3 tablespoons instant minced
onion

1/2 cup dry white wine
Salt to taste
1 teaspoon dry mustard
1 teaspoon paprika
1/4 teaspoon dried basil
1/4 teaspoon dried sage
1/8 teaspoon black pepper
3 tablespoons cornstarch
3 tablespoons water

Brown turkey thighs in heavy skillet or Dutch oven in heated oil and margarine.

Combine broth, mushrooms, onion, wine, salt, mustard, paprika, basil, sage and pepper. Pour over browned turkey pieces and bring to a boil. Reduce heat, cover and simmer for about 2 hours or until meat is tender.

Remove turkey to serving dish, cut in serving portions and keep hot. Skim off and discard any fat from cooking liquid. Mix cornstarch with water and stir into liquid in pan. Cook, stirring, until sauce boils and thickens. Serve over turkey.   Makes 6 servings.

Per Serving (approx):
Calories 885
Carbohydrate 7 gm

Protein 127 gm
Sodium 661 mg

Fat 38 gm
Cholesterol 381 mg

Turkey Jardiniere

1 pound turkey breast slices
1 teaspoon lemon pepper
2 medium carrots, cut into
   3-inch julienne strips

1 small zucchini, cut into
   3-inch julienne strips
1 small onion, chopped
1 cup water

Pound turkey between pieces of plastic wrap. Sprinkle turkey with lemon pepper; set aside.

Combine vegetables and water in saucepan. Bring to a boil; reduce heat, cover and simmer for 5 minutes or until tender-crisp.

Remove vegetables, reserving liquid in pan. Place vegetables on turkey. Roll up and secure with toothpicks. Cook turkey rolls in butter in skillet over medium heat for 15 minutes, turning frequently until evenly browned. Prepare sauce and serve over turkey.   Makes 4 servings.

WINE-LEMON SAUCE:
To 2/3 cup reserved liquid from vegetables, add 2 tablespoons white wine, 1 1/2 teaspoons cornstarch, 1 teaspoon lemon juice and 1/4 teaspoon grated lemon zest. Cook over medium heat, stirring constantly until thickened.

Per Serving (approx):
Calories 195
Carbohydrate 6 gm

Protein 28 gm
Sodium 309 mg

Fat 6 gm
Cholesterol 70 mg

Southern Fried Turkey with Gravy

2 pounds turkey wings
1/2 cup flour
1/2 teaspoon salt
1 teaspoon black pepper

1 egg, beaten
1 cup oil
1 cup milk

Cut turkey at joint to separate middle wing portion from wing drumette. Combine flour, salt and pepper in shallow dish. Reserve 1 tablespoon flour mixture for gravy. Coat turkey with egg, then with flour mixture.

Fry turkey in hot oil in skillet over medium-high heat for about 10 minutes, turning to brown evenly. Reduce heat to low. Cover and simmer for 1 hour.

Remove cover; increase heat to medium-high. Cook for 10 minutes more, turning occasionally to crisp. Place turkey on platter.

Make gravy by pouring all but 1 tablespoon oil out of skillet. Stir in reserved flour mixture. Cook and stir for 1 minute. Gradually add milk. Cook and stir over medium until thickened. Serve with turkey.

Makes 4 servings.

Per Serving (approx):
Calories 965
Carbohydrate 15 gm

Protein 49 gm
Sodium 437 mg

Fat 78 gm
Cholesterol 160 mg

Turkey Creole

3 tablespoons butter
1 pound turkey breast slices
1 green bell pepper, cut into chunks
2 stalks celery, sliced
1 medium onion, cut into wedges
2 tomatoes, cut into chunks

1 can (15 ounces) tomato sauce
1/4 teaspoon each dried thyme,
  black pepper, paprika
  and garlic powder
1/8 teaspoon cayenne pepper

Melt 1 tablespoon of the butter in skillet. When butter begins to brown, add half the turkey. Cook for 3 minutes; turn and cook for 2 minutes more. Place turkey on platter; cover to keep warm. Repeat with 1 more tablespoon butter and remaining turkey.

In same skillet melt remaining 1 tablespoon butter over medium heat. Add bell pepper, celery and onion. Cook for 3 minutes or until vegetables are tender-crisp, stirring frequently. Stir in tomatoes, tomato sauce and seasonings. Bring to a boil; reduce heat and simmer for 15 minutes. Serve over turkey and rice. Makes 4 servings.

Per Serving (approx):
Calories 510
Carbohydrate 62 gm

Protein 36 gm
Sodium 1191 mg

Fat 13 gm
Cholesterol 86 mg

> Technical advances in turkey genetics, production and processing have created a turkey which produces a pound of meat, using a smaller amount of feed, in less time than most other domestic meat-producing animals.

213

Almond-Crusted Turkey Steaks

1 turkey half breast
  (about 2 pounds)
1/2 cup raw almonds
1/4 cup grated Parmesan
  cheese
1/4 teaspoon dried basil

1/4 teaspoon paprika
Salt to taste
3 tablespoons each butter and
  oil, divided
1/2 cup white wine
2 teaspoons lemon juice

Remove skin from turkey and cut meat in half-inch slices parallel to top of breast. Place slices between sheets of waxed paper and pound to about 1/4 inch thickness.

Grind or grate almonds. Mix with cheese, basil, paprika and salt on sheet of waxed paper. Dip turkey slices, one at a time, into mixture, coating both sides.

Heat 1 tablespoon each butter and oil in 10-inch skillet. Add turkey slices to cover bottom of skillet; brown over medium heat, turning once. Cook each slice for about 4 minutes.

Remove turkey to heated serving platter. Add remaining butter and oil, and cook remaining turkey. Add wine and lemon juice to skillet and boil rapidly until very slightly thickened. Spoon over steaks.

Makes 4 to 6 servings.

Per Serving (approx):
Calories 648
Carbohydrate 4 gm

Protein 55 gm
Sodium 307 mg

Fat 43 gm
Cholesterol 151 mg

Turkey Slices Orangerie

Visions of duck a l'orange come to mind with this easy recipe for breast of turkey slices and a few simple ingredients. This dish takes just twenty minutes to prepare but is a classic in its own right.

1 to 1 1/4 pounds turkey
   breast slices
Salt and pepper to taste
1/3 cup flour
3 tablespoons butter
1 onion, chopped

3/4 cup chicken broth
1/3 cup sherry
2 tablespoons orange
   marmalade
1/4 cup whipping cream

Dredge turkey slices in seasoned flour. Brown turkey in butter in skillet over medium-high heat. Add onion, chicken broth and sherry to skillet. Cover and simmer for 15 minutes. Remove turkey from pan; set aside and keep warm.

Add orange marmalade and cream to pan juices; simmer for about 5 minutes or until thickened. Serve sauce over turkey slices.

Makes 4 servings.

Per Serving (approx):
Calories 388
Carbohydrate 21 gm

Protein 27 gm
Sodium 518 mg

Fat 19 gm
Cholesterol 98 mg

Turkey and Broccoli Stir-Fry

1 pound turkey breast cutlets,
   cut into 1/2-inch strips
1 tablespoon dry white wine
   or sherry
2 tablespoons reduced-sodium
   soy sauce
1 cup reduced-sodium
   chicken bouillon
1 tablespoon cornstarch

6 tablespoons slivered almonds
3 tablespoons oil
1/3 cup thinly sliced green
   onion
2 cloves garlic, minced
1 pound broccoli, cut
   into 1-inch pieces
1/2 pound mushrooms,
   sliced

In medium bowl combine turkey, wine and 1 tablespoon of the soy sauce. Set aside.

In small bowl, combine bouillon, remaining soy sauce and cornstarch. Set aside.

In wok or large skillet over medium-high heat, stir-fry almonds in 2 tablespoons of the oil, stirring to coat. Add turkey with marinade and stir-fry until turkey loses pink color and almonds are lightly browned. Remove from pan.

Add remaining oil to pan and stir-fry onion, garlic and broccoli until vegetables are tender-crisp. Add mushrooms and stir-fry for an additional minute. Fold in turkey and almonds. Add bouillon mixture and cook and stir until thickened.   Makes 6 servings.

*Per Serving (approx):
Calories 246
Carbohydrate 10 gm*

*Protein 23 gm
Sodium 286 mg*

*Fat 13 gm
Cholesterol 47 mg*

POT ROASTS & STEWS

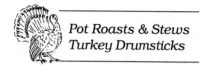
Drumsticks with Sauerkraut

In this main dish that serves four, it's the oven that does most of the work.

3 1/2 cups sauerkraut
1 apple, peeled, cored and sliced
1 medium onion, chopped
Brown sugar to taste
4 turkey drumsticks
   (about 3 pounds total)

Melted butter or margarine
Salt and pepper to taste
1/4 cup catsup
1 tablespoon Worcestershire
   sauce
Sweet potato or banana squash
   chunks (optional)

Drain sauerkraut and spread over bottom of large casserole or baking pan big enough to accommodate drumsticks. Mix in apple and onion. Taste; if too sour to suit you, add sprinkling of brown sugar.

Arrange drumsticks on top, pushing them down into mixture. Brush tops with butter and sprinkle with salt and pepper. Stir catsup and Worcestershire sauce together and spread over each drumstick. Cover pan with lid or foil.

Bake at 325 degrees for 1 hour. Uncover long enough to dot drumsticks with a little more butter, if necessary. Replace lid and bake for about 45 minutes longer or until meat is fork tender.

During last hour of baking, sweet potatoes or pieces of banana squash can be added to the casserole as it bakes, if you wish. Dinner, then, might be drumsticks and kraut, sweet potatoes or squash.

Makes 4 servings.

Per Serving (approx):
Calories 630
Carbohydrate 25 gm

Protein 71 gm
Sodium 1770 mg

Fat 27 gm
Cholesterol 215 mg

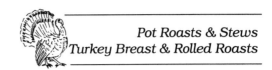

Cape Cod Turkey Roast

1 turkey breast (1 1/2 to 2 pounds)
2 cans (14 ounces each)
  chicken broth
1 bay leaf
1/2 teaspoon dried summer savory

2 medium onions, quartered
2 carrots, quartered
1/2 pound new potatoes, halved
1 cup fresh or frozen broccoli
  florets or

Place roast, broth and seasonings in 4-quart Dutch oven. Cover and simmer for 1 1/2 to 2 1/2 hours or until turkey is no longer pink and meat thermometer reaches 180 degrees. Add onions, carrots and potatoes; cook for 20 minutes more. Add broccoli; cook for 10 minutes. Slice roast; serve with vegetables and broth.　　　Makes 4 to 6 servings.

Per Serving (approx):
Calories 102
Carbohydrate 19 gm

Protein 4 gm
Sodium 823 mg

Fat 1 gm
Cholesterol 2 mg

Cranberry Turkey Roast

2 tablespoons flour
1/4 teaspoon black pepper
1 boneless turkey breast
2 tablespoons oil
1/4 cup chopped onion

1 1/2 cups fresh cranberries
  or canned whole berry
  cranberry sauce
1/2 cup orange juice
3 tablespoons sugar, or to taste*
1 teaspoon grated orange zest

On waxed paper combine flour and pepper. Coat turkey breast with flour mixture. In Dutch oven over medium heat, warm oil. Brown roast in oil until golden. Remove and set aside; pour off all but 1 tablespoon oil. In remaining oil over medium heat, cook onion for 3 minutes, stirring frequently. Add cranberries, orange juice, sugar and orange zest; bring to a boil. Cook for 2 to 3 minutes. Return turkey to Dutch oven and cover with cranberry mixture. Reduce heat to low, cover and simmer, turning turkey once or twice, for 30 to 40 minutes.　　　Makes 6 servings.

*Note: If using canned cranberry sauce, sugar may be omitted.

Per Serving (approx):
Calories 229
Carbohydrate 15 gm

Protein 27 gm
Sodium 163 mg

Fat 6 gm
Cholesterol 70 mg

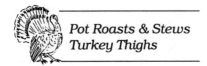

Dutch Oven Pot Roast

2 pounds turkey thighs,
  skin removed
2 small onions, quartered
1 tablespoon oil
1/2 cup reduced-sodium
  chicken bouillon
2 cloves garlic, minced
1/4 teaspoon salt
1/2 teaspoon dried basil
1/2 teaspoon black pepper

1/4 teaspoon dried thyme
4 small potatoes, peeled and
  cut in half
4 small carrots, cut into chunks
1/2 pound cabbage, cut into
  wedges
1 tablespoon cornstarch
1/4 cup cold water
2 tablespoons chopped parsley

In 5-quart Dutch oven over medium-high heat, brown turkey thighs and onions for 4 to 5 minutes in oil, turning thighs after 3 minutes. Add bouillon, garlic, salt, basil, pepper and thyme. Bring to a boil, reduce heat to low, cover and cook for 30 minutes or until turkey is tender.

Remove thighs from pan; add potatoes and carrots. Place turkey thighs over vegetables. Return mixture to a boil; reduce heat to low, cover and cook for 15 minutes or until vegetables are tender. Add cabbage; cover and cook for 8 to 10 minutes or until cabbage is fork tender.

Remove turkey and vegetables to platter. Keep warm. In small bowl combine cornstarch and water; stir into hot pan juices and cook for 1 minute over medium heat or until mixture is thickened.

To serve, pour sauce over turkey and vegetables. Garnish with parsley.
Makes 4 servings.

Per Serving (approx):
Calories 339
Carbohydrate 34 gm

Protein 30 gm
Sodium 340 mg

Fat 9 gm
Cholesterol 97 mg

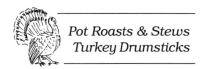

Italian Turkey with Vegetables

2 pounds turkey drumsticks
1 can (14 1/2 ounces) stewed
  tomatoes
1 teaspoon dried Italian seasoning
1/8 teaspoon garlic powder

1 package (16 ounces) frozen
  vegetable blend of your choice
2 tablespoons cornstarch
2 tablespoons grated Parmesan
  cheese

Rinse turkey and place in Dutch oven. Add tomatoes, herbs and garlic. Cover and bake in 350 degree oven for 1 1/2 hours. Add vegetables and re-cover. Bake for 30 minutes more. Remove pot from oven; remove turkey and keep warm. Blend a small amount of cooking liquid with cornstarch to form paste. Add to Dutch oven. Cook over medium heat, stirring constantly, until thickened. Serve with turkey; sprinkle with cheese.

Makes 4 servings.

Per Serving (approx):
Calories 453
Carbohydrate 26 gm

Protein 50 gm
Sodium 482 mg

Fat 17 gm
Cholesterol 137 mg

Pot Roast with Olives

3 pounds turkey drumsticks
  (2 or 3 drumsticks)
1/4 cup flour
2 tablespoons oil
2 large cloves garlic, thinly sliced
1 green bell pepper, chopped

2 medium onions, cut into
  wedges
1/2 cup minced parsley
2 cups dry white wine
1/2 cup sliced stuffed Spanish
  olives

Dip drumsticks into water; coat thickly with flour and brown in oil in Dutch oven. Drain off excess oil. Arrange garlic, bell pepper, onion and parsley around drumsticks. Pour in wine, cover and bring to a boil. Simmer for 2 to 2 1/4 hours until very tender, turning once or twice for even cooking. Add 1/2 to 1 cup water if necessary. Add olives during last 15 minutes. Separate meat from bones and serve with cooking liquid.

Makes 4 servings.

Per Serving (approx):
Calories 724
Carbohydrate 19 gm

Protein 70 gm
Sodium 624 mg

Fat 33 gm
Cholesterol 202 mg

Garden Fresh Turkey Skillet Dinner

Versatile turkey wings are joined by garden fresh vegetables in this very simple recipe. If you don't like zucchini, use some other vegetable!

4 turkey wings
    (about 3/4 pound each)
2 tablespoons butter or margarine
1 tablespoon oil
1 medium onion, thinly sliced
1 large clove garlic, minced
2 large ripe tomatoes, coarsely
    chopped (about 2 cups)

1/4 cup chopped parsley
2 teaspoons chopped fresh
    tarragon or 1/2 teaspoon
    dried, crushed
Salt and pepper to taste
2 medium zucchini, each cut
    into 8 chunks

Using sharp knife cut each turkey wing into 2 pieces at elbow joint. Rinse and pat dry. Melt butter with oil in large skillet. Sauté turkey wings until golden on all sides; remove from skillet. Lightly sauté onion and garlic. Add tomatoes, parsley and tarragon, stirring to combine. Bring to a boil.

Return turkey wings to skillet. Sprinkle with salt and pepper. Reduce heat, cover and simmer for 1 to 1 1/4 hours or until turkey is tender. Add zucchini and continue cooking, covered, for 20 minutes or until zucchini is tender.   Makes 4 servings.

Per Serving (approx):
Calories 535   *Protein 51 gm*   *Fat 32 gm*
Carbohydrate 10 gm   *Sodium 280 mg*   *Cholesterol 161 mg*

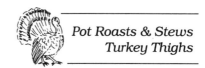

Country Pot Roast

2 turkey thighs (2 to 3 1/2
    pounds total)*
Salt and pepper to taste
1/2 cup finely chopped onion
2 cloves garlic, minced
1/2 teaspoon crumbled dried basil
1/4 teaspoon dried thyme
1 cup chicken or turkey broth

3 medium potatoes,
    peeled and halved
6 medium carrots,
    cut into chunks
1 tablespoon cornstarch
1/4 cup cold water
2 tablespoons chopped parsley

Rinse turkey and pat dry. Place skin side up in nonstick Dutch oven. Salt and pepper to taste. Bake in pre-heated 450 degree oven for 25 minutes or until skin is crisp. Drain and discard any fat.

Add onion, garlic, basil, thyme and broth to pot. Cover and simmer over low heat (or bake at 375 degrees) until turkey is nearly tender, about 1/2 hour. Add potatoes and carrots. Cover and cook until vegetables are tender, about 20 minutes.

Remove turkey and vegetables to platter and keep warm. Skim any fat from pan juices and discard. Mix cornstarch and cold water and stir into simmering pan juices. Cook, stirring, until sauce is thickened. Garnish with parsley.   Makes 4 servings.

*Note: Thighs may be boned before cooking.

Per Serving (approx):
Calories 143   *Protein 18 gm*   *Fat 5 gm*
Carbohydrate 8 gm   *Sodium 57 mg*   *Cholesterol 56 mg*

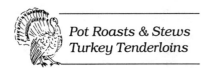
Poached Turkey Tenderloins

Make this recipe on a weekend and serve it when you have little time to cook. It stores nicely in the refrigerator for two days.

2 turkey breast tenderloins
   (1 1/4 to 1 1/2 pounds total)
1/2 cup chopped celery
   with leaves
1/4 cup sliced green onion

3 tablespoons chopped fresh
   tarragon or 1 teaspoon dried,
   crushed
1/4 teaspoon salt
1/4 teaspoon white pepper
3/4 cup white wine

In large skillet arrange tenderloins in single layer. Add celery, onion, tarragon, salt, pepper and wine. Add water to just cover tenderloins.

Cover skillet and simmer mixture over low heat for 40 minutes or until tenderloins are done. Remove tenderloins and keep warm. Increase heat under pan and reduce poaching liquid to about 1 cup. Serve over tenderloins, or store reserved poaching liquid, covered, in refrigerator.

Makes 4 servings.

Per Serving (approx):
Calories 180
Carbohydrate 0 gm

Protein 37 gm
Sodium 197 mg

Fat 2 gm
Cholesterol 97 mg

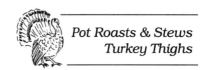

Garlic Slow-Cooker Turkey

1 1/4 pounds skinless,
    boneless turkey thighs
Salt and pepper to taste
1 tablespoon olive oil

1 head garlic, separated,
    and cloves peeled
1/2 cup dry white wine
1/2 cup reduced-sodium
    chicken broth

Season turkey lightly with salt and generously with pepper. In large skillet over medium-high heat, warm oil. Add thighs and brown for about 10 minutes.

Place turkey in slow cooker and add remaining ingredients. Cook on medium to high setting for 2 1/2 to 3 1/2 hours. Remove garlic cloves from pot. Crush and return to juices if desired. Serve juices over meat.

Makes 5 servings.

Per Serving (approx):
Calories 188
Carbohydrate 5 gm

Protein 24 gm
Sodium 165 mg

Fat 7 gm
Cholesterol 85 mg

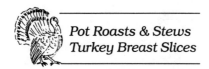

Turkey Creole with Mushrooms

We wanted a Creole recipe with a low cholesterol count, so we used turkey.
We think you'll be as pleased as we were with the results.

1 teaspoon corn oil
1/4 pound mushrooms, sliced
4 tablespoons dry white wine
1 onion, minced
1 clove garlic, minced
1 small bay leaf

1 green bell pepper, diced
1 can (16 ounces) chopped
   stewed tomatoes
1 pound boneless turkey breast
   slices, cutlets or tenderloin
   steaks, 1/4 to 1/2 inch thick

Preheat oil in nonstick skillet over high heat. Add mushrooms and cook until browned. Stir in remaining ingredients except turkey. Simmer, uncovered, for 5 to 6 minutes. Remove bay leaf.

Arrange turkey in single layer in shallow baking dish. Spoon sauce over top. Bake turkey, uncovered, in preheated 375 degree oven for about 15 minutes, basting occasionally. For cutlets that are thinner, cook less time. Makes 4 servings.

Per Serving (approx):
Calories 297
Carbohydrate 11 gm

Protein 40 gm
Sodium 223 mg

Fat 8 gm
Cholesterol 56 mg

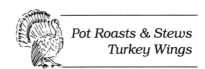

Oven-Barbecued Turkey Wings

So-very-inexpensive turkey wings become gourmet fare in this recipe.

4 turkey wings (about 3 pounds)
1/2 teaspoon smoke salt
2 tablespoons oil
1 can (15 ounces) tomato sauce
1/4 cup vinegar

1 teaspoon chili powder
1/4 teaspoon black pepper
1/8 teaspoon garlic powder
1 can (8 ounces) pineapple
  slices (liquid reserved)

Sprinkle turkey wings with smoke salt. Brown slowly on all sides in heated oil. Pour off and discard any fat in pan.

Combine tomato sauce, vinegar, chili powder, pepper, garlic powder and 1/4 cup syrup drained from pineapple slices. Pour over browned wings and bring to a boil.

Cover pan and bake at 350 degrees for about 1 1/4 hours, basting once or twice. Uncover, and skim off and discard any fat on sauce. Top each wing with pineapple slice. Bake, uncovered, for 15 minutes longer.

Makes 4 large servings.

Per Serving (approx):
Calories 667
Carbohydrate 17 gm

Protein 67 gm
Sodium 1131 mg

Fat 37 gm
Cholesterol 193 mg

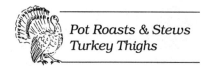
Turkey Navarin

The original French recipe calls for lamb. We use turkey thighs. Just as good? No, we think it is better.

1 3/4 pounds boneless
   turkey thighs
2 tablespoons oil
Black pepper to taste
2 tablespoons flour
1/4 teaspoon sugar
2 1/2 cups beef broth
1/2 cup white wine
1 tablespoon tomato paste
1 clove garlic, minced

1 or 2 sprigs fresh rosemary or
   1/4 teaspoon dried
1 or 2 sprigs fresh thyme or
   1/4 teaspoon dried
6 to 8 small potatoes,
   scrubbed but unpeeled
16 pearl onions, peeled
12 baby carrots, peeled
1 1/2 cups fresh or frozen peas
Salt and pepper to taste
1 tablespoon chopped parsley

Cut turkey into 1 1/2-inch cubes. In large skillet over medium-high heat, warm oil. Add turkey; sprinkle with pepper to taste. Cook for 6 to 8 minutes or until browned on all sides, turning occasionally.

Remove turkey from skillet and set aside. Reduce heat to medium; stir flour and sugar into drippings in pan. Cook for 2 to 3 minutes or until flour is a rich amber color, stirring constantly. Add beef broth, wine, tomato paste and garlic. Stir well, scraping bottom of pan to incorporate browned bits. Return turkey and any juices to pan. Tie herb sprigs together with kitchen string and add to skillet, or stir in dried herbs. Reduce heat to low; cover partially and simmer for 15 minutes.

Cut potatoes in halves or quarters: stir into pan with onions and carrots. Continue simmering, partially covered, for 20 minutes. Add peas and simmer for 6 to 8 minutes longer or until turkey and vegetables are tender. To serve, season with salt and pepper to taste and sprinkle with minced parsley.   Makes 4 servings.

Per Serving (approx):
Calories 880
Carbohydrate 98 gm

Protein 56 gm
Sodium 763 mg

Fat 18 gm
Cholesterol 112 mg

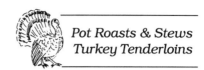

Light and Easy Turkey Tenderloin

1/2 cup carrot, julienne sliced
    to 1/4 inch
1 turkey breast tenderloin
    (approximately 1/2 pound)
2 green onions, sliced
2 slices red or green bell pepper

1/8 teaspoon garlic powder
1/8 teaspoon dried rosemary
1/8 teaspoon salt
Dash of black pepper
1 tablespoon white wine

On 12- by 16-inch foil rectangle, place carrots and top with tenderloin. Arrange onions and bell pepper slices over tenderloin. Sprinkle with garlic powder, rosemary, salt and black pepper.

Fold up edges of foil to form bowl shape. Pour wine over ingredients. Bring 2 opposite sides of foil together above food; fold edges over and down to lock fold. Fold short ends up and over.

Place foil bundle on small baking sheet and bake in preheated 400 degree oven for 20 to 25 minutes or until meat reaches 170 degrees. Check for doneness by opening foil bundle carefully to insert meat thermometer in thickest part of meat.   Makes 2 servings.

Per Serving (approx):
Calories 150
Carbohydrate 5 gm

Protein 27 gm
Sodium 226 mg

Fat 2 gm
Cholesterol 70 mg

The breast meat of roasted turkeys ranks higher in protein than any of the other cooked meats.

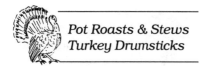

Pot Roasts & Stews
Turkey Drumsticks

Drumstick Dinner

4 turkey drumsticks
2 tablespoons oil
1 tablespoon butter
1 medium onion, sliced
1 can (16 ounces) stewed
  tomatoes
3 cubes chicken bouillon
1/2 teaspoon garlic salt
1/2 teaspoon dried oregano

1/2 teaspoon crumbled
  dried basil
8 small or 4 large potatoes
2 or 3 zucchini, sliced
  3/4 inch thick
1 tablespoon cornstarch
2 tablespoons warm water
2 tablespoons chopped parsley

Brown drumsticks on all sides in oil and butter in skillet. Remove to large baking pan and top with onion slices. In same skillet heat tomatoes with bouillon cubes and seasonings. Pour over drumsticks. Cover pan with foil, crimping to edge of pan. Bake for 2 hours at 325 degrees or until almost tender, basting once or twice.

Meanwhile, boil potatoes; slip off skins. Tuck potatoes and zucchini in and around meat and spoon liquid over them. Cover and bake for 30 minutes longer. Mix cornstarch and water and stir into hot sauce. Bake for 5 to 10 minutes to thicken slightly. Sprinkle with chopped parsley.

Makes 4 servings.

Per Serving (approx):
Calories 987
Carbohydrate 90 gm

Protein 79 gm
Sodium 1411 mg

Fat 35 gm
Cholesterol 216 mg

230

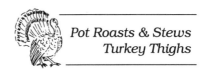

Aprés Ski Turkey Stew

1 1/2 pounds turkey thighs,
  boned, skinned and cut into
  1-inch cubes
1 tablespoon oil
1 cup peeled tomato, cut
into chunks
1 cup green bell pepper,
  thinly sliced
1 clove garlic, minced

2 tablespoons lemon juice
1 teaspoon dried Italian
  seasoning or 1/2 teaspoon
  dried basil and 1/2 teaspoon
  dried oregano
Salt and pepper to taste
2 1/2 teaspoons cornstarch
3 tablespoons cold water

In 3-quart saucepan over medium-high heat, sauté turkey in oil on all sides.

Add tomato, bell pepper, garlic, lemon juice, seasonings, salt and pepper. Cover, reduce heat to low, and simmer for about 12 minutes or until turkey is fork tender.

In small bowl mix cornstarch and cold water. Stir into hot turkey mixture and cook until thickened.

Serve over noodles, if desired. Makes 4 servings.

Per Serving (approx):
Calories 190
Carbohydrate 5 gm

Protein 23 gm
Sodium 100 mg

Fat 8 gm
Cholesterol 85 mg

> Tenderness depends on the age of the bird when processed. All birds marketed at retail are classified and labeled as "Young Turkey." The proper cooking method will yield a moist, juicy, turkey.

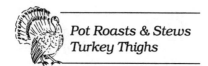

Hungarian Goulash

Americans have taken goulash and made it their own but often omit sauerkraut and sour cream, two of the most important ingredients in this famous Hungarian stew. Here it is—the original.

1 1/4 pounds boneless turkey thighs
2 tablespoons oil
3/4 cup chopped onion
4 teaspoons paprika
1 can (14 ounces) reduced-sodium chicken broth
2 tablespoons tomato paste

1 can (8 ounces) sauerkraut, drained
1/4 teaspoon caraway seeds
Salt and pepper to taste
1/2 cup sour cream
Buttered noodles
Chopped parsley (optional)

Trim thighs and cut into 2-inch pieces. In Dutch oven over medium heat, warm oil. Add turkey, in batches if necessary to avoid crowding; cook for 6 to 8 minutes or until well browned on all sides. Remove turkey and set aside.

Stir onion into pan; sauté for about 2 minutes or until softened. Add paprika and stir well. Stir in broth, tomato paste, sauerkraut and caraway seeds. Add salt and pepper to taste.

Toss turkey with sauerkraut. Cover pan partially with lid and reduce heat to very low; simmer for 40 to 50 minutes or until turkey is tender, stirring occasionally. Just before serving, stir in sour cream; do not boil.

Serve on bed of buttered noodles and sprinkle with parsley, if desired.

Makes 4 servings.

Per Serving (approx):
Calories 425
Carbohydrate 23 gm

Protein 34 gm
Sodium 603 mg

Fat 22 gm
Cholesterol 117 mg

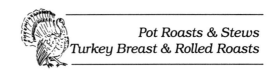

Herb-Sauced Turkey and Vegetables

This elegant one-dish meal is for company or for your family.

2 quarts turkey or chicken broth
1 turkey breast (2 1/2 pounds)
1 onion, chopped
1 cup chopped fresh basil
10 sprigs parsley
3/4 teaspoon dried thyme
1 pound new potatoes,
   quartered
1 pound pearl onions, peeled

2 bunches baby carrots,
   trimmed
3/4 pound green beans,
   trimmed and strings removed
4 tablespoons butter
2 tablespoons flour
1/3 cup each Dijon-style
   mustard and whipping cream
Salt and pepper to taste

Bring broth to a boil. Add turkey breast, onion, basil, parsley and thyme. Reduce heat; cover and simmer for 1 1/2 to 2 hours. Add potatoes and pearl onions during last 20 minutes. Add baby carrots and green beans during last 10 minutes. Drain turkey and vegetables; reserve broth. Remove skin from turkey. Slice turkey and arrange with vegetables on platter; keep warm.

Melt butter in saucepan; whisk in flour. Cook for 5 minutes. Add 2 cups reserved broth. Cook for 5 minutes, stirring constantly until thickened. Reduce heat; add mustard and cream. Season with salt and pepper. Serve turkey with vegetables and sauce. Makes 6 servings.

Per Serving (approx):
Calories 571
Carbohydrate 38 gm

Protein 49 gm
Sodium 671 mg

Fat 25 gm
Cholesterol 134 mg

233

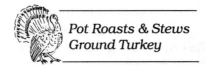

Turkey Tortilla Stew

1 1/2 pounds ground turkey
1 medium onion, finely chopped
2 cloves garlic, minced
2 teaspoons oil
2 1/2 cups water
1 can (16 ounces) no-salt-
    added tomatoes
1 can (15 ounces) pinto beans in
    chili sauce, undrained

1 can (10 ounces) reduced-
    sodium tomato soup
1 cup whole corn kernels
1 can (4 ounces) green chilies,
    chopped
1/4 teaspoon black pepper
12 corn tortillas (6 inch), cut
    into 1/4-inch strips
2 tablespoons oil

In large Dutch oven over medium-high heat, sauté turkey, onion and garlic in oil for 5 minutes or until turkey is no longer pink. Add water, tomatoes, beans, soup, corn, chilies and black pepper. Heat until mixture is bubbly; reduce heat to low and simmer for 30 minutes.

In large skillet over medium-high heat, sauté tortilla strips in the 2 tablespoons oil for 30 seconds or until lightly browned and crisp. Drain on paper towels. Add tortilla strips to turkey stew just before serving to let them soften.   Makes 6 servings.

Per Serving (approx):
Calories 497
Carbohydrate 55 gm

Protein 31 gm
Sodium 761 mg

Fat 17 gm
Cholesterol 82 mg

PASTAS & GRAINS

Meatballs in a Pasta Crown

The ring mold makes an "everyday" meal into a special occasion.

1 pound ground turkey
1 cup finely chopped onion
1 clove garlic, minced
3 tablespoons dried parsley flakes
1/2 cup seasoned bread crumbs
1/4 cup grated Parmesan cheese
Salt and pepper to taste

1 tablespoon oil
3 cups spaghetti sauce
8 ounces thin spaghetti
1/2 teaspoon dried Italian
   seasoning
1/2 cup grated mozzarella
   cheese

In medium bowl combine turkey, onion, garlic, 1 tablespoon of the parsley, the bread crumbs, Parmesan cheese, salt and pepper. Shape mixture into 12 meatballs.

In large skillet over medium-high heat, sauté meatballs in oil. Reduce heat to medium-low, cover skillet and cook for 6 to 8 minutes or until meatballs are no longer pink in center.

In large saucepan over low heat, warm spaghetti sauce. Prepare spaghetti according to package directions. Drain; do not rinse. Return spaghetti to cooking pan. Stir in remaining parsley, Italian seasoning and mozzarella cheese.

Arrange meatballs in bottom of lightly greased ring mold. Top with spaghetti, pressing firmly to mold spaghetti around meatballs. Allow mold to stand for 1 to 2 minutes. Invert mold onto large platter. Spoon spaghetti sauce into center of pasta crown.   Makes 6 servings.

*Per Serving (approx):
Calories 501
Carbohydrate 58 gm*

*Protein 26 gm
Sodium 1030 mg*

*Fat 19 gm
Cholesterol 59 mg*

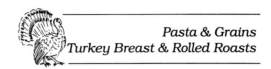

Turkey with Wild Rice

1 box (6 3/4 ounces) instant
   long-grain and wild rice mix
2 tablespoons slivered
   almonds

3 1/4 cups water
1 turkey breast (2 pounds)
1 box (10 ounces) frozen
   chopped broccoli, thawed

Combine seasoning packet from rice, almonds and 1 cup of the water in
3-quart casserole. Add turkey. Bake in 325 degree oven for 1 1/2 hours.
Stir in the remaining 2 1/4 cups hot water, rice and broccoli. Bake for
30 minutes or to internal temperature of 170 degrees. Let stand for 10
minutes before slicing. Wrap and refrigerate any remaining turkey and
rice.   Makes 4 servings.

Per Serving (approx):
Calories 515   *Protein 52 gm*   *Fat 16 gm*
Carbohydrate 41 gm   *Sodium 120 mg*   *Cholesterol 122 mg*

Per Capita Consumption of Turkey*			
Year	Pounds	Year	Pounds
1974	8.7	1985	11.6
1975	8.3	1986	12.9
1976	8.9	1987	14.7
1977	8.8	1988	15.7
1978	8.7	1989	16.6
1979	9.3	1990	17.6
1980	10.3	1991	18.0
1981	10.6	1992	18.0
1982	10.6	1993	18.1**
1983	11.0	1994	18.2**
1984	11.0		

**Statistical series revised by USDA in 1992 to reflect
inspected turkeys consumed*
**Estimated by NTF

Versatile Turkey Sauce

This sauce is good with pasta, noodles or rice. Add basil and oregano for Italian-style turkey spaghetti sauce, or add cumin and kidney beans for chili con turkey.

1 pound ground turkey
1 medium onion, chopped
1/2 medium green bell pepper, chopped
1/4 cup sliced celery
1 can (14 1/2 ounces) stewed tomatoes

1 can (12 ounces) tomato juice
1 can (6 ounces) tomato paste
1 tablespoon Worcestershire sauce
1/2 teaspoon salt
1/4 teaspoon garlic powder

Place turkey and fresh vegetables in large skillet. Cook over medium heat for 10 minutes, stirring and separating turkey as it cooks. Add remaining ingredients. Bring to a boil; reduce heat and simmer for 5 minutes, stirring occasionally. Serve over pasta or rice.

Makes 6 servings.

Per Serving (approx):
Calories 185
Carbohydrate 16 gm

Protein 16 gm
Sodium 666 mg

Fat 6 gm
Cholesterol 55 mg

Turkey Tetrazzini

Don't pass up this recipe. Sure, it takes some time and effort, but it's well worth it.

1 large turkey thigh
  (about 2 pounds) or
  2 small turkey thighs
  (about 1 pound each)
3/4 cup water
1 cube chicken bouillon
8 ounces medium noodles
  (about 4 cups cooked)
1/3 cup finely chopped
  onion
1/4 cup butter
1/4 cup flour

1 can (13 ounces) evaporated
  milk
1 can (4 ounces) sliced
  mushrooms, undrained
1/2 teaspoon salt
Dash each of ground nutmeg
  and black pepper
1/4 cup dry sherry
1 cup grated Swiss cheese
1/2 cup sliced almonds
1 cup buttered soft bread
  crumbs

Place turkey thigh in large pot with water and bouillon cube. Cover tightly and cook for 1 to 1 1/2 hours or until meat is tender. Let cool sufficiently to handle. Remove skin and bone; cut meat into bite-sized chunks. Measure cooking liquid (should be about 1 cup); add water if necessary to make this amount.

Cook noodles in boiling salted water according to package directions. Meanwhile, prepare sauce. Sauté onion lightly in butter. Blend in flour. Slowly stir in milk, the 1 cup cooking liquid and mushrooms. Cook, stirring, until sauce boils and thickens. Stir in salt, nutmeg, pepper and sherry. Drain noodles.

Place half the noodles in 2 1/2-quart baking dish. Add half the turkey, half the sauce and half the cheese. Sprinkle with 1/4 cup almond slices. Repeat layers, topping with buttered crumbs. Bake at 350 degrees for about 20 to 30 minutes or until hot and lightly browned on top.

Makes 6 servings.

Per Serving (approx):
Calories 731   *Protein 51 gm*   *Fat 33 gm*
Carbohydrate 54 gm   *Sodium 594 mg*   *Cholesterol 185 mg*

Spanish Rice with Turkey Sausage

1 pound turkey sausage links
1 cup chopped onion
1 red bell pepper, chopped
1 red bell pepper, chopped
1 can (14 1/2 ounces) no-salt-
  added stewed tomatoes

1 small can tomato sauce
1 1/4 cups water
1 cup uncooked white rice
1/4 teaspoon black pepper

Spray large skillet with nonstick cooking spray. Warm over medium-high heat for about 30 seconds. Add turkey breakfast sausage. Cook for 12 to 15 minutes or until lightly browned and no longer pink in center, turning occasionally. Remove from skillet and keep warm. Drain skillet.

Add onion and bell pepper to skillet. Cook, stirring, for 5 to 7 minutes or until vegetables are tender-crisp. Sir in stewed tomatoes, tomato sauce, 1 1/4 cups water, rice and black pepper. Heat until mixture just begins to boil.

Reduce heat to low. Cook, covered, for 15 to 20 minutes or until rice is tender and liquid is absorbed, stirring twice. Add sausage and stir gently. Cook until thoroughly heated. Makes 6 servings.

Per Serving (approx):
Calories 193
Carbohydrate 19 gm

Protein 13 gm
Sodium 362 mg

Fat 7 gm
Cholesterol 40 mg

A male turkey is a "tom," a female is a "hen," a baby is a "poult" and a large group of turkeys is a "flock."

Smoked Turkey Risotto

Tired of pasta? Try this turkey risotto. Although risotto is really just another rice dish, it has its own unique character. The rice absorbs the broth a little at a time, until each grain is plump and creamy yet firm to the bite.

1/2 cup chopped onion
1 tablespoon oil
4 tablespoons unsalted butter
2 cups Arborio rice
6 to 7 cups chicken or turkey
   stock

1/2 pound smoked turkey
   breast, cut into strips
2 cups chopped green apple
1/3 cup grated Parmesan cheese
3 tablespoons whipping cream
2 tablespoons chopped fresh
   basil or parsley

In heavy pot sauté onion in oil and 2 tablespoons of the butter until soft. Stir in rice, coating well with cooking fat. Heat stock to boiling. Begin adding stock in 1/2- to 3/4-cup increments, stirring continuously.* Allow all stock to be absorbed each time before adding more.

When rice is nearly cooked (about 20 minutes), stir in turkey and apple. When all stock has been added and rice is cooked to al dente stage (about 30 minutes), remove pan from heat. Stir in cheese, cream, basil and remaining 2 tablespoons butter. Serve immediately. Do not reheat.

Makes 6 servings.

*Note: Regulate heat so that liquid is absorbed steadily, neither too fast nor too slow.

Per Serving (approx):
Calories 450
Carbohydrate 61 gm

Protein 16 gm
Sodium 1160 mg

Fat 16 gm
Cholesterol 43 mg

Manicotti

So easy to make!

2 cups finely chopped cooked turkey
15 ounces ricotta cheese
1 egg, lightly beaten
1 package (10 ounces) frozen chopped spinach, thawed and well drained
1/4 cup grated Parmesan cheese

1/2 teaspoon ground nutmeg
3 cups marinara or spaghetti sauce
8 ounces manicotti shells, cooked
1/2 to 3/4 cup shredded mozzarella cheese

In medium bowl combine turkey, ricotta, egg, spinach, Parmesan and nutmeg. Into 9- x 12-inch baking pan, spoon thin layer of marinara sauce.

Fill manicotti shells with turkey mixture and arrange over sauce. Pour remaining sauce on top; sprinkle with mozzarella.

Bake for 25 to 30 minutes or until hot and bubbly.

Makes 4 to 6 servings.

Per Serving (approx):
Calories 505
Carbohydrate 45 gm

Protein 34 gm
Sodium 1033 mg

Fat 21 gm
Cholesterol 117 mg

Stuffed Turkey-Rice Roll

If you want an easy, inexpensive and elegant main course for entertaining, this is it.

2/3 cup long-grain white rice
1/4 teaspoon salt
1 1/3 cups boiling water
6 turkey breast cutlets
Salt and pepper to taste
2 cloves garlic, minced
4 green onions, sliced

2 green or red bell peppers,
   chopped
2 to 3 tablespoons olive oil
1/2 cup sliced ripe olives
3 tablespoons chopped fresh
   basil or 1 1/2 teaspoons dried
1 cup shredded Cheddar cheese

Stir rice and salt into boiling water; reduce heat and simmer, covered, for 20 minutes.

Pound turkey cutlets to 1/4 inch thick. On work surface overlap cutlets to make large rectangle; sprinkle with salt and pepper.

Sauté garlic, green onions and bell pepper in 2 tablespoons olive oil; combine with cooked rice, olives and basil. Spoon rice mixture onto cutlets, leaving half-inch border. Sprinkle with cheese. Roll up from long side. Brush with 1 tablespoon olive oil and bake at 350 degrees for 30 to 35 minutes. Allow to rest for 15 minutes before slicing. Serve warm or at room temperature with Fresh Tomato Salsa.   Makes 6 servings.

FRESH TOMATO SALSA:
Combine 4 tomatoes, peeled, seeded and chopped, 3 tablespoons chopped fresh basil or 1 1/2 teaspoons dried, 4 green onions, chopped, 1 clove garlic, minced, and 1 tablespoon olive oil. Let stand for about 1 hour for flavors to blend.

Per Serving (approx):
Calories 238
Carbohydrate 21 gm

Protein 6 gm
Sodium 398 mg

Fat 15 gm
Cholesterol 20 mg

Stuffed Pasta Shells Italiano

This is a good make-ahead recipe.

1 pound ground turkey
1 cup minced onion
1 cup grated peeled eggplant
2 cloves garlic, minced
1 tablespoon oil
1 can (28 ounces) tomatoes
1 can (8 ounces) tomato sauce
1 cup red wine or water

1 teaspoon each garlic salt,
   dried oregano and dried basil
1/2 teaspoon each dried
   tarragon and crushed red
   pepper flakes
1 package (12 ounces) jumbo
   pasta shells
1/2 cup grated Parmesan cheese
3/4 cup grated mozzarella cheese

Brown turkey, onion, eggplant and garlic in hot oil; do not burn. Set aside. Simmer tomatoes, tomato sauce, wine and seasonings for 15 minutes. Cook pasta shells until done but still firm; drain.

Combine turkey mixture and Parmesan cheese with half of tomato sauce mixture. Use to stuff shells*; place in 9- x 13-inch pan. Spoon remaining sauce over each and top with mozzarella cheese. Bake at 350 degrees for 30 minutes.   Makes 8 to 10 servings.

*Note: If shells are stuffed ahead of time and refrigerated, do not add sauce or grated cheese until just before baking, and increase cooking time by 8 to 10 minutes.

Per Serving (approx):
Calories 362
Carbohydrate 42 gm

Protein 22 gm
Sodium 450 mg

Fat 9 gm
Cholesterol 54 mg

Pesto Meatballs with Zucchini and Pasta

This is about as Italian as you can get with a pasta.

1 1/2 cups packed fresh basil
  leaves
1 1/2 pounds ground turkey
1 cup freshly grated
  Parmesan cheese
1 cup soft white bread crumbs
3 large cloves garlic, minced
1 egg, lightly beaten
1/4 teaspoon each salt and
  pepper

2 tablespoons olive oil
1 1/4 cups chicken or turkey
  broth
1 to 1 1/2 pounds fine egg
  noodles (2 to 3 ounces
  per person)
3 cups thinly sliced zucchini
8 sprigs basil, for garnish
Additional Parmesan cheese,
  for topping

Put basil leaves in food processor or blender and chop fine. Transfer to mixing bowl with turkey, 3/4 cup Parmesan cheese, bread crumbs, garlic, egg, salt and pepper. Mix ingredients with fork; do not mix with hands or meat becomes tough. Shape into balls (about the size of large walnut) with your hands.

Heat 1 tablespoon of the olive oil in 12-inch nonstick skillet; brown half the meatballs on all sides. Remove from pan with slotted spoon and repeat browning with remaining oil and meatballs. Return first batch of meatballs to skillet, pour in broth and bring to a boil. Reduce heat and simmer for 12 minutes.

Place noodles in boiling water and cook according to package directions. At the same time, add zucchini to meatballs and cook until tender-crisp; do not overcook. Serve meatballs and zucchini over cooked pasta in warmed shallow bowls. Garnish with sprigs of basil and pass remaining Parmesan cheese at the table.   Makes 8 servings.

Per Serving (approx):
Calories 319
Carbohydrate 23 gm

Protein 25 gm
Sodium 655 mg

Fat 15 gm
Cholesterol 110 mg

Cannellini Sauté

Smoked turkey breast sautéed with a medley of vegetables makes a quick and delicious one-dish meal.

1 1/2 to 2 pounds smoked
    turkey breast
1 clove garlic, minced
1 medium onion, chopped
1/2 green bell pepper, chopped
2 tablespoons olive oil
1/2 medium head red cabbage,
    thinly sliced
1 medium head Chinese cabbage,
    thinly sliced

2 tablespoons chopped fresh
    rosemary or 3/4 teaspoon
    dried
2/3 cup chicken stock
2 tablespoons red wine
1 can (28 ounces) plum
    tomatoes, drained and
    chopped
2 cans (15 ounces each)
    cannellini beans, drained
Salt and pepper to taste

Cut turkey breast into 1-inch cubes. In large skillet sauté garlic, onion and bell pepper in oil until soft, about 2 minutes. Add turkey cubes, cabbages and rosemary; sauté for 3 minutes. Add chicken stock, red wine, tomatoes, beans, salt and pepper; simmer for 5 minutes. Serve with pasta or rice in cabbage leaf cups, if desired.   Makes 8 servings.

Per Serving (approx):
Calories 334
Carbohydrate 31 gm

Protein 32 gm
Sodium 1640 mg

Fat 8 gm
Cholesterol 45 mg

Trattoria Eggplant Turkey Rolls

1 eggplant (1 1/4 pounds)
1/4 cup olive oil
2 tablespoons minced garlic
1/2 teaspoon dried basil
1/2 teaspoon dried oregano
6 to 8 ounces smoked or cooked
    turkey breast, thinly sliced

1 1/2 cups no-salt-added
    spaghetti sauce
6 ounces sliced Monterey jack
    cheese
4 servings hot pasta

Cut eggplant lengthwise into 1/2-inch-thick slices. Lay slices in single layer in lightly greased, shallow baking pans. Brush with half the olive oil. Sprinkle with half the garlic and herbs. Broil 2 inches from heat for 4 to 5 minutes or until cooked. Turn slices, brush with remaining oil and sprinkle with remaining garlic and herbs. Broil until done.

Top eggplant with turkey and roll up with meat inside. Place in baking dish, pour spaghetti sauce over and top with cheese. Bake uncovered at 425 degrees for 25 to 30 minutes or until hot and bubbly. Serve with hot pasta.
                                            Makes 4 servings.

Per Serving (approx):
Calories 540
Carbohydrate 35 gm

Protein 26 gm
Sodium 868 mg

Fat 33 gm
Cholesterol 78 mg

J. A. Brillalt-Savarin, in his book *The Physiology of Taste*, published in 1791, called the turkey "one of the most beautiful presents which the New World has made to the Old."

Turkey Fillets with Champagne-Mushroom Sauce

For a truly special and easy-to-make entree, serve this champagne and mushroom-sauced breast of turkey over your favorite pasta.

4 turkey fillets (approximately
  1 1/4 pounds)
3 tablespoons butter
3 shallots, chopped
2 cups Champagne
2 cups whipping cream

6 ounces assorted mushrooms,
  sliced*
2 tablespoons each capers and
  chopped chives
Salt and pepper to taste
8 ounces pasta, cooked and
  drained

Brown turkey fillets in butter for 3 to 4 minutes on each side. Add shallots and Champagne; cover and simmer for 10 minutes. Uncover; remove fillets and keep warm.

Increase heat to high and let Champagne reduce by half. Add remaining ingredients except pasta; simmer for 10 to 15 minutes or until slightly thickened. Slice fillets; serve on bed of pasta with sauce.

Makes 4 to 6 servings.

*Note: Any combination of wild or domestic mushrooms may be used.

*Per Serving (approx):
Calories 594
Carbohydrate 41 gm*

*Protein 16 gm
Sodium 337 mg*

*Fat 41 gm
Cholesterol 181 mg*

Turkey Sausage Ragout on Pasta

Here is a very different and interesting use of sausage.

2 cloves garlic, finely chopped
1 carrot, sliced
1 medium onion, chopped
1 green bell pepper, chopped
2 tablespoons oil
1/4 cup dry white wine (optional)

1 teaspoon dried basil
1 jar (14 ounces) spaghetti
  sauce
1/4 cup chopped parsley
Hot cooked pasta

Prepare Turkey Sausage.* In large skillet, cook sausage, garlic, carrot, onion and bell pepper in hot oil until sausage is no longer pink, about 5 minutes, stirring occasionally. Stir in remaining ingredients except parsley and pasta. Cover and simmer for 15 minutes, stirring occasionally. Stir in parsley. Serve over hot cooked pasta.   Makes 4 servings.

*Note: Or purchase 1 pound prepared turkey sausage.

TURKEY SAUSAGE:
Combine 1 pound ground turkey, 1 egg or 2 egg whites, lightly beaten, 1/3 cup dry bread crumbs, 2 green onions, minced, 1 clove garlic, minced, 1/2 teaspoon crushed fennel seed, 1/2 teaspoon each dried thyme and ground cumin, and 1 pinch each of red pepper flakes, salt and ground nutmeg.

Per Serving (approx):
Calories 345
Carbohydrate 19 gm

Protein 19 gm
Sodium 961 mg

Fat 21 gm
Cholesterol 61 mg

Peppercorn Turkey over Spinach Noodles

1 tablespoon crushed green
  peppercorns
4 turkey tenderloins
  (approximately 6 ounces each)
1 Granny Smith or tart apple,
  unpeeled, cored and thinly
  sliced
2 tablespoons margarine
1/4 cup sliced green onion
1 clove garlic, minced

1/2 cup sliced mushrooms
1 teaspoon crumbled dried
  rosemary
1/2 teaspoon celery seeds
1 tablespoon cornstarch
1/2 cup dry white wine or sherry
1/2 cup chicken broth
1 pound spinach noodles,
  prepared according to
  package directions

Press peppercorns into each side of turkey tenderloins; set aside.

In 12-inch nonstick skillet over medium-high heat, cook apples in 1 table-spoon of the margarine for 2 to 3 minutes or until tender-crisp. Remove apples from skillet; set aside.

In same skillet add turkey and remaining 1 tablespoon margarine and cook for 4 to 5 minutes on each side; remove tenderloins. Add onion, garlic, mushrooms, rosemary and celery seeds to skillet. Reduce heat and sauté for 2 to 3 minutes.

In small bowl dissolve cornstarch in wine and broth; add to vegetable mixture in skillet. Bring mixture to a boil, stirring constantly. Return tenderloins to skillet; reduce heat and simmer for 5 minutes or until sauce is slightly thickened.

To serve, slice turkey into medallions. Arrange noodles on 6 plates; top with apples and turkey and spoon vegetable mixture over top.

Makes 6 servings.

Per Serving (approx):
Calories 367
Carbohydrate 61 gm

Protein 11 gm
Sodium 185 mg

Fat 7 gm
Cholesterol 72 mg

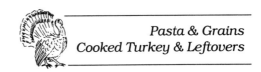

Spaghetti Pie

This is quite easy to make—and well worth the effort.

6 ounces spaghetti, cooked
   according to package
   instructions and drained
1 egg white, lightly beaten
1/3 cup grated Parmesan cheese
2 1/2 tablespoons margarine,
   melted
1 cup chopped onion
1 clove garlic, minced

1 package (10 ounces) frozen
   mixed vegetables, thawed
2 tablespoons flour
1 teaspoon dried poultry
   seasoning
1/8 teaspoon black pepper
1 1/2 cups skim milk
2 cups cubed cooked turkey

In medium bowl combine spaghetti, egg white, cheese and 1 tablespoon of the margarine. Press pasta mixture over bottom and up sides of well-greased 9-inch pie plate. Grease 10- by 12-inch piece of aluminum foil. Press foil, greased side down, next to pasta shell. Bake in preheated 350 degree oven for 25 to 30 minutes or until pasta shell is set and slightly browned on edges.

In medium saucepan over medium-high heat, sauté onion and garlic in remaining margarine for 2 to 3 minutes or until onion is translucent. Fold in vegetables and cook for 1 minute. Sprinkle flour, poultry seasoning and pepper over mixture, stirring to combine. Remove pan from heat.

Slowly pour milk over vegetable mixture, stirring constantly. Return saucepan to medium heat; cook and stir until mixture is thickened. Add turkey, reduce heat to medium-low and simmer for 5 minutes or until heated through. Pour mixture into cooked pasta shell.

To serve, cut spaghetti pie into 6 wedges.   Makes 6 servings.

Per Serving (approx):
Calories 325
Carbohydrate 35 gm

Protein 24 gm
Sodium 238 mg

Fat 9 gm
Cholesterol 41 mg

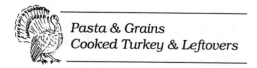

Tetrazzini Pasta Supper

This very elegant entree takes just a few minutes to make, thanks to its use of turkey leftovers.

6 quarts salted water
16 ounces tubular pasta, such
   as ziti or penne
2 tablespoons butter or
   margarine
3 green onions, minced
2 cloves garlic, minced
1 pound fresh shiitake
   mushrooms, stems removed
   and caps sliced, or fresh
   domestic mushrooms, sliced

3 tablespoons dry sherry
1/2 teaspoon dried tarragon
Salt and pepper to taste
2 to 3 cups coarsely chopped
   cooked turkey
1/2 cups part-skim ricotta
   cheese
3/4 cup freshly grated
   Parmesan cheese

In large saucepan over high heat, bring water to a boil. Cook pasta according to package directions until tender. Scoop out and reserve 1 cup cooking water from pasta. Drain pasta and place in large serving bowl.

Meanwhile, in large skillet over low heat, melt butter. Add onions and garlic; cook for about 1 minute or until tender, stirring constantly. Increase heat to high; add mushrooms, sherry, tarragon and 1/4 teaspoon each salt and pepper. Cook for about 5 minutes or until liquid is evaporated and mushrooms are browned, stirring constantly. Add turkey; cook for 1 minute longer or until heated through.

To serve, pour warm turkey mixture over hot pasta. Add ricotta and Parmesan cheeses with about 1/3 cup reserved hot cooking water. Toss and add additional cooking water, if necessary, to make creamy sauce. Season with additional salt and pepper; serve immediately.

Makes 6 servings.

Per Serving (approx):
Calories 704
Carbohydrate 99 gm

Protein 41 gm
Sodium 425 mg

Fat 16 gm
Cholesterol 130 mg

ROASTING BREASTS
& ROLLED ROASTS

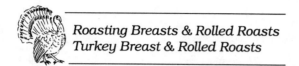

Turkey Della Robbia

The ring of fruit around the turkey half breast on the platter makes a spectacular dish, with very little special effort on your part.

1 turkey half breast
  (1 1/2 pounds)
Oil, as needed
Salt and pepper to taste
1/3 cup peach or apricot
  preserves
	2 nectarines or peaches
	4 plums
	2 tablespoons sugar
	2 tablespoons grated lemon zest
	1 tablespoon lemon juice
	1 pound seedless grapes

Place turkey bone side down on rack in roasting pan. Brush with oil and sprinkle with salt and pepper. Roast at 450 degrees for 20 minutes. Spoon preserves over turkey, cover pan with foil and reduce oven heat to 350 degrees. Roast for 45 minutes longer or until thermometer registers 170 degrees.

When roast is nearly done, quarter nectarines and plums and combine in large saucepan with sugar, lemon zest and lemon juice. Cook, stirring gently, for 5 minutes or until juices collect and fruit is tender but not mushy. Add grapes and heat through.

To serve, transfer turkey to serving platter. Lift fruit from juice with slotted spoon and place in ring around turkey. For sauce, pour pan drippings into cup. Remove fat on top, then combine with juice from fruit. Serve as sauce with turkey. **Makes 4 servings.**

Per Serving (approx):
Calories 577	*Protein 46 gm*	*Fat 17 gm*
Carbohydrate 59 gm	*Sodium 211 mg*	*Cholesterol 130 mg*

Pineapple-Mustard-Glazed Turkey Breast

1 turkey half breast, bone in
   (2 1/2 pounds)
1/3 cup pineapple preserves

1 teaspoon lemon juice
2 teaspoons Dijon-style
   mustard

Prepare grill for indirect-heat cooking. Place turkey, skin side up, on rack over drip pan. Cover and grill turkey breast for 1 to 1 1/4 hours, or until meat thermometer inserted in thickest portion of breast registers 170 degrees.

In small bowl combine preserves, lemon juice and mustard. Brush glaze on breast 1/2 hour before end of grilling time. At end of cooking time, remove turkey breast from grill and let stand for 15 minutes. To serve, slice breast and arrange on platter.   Makes 6 servings.

Per Serving (approx):
Calories 295
Carbohydrate 13 gm

Protein 37 gm
Sodium 134 mg

Fat 10 gm
Cholesterol 96 mg

Indirect-Heat Cooking

"Indirect" grilling over a drip pan with hot coals on the outside is recommended for whole birds and large turkey parts such as the whole breast. This slower cooking method allows time for the meat to cook through to the center without burning on the outside.

Spread one layer of charcoal in an outdoor grill; pile charcoal in the center to form a pyramid. Light and let burn to white-coal, slow-heat stage, about one-half hour. Divide glowing coals in half, arranging along both sides of grill, leaving the center open. Place foil drip pan in the center of the grill. Place the turkey on a rack over a drip pan. Cover the grill, either with its own top or with a "tent" of heavy-duty aluminum foil. (If using foil, punch four vent holes in the center and seal edges, leaving four to six openings around the rim of the grill.)

255

Roasting Breasts & Rolled Roasts
Turkey Breast & Rolled Roasts

Turkey Breasts Verde

1 turkey breast (2 to 4 pounds)
1 cup extravirgin olive oil
1/4 teaspoon black pepper
Juice of 1 lemon
2 cloves garlic

3 cups chopped fresh basil
   and/or parsley
3 tablespoons grated Parmesan
   cheese
2 tablespoons pine nuts

Rub turkey with 1/2 cup of the olive oil and sprinkle with black pepper. Place turkey in baking dish. Cover and bake in preheated 350 degree oven for 45 minutes or until lightly browned.

Meanwhile, combine lemon juice, remaining olive oil, garlic, basil and cheese in electric blender and blend until smooth. Serve turkey covered with this sauce. Sprinkle with pine nuts.   Makes 4 servings.

Per Serving (approx):
Calories 716
Carbohydrate 6 gm

Protein 28 gm
Sodium 142 mg

Fat 65 gm
Cholesterol 65 mg

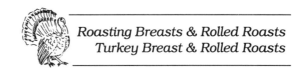

Roast Turkey Breast
with Spiced Cherry Sauce

This delicious entree is low in calories, sodium and cholesterol.

1 turkey breast, bone in
  (4 to 6 pounds)
1 can (16 ounces) dark pitted
  cherries, drained, juice
  reserved
1/4 cup sugar

2 tablespoons vinegar
1/8 teaspoon ground cloves
1/2 teaspoon ground cinnamon
1 1/2 tablespoons cornstarch
2 tablespoons brandy
  (optional)

Wipe turkey with damp paper towel. Place breast on rack in shallow roasting pan. Place in preheated 325 degree oven and roast for 1 1/2 to 2 1/4 hours or until meat thermometer inserted into thickest part, not touching bone, registers 170 degrees.

While breast is roasting, in small saucepan combine all but 3 tablespoons cherry juice, sugar, vinegar, cloves and cinnamon. Bring to a boil; reduce heat and cook for 10 minutes. Mix reserved cherry juice with cornstarch. Stir into hot liquid, stirring constantly until thickened. Add cherries and heat through. Stir in brandy, if desired.

Remove turkey breast from oven and allow to stand for 10 to 15 minutes. Remove skin from breast and slice breast. Serve 2 tablespoons warm sauce over each serving of breast.   Makes 16 servings.

Per Serving (approx):
Calories 144
Carbohydrate 32 gm

Protein 27 gm
Sodium 45 mg

Fat 1 gm
Cholesterol 56 mg

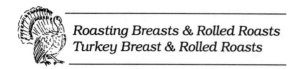

Turkey Breast with Southwestern Corn Bread Dressing

5 cups coarsely crumbled corn bread
4 English muffins, coarsely crumbled
3 mild green chilies, roasted, peeled, seeded and chopped
1 red bell pepper, roasted, peeled, seeded and chopped
3/4 cup pine nuts, toasted
1 tablespoon chopped cilantro
1 tablespoon chopped parsley
1 1/2 teaspoons chopped fresh basil
1 1/2 teaspoons chopped fresh thyme
1 1/2 teaspoons chopped fresh oregano
1 pound bulk turkey sausage
3 cups chopped celery
1 cup chopped onion
2 to 4 tablespoons turkey broth or water, or as needed
1 turkey breast (5 to 6 pounds), bone in
2 tablespoons chopped garlic
1/2 cup chopped cilantro

In large bowl combine corn bread, muffins, chilies, bell pepper, pine nuts, cilantro, parsley, basil, thyme and oregano.

In large skillet over medium-high heat, sauté sausage, celery and onion for 8 to 10 minutes or until sausage is no longer pink and vegetables are tender. Combine mixture with corn bread mixture. Add broth if mixture is too dry. Set aside.

Loosen skin on both sides of turkey breast, being careful not to tear skin and leaving it connected at breast bone. Spread 1 tablespoon garlic under loosened skin over each breast half. Repeat procedure with 1/4 cup cilantro on each side.

Place turkey breast in lightly greased 13- x 9- x 2-inch roasting pan. Spoon half of stuffing mixture under breast cavity. Spoon remaining stuffing into lightly greased 2-quart casserole; set aside.

Roast turkey breast, uncovered, for 2 to 2 1/2 hours or until meat thermometer registers 170 degrees in deepest portion of breast. Bake remaining stuffing, uncovered, along with turkey breast during last 45 minutes.   Makes 12 servings.

Per Serving (approx):
Calories 422
Carbohydrate 26 gm

Protein 45 gm
Sodium 677 mg

Fat 16 gm
Cholesterol 128 mg

258

Rolled Turkey Breast
with Fruit Sauce

1 turkey breast, boned and
   butterflied (approximately
   3 pounds)

Salt and pepper to taste
1/4 cup chopped dried apricots
1/4 cup cranberry relish

Season turkey breast with salt and pepper. Spread dried fruit and cranberry relish over surface of breast. Roll up and tie. Roast in 450 degree oven for approximately 40 to 45 minutes. Slice and serve with Fruit Sauce.

Make 10 servings.

FRUIT SAUCE:
In large heavy saucepan, carmelize 1/4 cup sugar. Add 1/2 cup raspberry vinegar, 1 cup orange juice and 1/2 cup Riesling wine. Reduce to thick and syrupy consistency. Add 2 cups turkey stock; bring to a boil and reduce consistency of sauce.

Per Serving (approx):
Calories 248
Carbohydrate 11 gm

Protein 30 gm
Sodium 391 mg

Fat 8 gm
Cholesterol 73 mg

> The new broad-breasted turkeys are so tender they require only about half as long roasting as those in our grandmother's day.

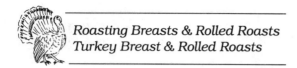

Foil-Baked Turkey Roast with Raspberry Sauce

1 turkey breast (1 1/2 to 2 pounds)
1 tablespoon margarine, cut
   into small pieces

1/4 teaspoon each dried dill
   weed, crushed dried basil
   and black pepper

Place turkey on sheet of aluminum foil. Top with margarine. Sprinkle with seasonings. Bring edges of foil together up and over meat and fold over twice. Fold edges in twice to seal. Place packet in shallow pan.

Bake in 350 degree oven for about 1 1/2 to 2 hours or until turkey is no longer pink in center and meat thermometer reaches 180 degrees. Open foil carefully. Slice meat and serve with juices or Raspberry Sauce.

Makes 4 to 6 servings.

RASPBERRY SAUCE:
In small saucepan over medium heat, combine 1/4 cup butter, 1/2 cup raspberry or currant jelly, 1/4 cup red wine, 2 tablespoons lemon juice, 2 tablespoons cider vinegar, and 2 teaspoons prepared mustard. Bring to a boil; cook for 3 minutes. Reduce heat to low and add 1 tablespoon cornstarch dissolved in 1 tablespoon cold water; stir until thickened.

Per Serving (approx):
Calories 349
Carbohydrate 25 gm

Protein 24 gm
Sodium 185 mg

Fat 16 gm
Cholesterol 81 mg

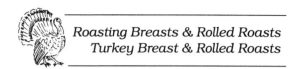

Golden Delicious Turkey Roast

1 turkey breast (1 1/2 to 2 pounds)
1 cup unsweetened apple cider
  or apple juice
2 tablespoons soy sauce

2 tablespoons cornstarch
  dissolved in 2 tablespoons
  cold water

Place turkey, cider and soy sauce in roasting pan; cover tightly with foil. Roast at 325 degrees for 1 1/2 to 2 hours or until meat thermometer reaches 180 degrees and turkey is no longer pink in center.

Pour liquid from pan into small saucepan; stir in cornstarch mixture. Bring to a boil; simmer until sauce begins to thicken. Serve turkey with sauce.   Makes 4 to 6 servings.

Per Serving (approx):
Calories 183
Carbohydrate 6 gm

Protein 25 gm
Sodium 1117 mg

Fat 7 gm
Cholesterol 60 mg

Herb-Roasted Turkey and Potatoes

1 turkey breast (1 1/2 pounds)
1 clove garlic, thinly sliced
4 red potatoes
3/4 teaspoon onion salt

3/4 teaspoon dried oregano
2 tablespoons margarine,
  melted
Paprika

Make cuts in surface of turkey and insert garlic slices. Place turkey, skin side up, in 9- x 9-inch pan. Quarter potatoes and place around roast. Combine onion salt and oregano. Sprinkle roast with two-thirds of the onion-oregano mixture. Drizzle margarine over potatoes and sprinkle with remaining onion-oregano mixture and paprika. Bake in 350 degree oven for 1 1/2 hours or to internal temperature of 170 degrees.   Makes 4 servings.

Per Serving (approx):
Calories 339
Carbohydrate 33 gm

Protein 28 gm
Sodium 115 mg

Fat 11 gm
Cholesterol 61 mg

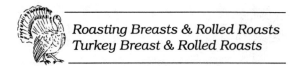

Roasting Breasts & Rolled Roasts
Turkey Breast & Rolled Roasts

Pineapple Minted Turkey Breast

Salt to taste
1 turkey breast (4 to 6
   pounds), bone in, skin removed
1 can (20 ounces) pineapple chunks
   in natural juice

1/2 cup pineapple or apple
   juice
1 1/2 tablespoons cornstarch
2 teaspoons dried mint

Salt breast to taste and place on rack in shallow roasting pan; cover with aluminum foil. Place in preheated 325 degree oven and roast for 1 1/2 to 2 1/4 hours or until meat thermometer registers 170 degrees when inserted into thickest part, not touching bone.

During roasting time, drain pineapple chunks; set aside. To juice add additional pineapple or apple juice to measure 1 1/2 cups. In medium saucepan stir together cornstarch, mint and salt. Gradually stir in juice until smooth. Stirring constantly, bring to a boil over medium heat and boil for 1 minute. Remove from heat. Remove 1/2 cup of mixture for glaze. Stir pineapple chunks into remaining mixture for sauce; keep warm.

Remove turkey breast from oven 45 minutes before done. Brush with glaze. Return to oven, uncovered, and continue roasting, brushing frequently with glaze until breast tests done.

Remove turkey breast from oven and allow to stand for 10 to 15 minutes before slicing. Heat sauce and serve 1 1/2 tablespoons over each serving of sliced turkey.   Makes 16 servings.

Per Serving (approx):
Calories 143
Carbohydrate 20 gm

Protein 26 gm
Sodium 76 mg

Fat 1 gm
Cholesterol 56 mg

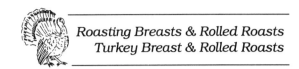

Half Turkey Breast, Southwest Style

This self-basting turkey (the stuffing does the basting) is very reminiscent of the Southwest.

1 turkey half breast (approximately
   1 1/2 pounds)
3 slices bacon, chopped
2 cloves garlic, minced
1/3 cup minced onion
1 teaspoon dried basil
1/2 teaspoon dried thyme

1 bay leaf, crushed
1/3 cup butter, melted
2 cloves garlic, minced
3 red or green bell peppers,
   quartered
3 leeks, halved

Guide knife-sharpening steel through thickest part of breast. Combine bacon, garlic, onion and herbs; pack into hole created by knife steel.* Brush with combined butter and garlic; grill in covered barbecue for about 1 hour and 20 minutes, basting occasionally. After 1 hour, place pepper quarters and leeks on grill, basting and turning until done. Or roast turkey breast in 350 degree oven for about 1 1/2 hours, basting with garlic butter. Place peppers and leeks around breast for last 30 minutes.   Makes 4 to 6 servings.

*Note: If knife-sharpening steel is unavailable, lift skin and pack season-ing under skin.

Per Serving (approx):
Calories 267
Carbohydrate 19 gm

Protein 5 gm
Sodium 275 mg

Fat 19 gm
Cholesterol 48 mg

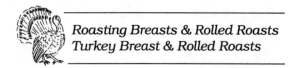

Stuffed Turkey Breast
with Pesto Sauce

1 turkey breast (4 to 6 pounds), boned
   and butterflied

Prepare stuffing, Marmalade Glaze and Pesto Sauce. Spoon stuffing over each breast. Bring sides together to encase stuffing; fasten with skewers. In 11- x 9- x 1-inch roasting pan, place breast skewered side down on meat rack. Bake in preheated 350 degree oven for 2 to 2 1/2 hours or until breast meat reaches 170 to 175 degrees. Brush with glaze 2 or 3 times during last 30 minutes of baking. To serve, slice turkey breast across roll and offer Pesto Sauce with each serving, if desired.

Makes 16 servings.

STUFFING:

In large skillet over medium-high heat, sauté 1 pound turkey sausage and 1/4 cup chopped onion, stirring to break up meat, until meat is no longer pink and onion is translucent. Drain and set aside. In large bowl combine 1 can (8 ounces) mushroom stems and pieces, drained, 2 1/2 cups French bread cut into 1/2-inch cubes, 1/4 cup pine nuts, toasted, 1 egg, 1/8 teaspoon cayenne pepper and 2 tablespoons Pesto Sauce. Add sausage mixture and stir to combine. Makes 3 cups.

GLAZE:

In small bowl combine 1/4 cup marmalade, 1 tablespoon margarine, melted and 1/4 teaspoon ginger. Use as a basting sauce for turkey breast.

Makes 1/4 cup.

PESTO SAUCE:

In electric blender container (or food processor bowl fitted with metal blade) combine 2/3 cup olive or oil, 2 cups tightly packed parsley, 1/2 cup grated Parmesan cheese, 2 cloves garlic, 4 teaspoons dried basil, 1 tablespoon capers and 1/8 teaspoon black pepper. Blend or process for 30 seconds or until mixture is smooth. Place in covered container and refrigerate. May be kept up to 1 week. Makes 1 cup.

Per Serving (approx) excluding additional Pesto Sauce:
Calories 323	*Protein 40 gm*	*Fat 15 gm*
Carbohydrate 6 gm	*Sodium 296 mg*	*Cholesterol 121 mg*

Cranapple Roasted Turkey Breast I

Here's a delicious turkey and dressing idea for a small holiday gathering.

1 onion, chopped
2 ribs celery with leaves, chopped
1 green apple, cored and chopped
6 tablespoons butter
1 cup chopped fresh
   cranberries
1 cup reduced-sodium turkey or
   chicken broth

5 slices rye bread, torn into
   small pieces
1 egg, lightly beaten
Salt and pepper to taste
1 turkey breast, bone in
   (about 3 pounds)
1/4 cup apple brandy

Sauté onion, celery and apple in 4 tablespoons of the butter until tender-crisp, about 3 minutes. Add cranberries, broth, bread pieces, egg, salt and pepper. Mix gently; mound on greased baking sheet.

Place turkey breast, skin side up, over dressing. Melt remaining 2 tablespoons butter with apple brandy. Baste turkey breast with butter mixture.

Roast in preheated 350 degree oven, basting occasionally, until meat thermometer inserted in thickest part of breast registers 170 degrees, about 1 hour and 15 minutes.   **Makes 6 servings.**

Per Serving (approx):
Calories 579	*Protein 47 gm*	*Fat 25 gm*
Carbohydrate 35 gm	*Sodium 634 mg*	*Cholesterol 169 mg*

The Voyage of Turkey

When Neil Armstrong and Edwin Aldrin sat down to eat their first meal on the moon, their food packets contained roasted turkey and all the trimmings.

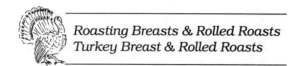
Cranapple Roasted Turkey Breast II

Like version "I," this is perfect for a small holiday dinner.

1 turkey breast (2 pounds)
1 cup apple juice
Salt and pepper to taste
2 cups fresh or canned whole
    cranberries
1 apple, chopped

1/4 cup sugar
1 tablespoon cornstarch
    dissolved in 1 tablespoon
    cold water
1/4 cup strawberry jam

Place turkey in 9- x 9-inch baking pan. Pour apple juice over turkey; season with salt and pepper. Bake in preheated 350 degree oven, basting occasionally, for 1 hour and 15 minutes.

Combine cranberries, apple and sugar. Place around turkey. Bake for 15 to 30 minutes longer or until turkey is no longer pink and meat thermometer registers 170 degrees. (Total cooking time is 20 to 25 minutes per pound.) Remove roast to platter; keep warm.

Stir cornstarch mixture and jam into cranberry mixture in pan. Heat for 5 minutes longer or until sauce thickens and fruit is soft. Serve fruit sauce over sliced turkey.   **Makes 6 to 8 servings.**

Per Serving (approx):
Calories 260
Carbohydrate 25 gm

Protein 25 gm
Sodium 100 mg

Fat 7 gm
Cholesterol 61 mg

Repeated History

President Lincoln proclaimed Thanksgiving a national holiday in 1863, in response to a campaign organized by magazine editor Sara Josepha Hale.

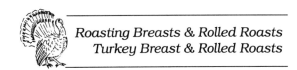

Cranberry Turkey

1 turkey half breast (approximately 4 pounds)   Salt and pepper to taste

Season turkey with salt and pepper. Place in open roasting pan. Bake in 325 degree oven for 1 1/2 hours.

Prepare sauce. Spoon some over turkey. Bake for about 30 minutes more or to internal temperature of 170 degrees. Let turkey stand for 10 minutes before slicing. Meanwhile, heat remaining sauce; serve with turkey.

Makes 8 servings.

SAUCE:
Combine 1 can (16 ounces) whole berry cranberry sauce, 1/4 teaspoon ground cloves and 1/2 cup firmly packed brown sugar.

Per Serving (approx):
Calories 386
Carbohydrate 29 gm

Protein 54 gm
Sodium 135 mg

Fat 6 gm
Cholesterol 125 mg

Feathers, Feathers, and More Feathers

It's estimated that turkeys have approximately 3,500 feathers at maturity. • The bulk of turkey feathers are disposed of; however, some feathers may be used for special purposes. • For instance, dyed feathers are used to make American Indian costumes or as quills for pens. • The costume that "Big Bird" wears on "Sesame Street" is rumored to be made of turkey feathers. • Turkey feather down has been used to make pillows. • And recently turkey and chicken feathers have been found to be effective in absorbing oil spills at sea.

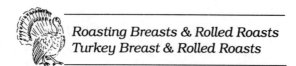

Easy Baked Turkey Breasts

1 turkey breast (2 to 4 pounds)
1/2 cup extravirgin olive oil
4 large potatoes, peeled and
   cut into eighths
1 cup coarsely chopped
   tomato

1/2 teaspoon black pepper
1 teaspoon dried oregano
6 large mushrooms, sliced
1 tablespoon chopped parsley

Preheat oven to 350 degrees. Place turkey in oven-proof casserole. Add olive oil, potatoes, tomatoes, pepper, oregano and mushrooms. Bake, uncovered, for 1 hour. Baste with sauce from casserole every 20 minutes. Remove from oven and sprinkle with parsley.   Makes 4 servings.

Per Serving (approx):
Calories 778
Carbohydrate 83 gm

Protein 34 gm
Sodium 83 mg

Fat 34 gm
Cholesterol 61 mg

ROASTING WHOLE & HALF TURKEYS

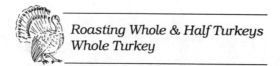

Roast Turkey with Peanut Sauce

Don't let the peanut butter in the ingredients stop you from making this version of "satay," a traditional Indonesian dish.

1 turkey (about 10 pounds)
2 lemons
Garlic salt and black pepper
   to taste

1/4 cup butter, melted
12 carrots, cut in
   pieces
2 onions, sliced

Preheat oven to 400 degrees. Pierce rinds of lemons and place inside turkey cavity; truss bird. Sprinkle turkey with garlic salt and pepper; place on rack in roasting pan. Reduce oven to 325 degrees; place turkey in oven. Baste with melted butter throughout cooking. If skin gets too dark, cover lightly with foil tent.

Cook turkey for 15 to 20 minutes per pound or until meat thermometer inserted into breast measures 175 degrees. Put carrots and onions around turkey during last 30 minutes of cooking; stir occasionally.

Slice turkey. Serve with carrots, onions and Peanut Sauce.

Makes 12 to 14 servings.

THAI PEANUT SAUCE:
Heat 2 tablespoons vegetable oil. Sauté 1 onion, chopped and 2 cloves garlic, minced. Reduce heat; add 1 tablespoon brown sugar. Cook for 3 minutes. Add 1 can (14 1/2 ounces) chicken broth and 1 cup creamy peanut butter. Cook and stir until smooth. Remove from heat; stir in 3 tablespoons soy sauce and 1 to 2 tablespoons red pepper flakes.

Per Serving (approx):
Calories 858
Carbohydrate 19 gm

Protein 91 gm
Sodium 740 mg

Fat 46 gm
Cholesterol 256 mg

> Turkeys today are available as boneless roasts, halves, quarters, or cut-up parts; also as precooked rolls.

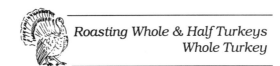

Roast Turkey with Giblet Stuffing and Gravy

For a traditional festive occasion, this classic recipe—turkey with a giblet stuffing and gravy—is quite simple to make.

1 turkey (12 to 14 pounds),
  with giblets
1 onion, quartered
2 stalks celery, chopped

Packaged seasoned stuffing
  mix (enough for 12- to
  14-pound turkey)
Salt and pepper to taste
5 tablespoons flour

Remove giblets from turkey. Place giblets in medium saucepan with onion and celery. Add water to cover. Bring to a boil; reduce heat, cover and simmer for 45 minutes to 1 hour or until giblets are done. Let cool enough to handle; remove giblets and chop, reserving cooking liquid for gravy. Prepare seasoned stuffing mix according to package directions, adding chopped giblets.

Rub salt and pepper into turkey neck and body cavities. Lightly spoon stuffing into neck cavity; close with skewer. Fill body cavity. Secure drumsticks lightly with string. Roast uncovered on roasting rack in 325 degree oven for 20 to 22 minutes per pound or to internal temperature of 175 to 180 degrees. Because of variations in turkeys, begin checking for doneness about one hour ahead. Any extra stuffing may be baked in covered casserole along with turkey during last hour of roasting. Uncover stuffing during final 10 minutes of cooking. Remove turkey to platter and let stand for at least 20 minutes before carving.

Meanwhile, make gravy by pouring off all but 6 tablespoons drippings from roasting pan. Over low heat, stir in flour until thickened. Let flour cook for about 30 seconds or until bubbly. Measure reserved giblet cooking liquid; add water to make 2 1/2 cups. Add to roasting pan, stirring until smooth.   Makes 10 to 12 servings.

Per Serving (approx):
Calories 735
Carbohydrate 10 gm

Protein 98 gm
Sodium 400 mg

Fat 34 gm
Cholesterol 282 mg

271

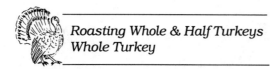

Port-Sauced Turkey

good

We're not sure whether this recipe originated in Spain or in England, but it is an exciting change of pace for roast turkey.

1 orange, unpeeled
1 turkey (10 to 12 pounds)
Salt and pepper to taste
1/2 cup butter, melted
1 large onion, cut in wedges
3/4 pound white boiling
   potatoes, quartered
1/2 cup sliced mushrooms

1/2 cup sliced leeks
3 carrots, cut in 2-inch chunks
1/4 cup flour
1/4 cup balsamic vinegar*
   or malt vinegar
1 1/2 cups ruby Port wine
4 cups chicken broth

Pierce rind of orange in several places with fork and place in cavity of turkey. Salt and pepper outside of turkey; place in deep roasting pan. Baste with 1/4 cup of the butter. Roast in 350 degree oven.

Meanwhile, sauté onion, potatoes, mushrooms, leeks and carrots in remaining 1/4 cup butter for 3 minutes. Sprinkle flour over vegetables and stir in. Add remaining ingredients and bring to a boil.

After turkey has roasted for 45 minutes, spoon vegetables and liquid over turkey, making sure vegetables are well covered with liquid. Continue cooking for about 1 1/2 hours longer or until meat thermometer placed in the thickest part of breast registers 175 degrees. Serve with braised vegetables and some of braising liquid.* Makes 8 to 10 servings.

*Note: Remaining braising liquid makes an excellent soup base.

Per Serving (approx):
Calories 1150
Carbohydrate 21 gm

Protein 129 gm
Sodium 1219 mg

Fat 56 gm
Cholesterol 399 mg

"For turkey braised, the Lord be praised"—from a 19th Century Guide to Food Preparation.

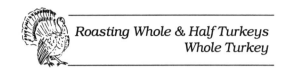

Roast Turkey with Oyster Stuffing

It was probably the Pilgrims who came up with the idea of stuffing turkey with oysters . . . and a very good idea it was, and still is.

1 turkey (12 to 14 pounds)   Salt and pepper to taste

Prepare Oyster Stuffing. Rub salt and pepper into neck and body cavities. Lightly spoon Oyster Stuffing into neck cavity; close with skewer. Fill body cavity. Secure drumsticks lightly with string. Roast uncovered on roasting rack in 325 degree oven for 20 to 22 minutes per pound or to internal temperature of 170 to 180 degrees, thick part of drumstick feels soft when pressed with thumb and forefinger, or when drumstick moves easily. Any remaining stuffing may be baked, in covered casserole, along with turkey during last hour of roasting. Uncover dressing during final 10 minutes of cooking. Let turkey stand for at least 20 minutes before carving.   Makes 12 servings.

OYSTER STUFFING:
Dry 1 loaf (1 pound) white bread slices overnight in open air, or on rack in 250 degree oven for 1 to 1 1/4 hours.

In skillet sauté 2 cups finely chopped celery and 2 cups finely chopped onion in 3/4 cup butter or margarine until tender. Warm 1/2 cup milk over low heat in small saucepan. Tear bread into 1/2-inch pieces, making about 11 cups; place in large mixing bowl. Sprinkle warm milk over bread and toss lightly. Add onion mixture and 3 containers (8 ounces each) fresh or frozen oysters, drained* to bread; toss to mix well. Sprinkle with 1 teaspoon lemon juice, 1/4 teaspoon ground nutmeg, 3/4 teaspoon dried poultry seasoning, 1/4 teaspoon salt and 1/4 teaspoon pepper; mix thoroughly.

*Note: If desired, canned oysters may be substituted.

Per Serving (approx):
Calories 918   *Protein 97 gm*   *Fat 46 gm*
Carbohydrate 30 gm   *Sodium 833 mg*   *Cholesterol 339 mg*

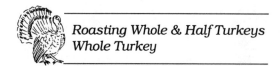
Turkey Southwest Style with Sage Corn Bread Stuffing and Chile Gravy

1 turkey (12 to 14 pounds)   1/2 teaspoon dried sage
1/4 cup butter

Prepare Sage Corn Bread Stuffing. Spoon stuffing into turkey cavity and truss. Melt butter and add sage; brush over turkey.

Roast at 325 degrees for 3 to 3 1/2 hours or until meat thermometer registers 170 to 180 degrees, thick part of drumstick feels soft when pressed with thumb and forefinger, or when drumstick moves easily. Let stand for 20 minutes before carving; reserve drippings for Chile Gravy.

Makes 10 to 12 servings.

SAGE CORN BREAD STUFFING:
Sauté 1 cup chopped onion and 3/4 cup chopped celery in 1/4 cup butter until soft. Combine with 3 cups corn bread stuffing mix, 1 cup chicken broth, 1 cup corn kernels (fresh, frozen or canned), 1/4 cup diced green chilies, 1/2 cup chopped walnuts, toasted, 1 egg, lightly beaten, 1 teaspoon dried sage, salt and pepper to taste.

CHILE GRAVY:
Pour fat and drippings into 4-cup measure. Skim off and reserve 1/3 cup fat. Discard remaining fat, reserving drippings. Add enough broth to drippings to measure 4 cups. Melt fat in saucepan; stir in 1/2 cup flour until smooth. Cook for 2 minutes, stirring. Gradually add broth, 1/4 diced green chilies, 1 teaspoon dried sage and dash of pepper. Bring to a boil. Reduce heat; simmer, covered, until thickened slightly, for about 5 minutes.

Per Serving (approx):
Calories 917   *Protein 105 gm*   *Fat 49 gm*
Carbohydrate 14 gm   *Sodium 791 mg*   *Cholesterol 341 mg*

Roast Turkey with Dried Fruit Stuffing

Make it a Scandinavian Christmas with this very different recipe.

1 turkey (10 to 12 pounds)   Salt and pepper to taste

Rub salt and pepper into turkey neck and body cavities. Secure drumsticks lightly with string. Insert meat thermometer into center of thigh next to body, but not touching bone. Roast uncovered on roasting rack in 325 degree oven for 20 to 22 minutes per pound. Turkey is done when meat thermometer registers 170 to 180 degrees, thick part of drumstick feels soft when pressed with thumb and forefinger, or when drumstick moves easily.

Prepare Dried Fruit Stuffing. When turkey is done, remove from oven and let stand for 20 to 30 minutes before carving. Meanwhile, increase oven temperature to 350 degrees. Add hot water to baking pans with ramekins to depth of 1/4 to 1/2 inch. Cover pans with aluminum foil. Bake stuffing for 20 minutes; uncover and bake for an additional 10 minutes. To serve, carve turkey. Run spatula around inside of each ramekin; turn out individual servings of stuffing.   Makes 12 servings.

DRIED FRUIT STUFFING:
Bake 16 slices white bread in single layers on baking sheets for 25 mintues, turning once. Set aside; cool. Cut cooled bread into 1/4-inch pieces. Sauté 1 large onion, finely minced and 1 cup finely minced celery in 1/2 cup butter or margarine. Combine with 2 cups finely minced and peeled apple, 3 cups finely chopped pitted prunes and bread in large mixing bowl. Combine 1 can (14 1/2 ounces) chicken broth and 1/3 cup orange juice; add to bread mixture, tossing lightly to moisten thoroughly. Place in 12 greased ramekins, 3 1/2 inches each. Place ramekins in 2 baking pans, 9 x 13 inches each.*

*Note: If desired, stuffing may be baked instead 9- x 13-inch baking pan. Cover baking pan with aluminum foil and bake for 30 minutes at 350 degrees.

Per Serving (approx):
Calories 910   *Protein 89 gm*   *Fat 39 gm*
Carbohydrate 51 gm   *Sodium 725 mg*   *Cholesterol 267 mg*

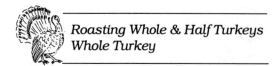

Butterflied Chile-Buttered Turkey

1 turkey (10 to 12 pounds)

Spread turkey as flat as possible (have butcher saw through backbone).
Arrange skin side up on rack in baking pan. Prepare Chile Butter.

Roast turkey at 325 degrees for 2 1/2 to 3 hours, basting every 20 minutes with Chile Butter. Makes 8 servings.

CHILE BUTTER:
Combine 3/4 cup butter, 2 cloves garlic, minced, 1 small green chile,
seeds removed, minced, 1 teaspoon dried coriander or 1 tablespoon
chopped cilantro, and 1 teaspoon ground cumin.

Per Serving (approx):
Calories 1064   *Protein 127 gm*   *Fat 61 gm*
Carbohydrate 2 gm   *Sodium 483 mg*   *Cholesterol 415 mg*

Turkey in an Oven-Roasting Bag

*If you want to serve this turkey with stuffing, we suggest that you bake your
stuffing separately. We have not had great success with stuffed poultry of
any kind in an oven-roasting bag.*

2 tablespoons flour   Salt and pepper to taste (optional)
1 turkey (8 to 12 pounds)

Place flour in oven-roasting bag and shake. Season turkey with salt and
pepper, if desired. Place turkey in bag; place bag in baking dish.

Close bag with tie and make six 1/2-inch slits in top of bag. Cook in
preheated 350 degree oven for 2 to 2 1/2 hours. Let stand for 20 minutes. Slice and serve with your favorite sauce.   Makes 8 to 12 servings.

Per Serving (approx):
Calories 603   *Protein 84 gm*   *Fat 29 gm*
Carbohydrate 1 gm   *Sodium 236 mg*   *Cholesterol 245 mg*

276

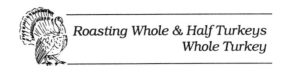

Roast Turkey Athena

Here is a very interesting alternative to a bread stuffing, compliments of Greece.

1 turkey (12 to 15 pounds)
Salt and pepper to taste
1 onion halved
2 sprigs parsley plus
    more for garnish
1/4 cup olive oil

2 tablespoons lemon juice
1/2 teaspoon dried basil,
    finely crushed
Poached peach and pear halves,
    for garnish

Season inside cavity of turkey with salt and pepper, and tuck in onion and 2 parsley sprigs. Fasten neck skin to back; truss and tie wings and drumsticks to bird. Place turkey, breast side up, on rack in shallow pan. Combine oil, lemon juice and basil. Brush over skin of turkey. Insert meat thermometer so bulb is in center of inside thigh muscle or thickest part of breast (do not allow to touch bone).

Roast, uncovered, in 325 degree oven, for about 4 1/2 to 5 hours for unstuffed turkey (about 170 to 180 degrees on meat thermometer). Baste occasionally with pan drippings. Make Bulgur Wheat Stuffing. When ready to serve, garnish turkey with peach and pear halves and parsley. Serve Bulgur Wheat Stuffing separately.   Makes 10 servings.

BULGUR WHEAT STUFFING:
Cook 1 cup chopped onion and 1 cup sliced celery in 1/2 cup butter or margarine just until vegetables begin to soften. Stir in 2 cups uncooked bulgar wheat, 1/2 teaspoon salt, 1/4 teaspoon herb seasoned pepper and 1/2 teaspoon dried poultry seasoning. Add 2 cans (10 3/4 ounces each) condensed chicken broth, 1 cup water and 1 tablespoon lemon juice. Cover and bring to a boil. Reduce heat and simmer for 15 to 20 minutes or just until vegetables are tender and liquid is absorbed. Stir in 1 cup small wedges ripe olives and 1/4 cup finely chopped parsley.

Per Serving (approx):
Calories 1129
Carbohydrate 44 gm

Protein 115 gm
Sodium 1055 mg

Fat 55 gm
Cholesterol 338 mg

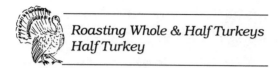

Roasting Whole & Half Turkeys
Half Turkey

Maple-Glazed Turkey with Apple-Pecan Stuffing

This came to us from maple syrup country. It has an interesting, subtle sweet flavor.

1 half turkey (5 to 6 pounds)
Salt and pepper to taste
4 tablespoons butter or margarine, melted

1/3 cup maple or maple-flavored syrup
1/3 cup dark corn syrup

Rinse turkey; drain and pat dry. Rub salt and pepper into neck and body cavities. Tie leg to tail with string. Lay wing flat over white meat and tie string around breast to hold wing down. Skewer skin to meat along cut edges to prevent shrinking. Place turkey on rack in shallow roasting pan, skin side up. Brush skin with 2 tablespoons of the melted butter. Insert meat thermometer into inside thigh muscle, not touching bone. Roast in 325 degree oven for 2 to 2 1/2 hours or to an internal temperature of 170 to 180 degrees.

Meanwhile, combine the remaining 2 tablespoons melted butter with the maple and corn syrups. Brush over turkey during last hour of roasting, basting several times to use all of glaze.

When turkey is done, remove from oven and let stand for 20 to 30 minutes before carving. Meanwhile, cover stuffing casserole and bake for 25 to 30 minutes at 325 degrees. Uncover during last 5 to 10 minutes of baking.   Makes 6 servings.

APPLE-PECAN STUFFING:
Tear 8 slices soft white bread into small, 1/4-inch pieces to make 6 cups. Sauté 1 small onion, chopped, and 1/2 cup chopped celery with leaves in 1/4 cup melted butter or margarine. Combine onion mixture with bread, 1 large apple, peeled, cored and chopped, and 1/2 cup pecans. Beat together 1/2 cup turkey or chicken stock, 1 egg, 3/4 teaspoon dried sage, 1/2 teaspoon salt and 1/8 teaspoon pepper. Slowly add to bread mixture, tossing lightly to mix well. Add additional stock if more moist dressing is desired. Place in greased 2-quart casserole.

Per Serving (approx):
Calories 1000
Carbohydrate 52 gm

Protein 83 gm
Sodium 755 mg

Fat 51 gm
Cholesterol 304 mg

278

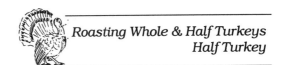

Turkey a la Jamaica

*This is a mild version of Caribbean cooking. Want it closer to the original?
Add your favorite chili sauce and/or chile peppers.*

2 tablespoons dried onion
3 teaspoons ground thyme
2 teaspoons each onion powder
  and sugar
1 teaspoon ground allspice
1 teaspoon black pepper

1/2 teaspoon cayenne pepper
1/4 teaspoon each ground
  nutmeg and ground cinnamon
1 half turkey
1 cup water

In small bowl combine seasonings. Rub on top and bottom and under edges of skin of turkey. Place turkey on rack in baking dish, skin side up. Add water to dish. Cover with foil. Cook for 60 minutes. Remove foil and cook for 45 to 60 minutes more. Let stand for 20 minutes before slicing.   Makes 12 servings.

Per Serving (approx):
Calories 309
Carbohydrate 2 gm

Protein 42 gm
Sodium 103 mg

Fat 15 gm
Cholesterol 123 mg

Handle with Care

- Do not leave turkey at room temperature.
- Refrigerate turkey at 40 degrees F. or below
- Cook ground or boneless turkey to a minimum internal temperature of 160 degrees F.
- Cook bone-in turkey to a minimum internal temperature of 170 degrees F.
- Cook whole turkey to an internal temperature of 180 degrees F. in inner thigh.
- Cool food rapidly. Store in small, shallow containers.
- Keep hands, utensils and work areas clean.

279

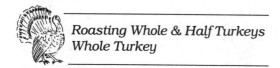

Roast Turkey with Jalapeño Corn Bread Stuffing

1 turkey (10 to 12 pounds),
   with giblets

1 cube chicken bouillon
2 1/2 cups water

Remove giblets from turkey. Rinse giblets and place, with chicken bouillon cube, in saucepan with water. Bring to a boil; cover and simmer until tender, about 1 hour. Set giblets aside for later use in gravies or soups. Reserve broth; let cool. Prepare Jalapeño Corn Bread Stuffing.

Lightly spoon stuffing into neck cavity; close with skewer. Fill body cavity. Secure drumsticks lightly with string. Roast uncovered on roasting rack in 325 degree oven for 20 to 22 minutes per pound or to internal temperature of 170 to 180 degrees.

Remaining stuffing may be baked, in covered 1 1/2-quart casserole dish, along with turkey during last hour of roasting. Uncover stuffing during final 10 minutes of cooking. Let turkey stand for at least 20 minutes before carving.   Makes 10 to 12 servings.

JALAPEÑO CORN BREAD STUFFING:
To make corn bread, combine 1 1/3 cups cornmeal, 2/3 cup flour, 2 tablespoons sugar and 1 tablespoon baking powder in medium bowl. Beat 1 egg with 1 cup milk; add to dry ingredients, mixing just until moistened. Stir in 1/4 cup melted butter or margarine. Pour batter into greased 8-inch-square baking pan. Bake at 425 degrees for 20 to 25 minutes, or until golden. Remove from oven and cool.

Make stuffing by crumbling corn bread into a large bowl. Add 6 cups dry bread cubes. Sauté 1 pound turkey sausage with 1 cup chopped onion and 1 1/2 cups chopped celery in skillet until sausage loses red color and is crumbly. Drain off all but 1/4 cup fat from sausage in skillet. Add 1 teaspoon salt, 1 teaspoon dried poultry seasoning and 1/4 cup chopped, seeded jalapeño peppers to sausage. Combine sausage mixture with bread mixture, tossing to mix well. Beat together 1 cup reserved broth from cooking giblets with 2 eggs; add to stuffing. (Add additional reserved giblet broth if desired for a more moist stuffing.)

Per Serving (approx):
Calories 859
Carbohydrate 44 gm

Protein 88 gm
Sodium 1213 mg

Fat 36 gm
Cholesterol 303 mg

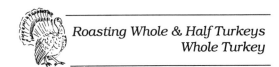

Maple-Basted Roast Turkey with New England Stuffing

1 turkey (10 to 16 pounds),
  with giblets
1 1/2 teaspoons dried poultry
  seasoning
Salt and pepper to taste

1/2 cup light maple syrup
1/2 to 1 cup reduced-sodium
  chicken broth
5 tablespoons flour
1/2 cup cranberry juice

Remove giblets from cavity of turkey; set aside for another use. Season turkey with poultry seasoning, salt and pepper.

Truss turkey and place in large roasting pan. Roast turkey in preheated 325 degree oven, allowing 14 to 18 minutes per pound (3 to 4 hours), until juices run clear (larger birds need less cooking time per pound). Baste with maple syrup during last hour. While turkey is roasting, prepare New England Stuffing. Place in oven with turkey for last 30 minutes of cooking time. Remove cooked turkey to serving platter; skim off and discard all fat from pan juices.

To prepare gravy, pour degreased pan juices into heatproof measuring cup and add enough chicken broth to measure 5 cups. Return juices to roasting pan and stir to incorporate any browned bits. In measuring cup stir flour into cranberry juice to dissolve; whisk into juices into roasting pan. Place over medium heat and cook for 5 to 10 minutes or until gravy thickens, stirring constantly. Season gravy to taste with salt and pepper. To serve, carve turkey, discarding skin. Spoon gravy over slices and accompany with stuffing.   Makes 12 to 18 servings.

NEW ENGLAND STUFFING:
Cube 10 slices dried bread into large bowl. In large skillet over medium-low heat, melt 1/4 cup low-fat margarine. Add 1 cup chopped onion, 1/2 cup chopped celery and 1 teaspoon dried poultry seasoning. Sauté for 8 to 10 minutes until vegetables are softened. Add vegetables and 1/2 cup dried cranberries, cherries or mixed fruit bits to bread cubes; toss to combine. Stir in 1 1/2 cups reduced-sodium chicken broth and season with salt and pepper to taste. Transfer to greased baking dish.

Per Serving (approx) including stuffing and gravy:
Calories 425   *Protein 59 gm*   *Fat 11 gm*
Carbohydrate 18 gm   *Sodium 390 mg*   *Cholesterol 150 mg*

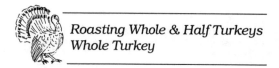

Roasting Whole & Half Turkeys
Whole Turkey

Southwest Turkey Roast

1 turkey (12 to 14 pounds)

Prepare Southwestern Rice Stuffing and Orange Glaze.

Spoon stuffing into turkey cavity and truss. Roast for 20 minutes per pound at 325 degrees (or use Grill Method, below), basting with Orange Glaze. Cover with foil if skin gets too dark. Let stand for 20 to 30 minutes before carving. Serve with stuffing.   Makes 12 to 14 servings.

SOUTHWESTERN RICE STUFFING:
Stir 1 1/2 cups long-grain rice, 1 tablespoon butter and 1/4 teaspoon salt into 3 cups boiling water; reduce heat and simmer, covered, for 20 minutes. Sauté 3 cloves garlic, minced, 3 medium red or green bell peppers, chopped, 1 large red onion, chopped, 5 jalapeño chilies, seeded and finely chopped, and 3 ears corn, kernels cut off cob, or 1 package (10 ounces) frozen whole kernel corn, thawed, in 3 tablespoons olive oil; combine with rice and 1/4 cup chopped cilantro or 2 teaspoons dried coriander and 1/4 teaspoon chili powder.

ORANGE GLAZE:
Sauté 2 cloves garlic, chopped, in 1/4 cup melted butter until soft. Add 1/2 cup orange marmalade and 1/2 teaspoon ground cumin. Heat through.

GRILL METHOD:
Do not stuff turkey. Roast in covered grill, using indirect method,* for 10 to 15 minutes per pound to 180 to 185 degrees internal temperature at thigh. Bake stuffing in uncovered casserole at 375 degrees for 30 to 35 minutes, moistening occasionally with juices caught in drip pan.

*Note: For information on indirect-heat cooking, see page 255.

Per Serving (approx) including glaze:
Calories 796   *Protein 85 gm*   *Fat 37 gm*
Carbohydrate 30 gm   *Sodium 439 mg*   *Cholesterol 258 mg*

282

BARBECUING & GRILLING

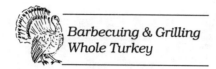

Turkey Grill

Marinate a butterflied whole turkey in fruit juices and wine for a delectable dinner party main course.

1 quart each cranberry juice
    and orange juice
1 bottle Sauvignon Blanc
    (reserve 1/4 cup for glaze)
2 teaspoons each chopped
    fresh rosemary and thyme
    or 1 teaspoon each dried

1 cup chopped onion
Salt and pepper to taste
1 turkey, butterflied
    (about 12 pounds)

Combine all ingredients except turkey. Place turkey in marinade for 2 hours; turn turkey halfway through. Place turkey on grill with cover, breast side up, and cook for approximately 15 to 20 minutes per pound. (Internal temperature should be 170 degrees). Brush with Rosemary-Wine Glaze last 15 minutes of cooking time.   Makes 8 to 10 servings.

ROSEMARY-WINE GLAZE:
Blend together 3/4 cup honey, 1/4 cup each Sauvignon Blanc and lemon juice, and 1 tablespoon chopped fresh rosemary.

Per Serving (approx):
Calories 1225
Carbohydrate 59 gm

Protein 128 gm
Sodium 499 mg

Fat 44 gm
Cholesterol 368 mg

Direct-Heat Cooking

Remove top grill rack; open all vents. Mound 40 to 50 briquettes in center of lower grill rack or bottom of grill; ignite briquettes. When coals become ash gray (about 20 to 40 minutes), spread them evenly over lower grill rack or bottom of grill. Lightly grease top grill rack and reposition it over hot coals; place turkey on grill rack.

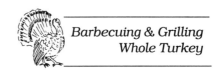

Southwestern Butterflied Turkey with Roasted Garlic

Never grilled a whole turkey? One good way is to split it down the back and lay it flat. Makes the grilling quick and easy.

1 turkey (10 to 12 pounds)
3/4 cup butter, melted
2 tablespoons chopped cilantro or
   1 teaspoon dried coriander

1 teaspoon red pepper flakes
1 teaspoon ground cumin
Salt to taste

Ask butcher to saw turkey through backbone, leaving breast attached. Spread turkey flat. Prepare medium-hot charcoal fire. When coals are gray, arrange around perimeter of barbecue. Put turkey on grill, skin side up. Combine butter, cilantro, pepper flakes, cumin and salt. Baste turkey with seasoned butter. Cover, leaving vents partly open, and grill for about 2 hours, adding fresh briquettes as needed. Baste every 20 minutes. About 1 hour before turkey is done, prepare Roasted Garlic and corn. Serve turkey with Roasted Garlic and Grilled Corn, squeezing cloves of garlic over turkey as you eat.   Makes 10 servings.

ROASTED GARLIC:
Select 8 to 10 medium heads garlic. Cut across top of each to expose cloves; do not peel. Place each on sheet of aluminum foil; drizzle with olive oil. Sprinkle with chopped herbs, if desired. Close foil packets and place around turkey about 1 hour before turkey is done.

GRILLED CORN WITH SAVORY BUTTER:
To grill corn in husk, peel back husk and remove silk. Pull husk back up and tie with string. Soak corn in water for 15 minutes. Grill for 15 to 20 minutes, turning occasionally. Serve with melted butter flavored with minced fresh herbs (1 tablespoon per 1/2 cup butter) or spices (2 teaspoons chili powder to 1/2 cup butter, for example).

Per Serving (approx) excluding garlic and corn:
Calories 1056   *Protein 126 gm*   *Fat 61 gm*
Carbohydrate 0 gm   *Sodium 530 mg*   *Cholesterol 415 mg*

Sonoma Turkey Barbecue

Some of the best wines and some of the best turkeys share a common heritage: Sonoma County, California. Everyone knows that Sonoma County produces premium wines, but, unknown to most, Sonoma County is also home to the largest turkey breeding operation in the world. The Nicholas Turkey Breeding Farms ships more than 300 million turkey eggs each year to growers in Europe, Asia and throughout the United States. You'll enjoy this classic Sonoma County turkey barbecue.

1/3 cup tomato paste
1/2 cup White Zinfandel
1/2 cup each chopped red
   onion and cilantro
2 teaspoons each chili powder
   and cumin

Salt and pepper to taste
1 half breast turkey
   (2 to 3 pounds)
1 to 2 tablespoons oil

Mix together tomato paste, wine, onion, cilantro, chili powder, cumin, salt and pepper. Rub turkey breast with oil.

Grill in covered barbecue, using indirect method,* for 10 to 15 minutes per pound to 170 degrees internal temperature. Brush with some sauce during last 1/2 hour of cooking time. Thin remaining sauce to desired consistency, bring to a boil and serve with sliced turkey.

Makes 4 to 6 servings.

*Note: For information on indirect-heat cooking, see page 255.

Per Serving (approx):
Calories 484
Carbohydrate 7 gm

Protein 63 gm
Sodium 249 mg

Fat 21 gm
Cholesterol 153 mg

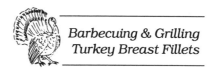

Thai Turkey Kabobs

Thailand and California are joined in this recipe with the blending of Asian ingredients with wine.

1 1/2 pounds turkey breast fillets
  or tenderloins
1 cup Chardonnay wine
1/3 cup soy sauce

1 tablespoon minced fresh ginger
  or 1 teaspoon ground
3 cloves garlic, minced

Cut turkey into 1-inch cubes. Combine wine, soy sauce, ginger and garlic. Pour over turkey and let marinate for 2 hours in refrigerator. Remove turkey; reserve 1/2 cup marinade and prepare Thai Peanut Sauce.

Thread turkey on skewers. Brush with half the sauce. Grill over medium coals for 10 to 15 minutes or until done; turn frequently. Heat remaining sauce thoroughly, thinning with Chardonnay if necessary, and serve with turkey kabobs. Makes 6 servings.

THAI PEANUT SAUCE #2:
Sauté 1/2 cup chopped onion in 1 tablespoon each sesame oil and vegetable oil until soft. Add 1/2 cup reserved marinade, 1/3 cup peanut butter, 2 tablespoons each brown sugar and catsup, 1/2 teaspoon ground coriander and dash of red pepper flakes. Whisk together.

Per Serving (approx):
Calories 342
Carbohydrate 11 gm

Protein 31 gm
Sodium 1042 mg

Fat 16 gm
Cholesterol 69 mg

Roman-Style Grilled Turkey Breast

2 tablespoons lemon juice
2 tablespoons olive oil
2 tablespoons minced fresh
   oregano or 2 teaspoons dried
2 to 3 cloves garlic, minced

1 teaspoon red pepper flakes
1 teaspoon black pepper
1 teaspoon salt
1 turkey breast (4 to 6 pounds)

Prepare covered grill for indirect-heat cooking.* When coals are hot, arrange in double layer around drip pan, with 8 to 10 unlit coals at outer edge of fire. Add 1 cup water to drip pan and open all vents.

In small bowl combine lemon juice, 1 tablespoon of the oil, oregano, garlic, red pepper flakes, 3/4 teaspoon of the black pepper and 1/2 teaspoon of the salt.

Working from broad "neck end" of breast, carefully run fingers under skin to loosen. Leave skin attached at base of breast to hold in seasonings. Spread combined seasonings under skin and rub into flesh. Rub outside of skin with remaining oil and sprinkle with remaining salt and black pepper.

Place turkey breast on grill over drip pan; cover and grill for 15 to 30 minutes per pound or until meat thermometer inserted in thickest part of breast registers 170 to 175 degrees. Turn breast every 30 minutes to brown evenly; let stand for 10 minutes before carving.

Makes 8 to 10 servings.

*Note: For information on indirect-heat cooking, see page 255.

Per Serving (approx):
Calories 374
Carbohydrate 1 gm

Protein 82 gm
Sodium 377 mg

Fat 5 gm
Cholesterol 226 mg

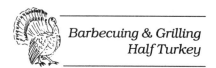

Teriyaki Turkey Luau

Hawaii is in your own backyard with this luau recipe, the aromas from which will probably bring out grass skirts and ukuleles.

1 half turkey (5 to 6 pounds)
Salt to taste
4 sweet potatoes
Oil
2 tablespoons butter or
 margarine
2 tablespoons dark brown sugar,
 firmly packed

2 tablespoons honey
1 tablespoon soy sauce
3 tablespoons lime juice
Dash of ground ginger
4 slices pineapple, canned or
 fresh

Skewer turkey skin to meat along cut edges to prevent shrinking during roasting. Rub cavity lightly with salt. Tie leg to tail with string. Lay wing flat over white meat and tie string around breast end to hold wing down.

Prepare grill for indirect-heat cooking.* Slowly cook turkey for about 20 minutes per pound or until meat thermometer inserted in thickest part of breast registers 170 to 175 degrees. Add more charcoal as needed to maintain heat (about every 30 minutes).

Meanwhile, scrub sweet potatoes; pat dry, then prick each with fork and brush with vegetable oil. Wrap each in a square of aluminum foil, over-lapping ends. Bake along with turkey, turning occasionally during final hour of cooking.

For basting sauce, melt butter in small saucepan. Add brown sugar, honey, soy sauce, lime juice and ginger, stirring to combine. Heat through. Brush on turkey during last hour of roasting.

When turkey is done, remove from grill and let stand for 20 minutes before carving. Continue cooking potatoes. Grill pineapple slices, brushing with remaining sauce and turning once. Carve turkey. Serve with sweet potatoes and pineapple slices.   Makes 4 generous servings.

*Note: For information on indirect-heat cooking, see page 255.

Per Serving (approx):
Calories 1072
Carbohydrate 46 gm

Protein 114 gm
Sodium 710 mg

Fat 48 gm
Cholesterol 325 mg

Mesquite-Grilled Turkey

1 cup mesquite chips
2 pounds turkey breast
   tenderloins or fillets

Black pepper to taste
Salsas, for accompaniment

In small bowl cover mesquite chips with water and allow to stand for 2 hours. Preheat charcoal grill for direct-heat cooking.* Drain water from mesquite chips and add chips to hot coals.

Sprinkle tenderloins with pepper and grill for 15 to 20 minutes or until turkey is no longer pink in center and registers 170 degrees on meat thermometer. Turn turkey halfway through grilling time. Allow to stand 10 minutes before serving.

To serve, slice turkey into 1/2-inch-thick medallions and arrange on serving plate. Top with choice of salsas.   Makes 8 servings.

*Note: For information on direct-heat cooking, see page 284.

Per Serving (approx) using tenderloins:
Calories 129	*Protein 27 gm*	*Fat 2 gm*
Carbohydrate 0 gm	*Sodium 76 mg*	*Cholesterol 70 mg*

Turkey a l'Orange

1 pound turkey breast
   tenderloins
1 tablespoon brown sugar
2 teaspoons cornstarch

1/2 cup orange juice
1 1/2 teaspoons lemon juice
1 teaspoon butter
1 tablespoon brandy (optional)

Place turkey on broiler pan. Move oven rack so top of turkey is 5 inches from heat. Broil 10 minutes; turn. Broil for 10 minutes on each side.*

Meanwhile, combine sugar and cornstarch in saucepan; add juices and butter. Cook over medium heat, stirring constantly until thickened. Serve over turkey.   Makes 2 to 4 servings.

TO FLAME:
Heat brandy in small pan over low heat until it begins to sizzle along sides of pan when tilted. Remove from heat. Using long match, light brandy; pour over turkey and sauce.

MICROWAVE METHOD:
Place turkey in glass baking dish; cover with plastic wrap, turning back corner to vent. Microwave on high for 4 minutes. Turn turkey over. Cover. Microwave on high for 2 to 5 minutes more or until no longer pink. Combine sugar, cornstarch, juices, butter and brandy (if used) in 2-cup glass measure. Microwave on high for 2 minutes, stirring halfway through cooking.

*Note: Recipe is written for large (2 per package) turkey breast tenderloins. Decrease total cooking time to 10 minutes if small (3 or 4 per package) tenderloins are used.

Per Serving (approx):
Calories 178
Carbohydrate 5 gm

Protein 27 gm
Sodium 74 mg

Fat 6 gm
Cholesterol 72 mg

Zesty Grilled Turkey Wings

For a delicious, economical barbecue, this dish scores high.

4 turkey wings
3 cans beer or
   4 cups chicken broth
1/2 teaspoon salt
1/2 teaspoon black pepper
1 can (16 ounces) Italian-style
   tomatoes, drained
1/2 cup each cider vinegar,
   beef broth and melted butter

1/2 cup chopped onion
2 tablespoons each
   Worcestershire sauce
   and brown sugar
1/2 teaspoon each curry
   powder and chili powder

Simmer turkey wings in beer, salt and pepper for 30 minutes. Place all remaining ingredients in blender or food processor; blend to make sauce. In pan, cook sauce for 20 minutes over medium heat or until slightly thickened. Grill wings, basting liberally with sauce, for about 30 minutes.* Serve any remaining sauce with wings.   Makes 4 servings.

*Note: Wings can be baked in 350 degree oven, for 1 hour, basting with sauce occasionally.

Per Serving (approx):
Calories 771
Carbohydrate 22 gm

Protein 51 gm
Sodium 682 mg

Fat 46 gm
Cholesterol 207 mg

Pineapple and Turkey on Skewers

1 pound turkey steaks
1 can (16 ounces) pineapple
  chunks with juice
2 tablespoons regular or
  reduced-calorie Italian
  salad dressing

1 tablespoon soy sauce or
  Worcestershire sauce
1/4 teaspoon ground cinnamon
  or apple pie spice
Salt and pepper to taste

Cut turkey into 1 1/2-inch cubes. Thread on skewers, alternating with pineapple. Reserve pineapple juice. Brush turkey with salad dressing. Broil or barbecue 3 inches from heat source, turning frequently, for approximately 15 minutes. Meanwhile, combine reserved pineapple juice, soy sauce and spice in small saucepan. Simmer, uncovered, to thicken glaze. Spoon over turkey just before serving. Makes 4 servings.

Per Serving (approx):
Calories 300
Carbohydrate 25 gm
Protein 38 gm
Sodium 330 mg
Fat 5 gm
Cholesterol 25 mg

Mustard-Topped Turkey Steaks

1 pound turkey steaks
2 teaspoons vegetable oil
2 tablespoons reduced-calorie
  mayonnaise
1 tablespoon white wine

1 1/2 tablespoons bread
  crumbs
1 1/2 teaspoons Dijon-style
  mustard
1/4 teaspoon sugar

Preheat broiler. Brush turkey steaks with oil on both sides. In small bowl combine remaining ingredients; set aside. Place turkey on boiler rack. Broil 5 to 6 inches from heat for 5 minutes on each side. Spread mustard mixture over turkey; broil for 1 1/2 to 2 minutes longer or until topping is hot and golden brown. Slice to serve. Makes 4 servings.

Per Serving (approx):
Calories 183
Carbohydrate 3 gm
Protein 27 gm
Sodium 247 mg
Fat 6 gm
Cholesterol 73 mg

Island Grilled Turkey Breast

1 half breast turkey
  (approximately 4 pounds)

Place foil drip pan on bottom of kettle grill surrounded by hot coals. Place turkey on rack over drip pan. Cover. Cook for 2 to 2 1/2 hours or to internal temperature of 170 degrees. (Add coals during cooking to maintain heat.) Meanwhile, combine Island Sauce ingredients. Brush turkey with sauce frequently during last 30 minutes of grilling.

Makes 8 servings.

ISLAND SAUCE:
Combine 1/4 cup butter, melted, 1/3 cup honey, 1 tablespoon Dijon mustard, 1 teaspoon curry powder and 1/4 teaspoon garlic powder.

Per Serving (approx):
Calories 371	*Protein 55 gm*	*Fat 12 gm*
Carbohydrate 12 gm	*Sodium 223 mg*	*Cholesterol 141 mg*

Glazed Sesame Turkey

1 turkey breast (2 to 3 pounds)   1 teaspoon sesame seeds

Prepare grill for indirect-heat cooking.* Put foil drip pan on bottom of kettle grill surrounded by hot coals. Place turkey on rack over drip pan. Cover. Cook for 1 hour. (Add coals during cooking to maintain heat.) Prepare Orange-Apricot Sauce. Brush turkey with sauce and sprinkle with sesame seeds. Cook for 30 minutes more to internal temperature of 170 degrees. Serve with remaining sauce.   Makes 2 to 4 servings.

ORANGE-APRICOT SAUCE:
Combine 1 cup orange marmalade, 1/2 cup apricot nectar, 1 tablespoon soy sauce and 1 tablespoon cornstarch. Cook, stirring frequently, until thickened.

*Note: For information on indirect-heat cooking, see page 255.

Per Serving (approx):
Calories 518	*Protein 53 gm*	*Fat 6 gm*
Carbohydrate 63 gm	*Sodium 381 mg*	*Cholesterol 120 mg*

Midsummer Turkey Kabobs

3 ears corn, cut into 1-inch
   slices
2 medium zucchini, cut into
   3/4-inch pieces
2 red bell peppers, cut into
   1-inch cubes

2 turkey tenderloins
   (approximately 1 pound),
   cut into 1-inch cubes
1/3 cup reduced-calorie
   Italian salad dressing

In medium saucepan over high heat, parboil corn for about 1 to 2 minutes. Remove from water and plunge into cold water.

In large bowl place corn, zucchini, peppers, turkey and dressing. Cover and refrigerate for 1 to 2 hours.

Drain turkey and vegetables, discarding marinade. Alternately thread turkey cubes and vegetables on eight 9-inch skewers, leaving 1/2-inch space between turkey and vegetables.

On charcoal grill, cook kabobs for 18 to 20 minutes total, brushing with additional dressing. Turn skewers after first 10 minutes.

Makes 4 servings.

Per Serving (approx):
Calories 218
Carbohydrate 18 gm

Protein 30 gm
Sodium 381 mg

Fat 4 gm
Cholesterol 70 mg

Chutney-Curry Grill

It took us 3 years to get the recipe for the best-ever chutney that makes up the glaze. It comes from Partner/Chef Danny at Ella's, a thirty-seven seat restaurant in San Francisco.

2 teaspoons chopped fresh mint
1 teaspoon each black pepper
  and minced garlic

Salt to taste
2 cups plain yogurt
4 to 6 turkey thighs

Combine mint, pepper, garlic and salt with yogurt; mix well. Brush over turkey; let stand in refrigerator for 2 hours. Grill over medium-hot coals to 170 degrees internal temperature, about 45 minutes. Turn and baste with glaze during last 15 minutes of grilling.   Makes 4 to 6 servings.

GLAZE:
Mix together 1 cup chutney, 1/2 cup Gewürztraminer wine and 2 teaspoons curry powder.

CHUTNEY:
Bring 1 package (1 pound) brown sugar and 1 1/2 cups cider vinegar to a boil. Add 3 cups peeled green apples cut into little cubes and return to a boil. Add 1 lemon, very thinly sliced, 2 cloves garlic, minced, 3/4 cup diced red bell pepper, 1 cup diced onion, 1 1/2 cups raisins, 1 teaspoon salt and 2 teaspoons cayenne pepper. Boil until thick, stirring consistently.

Per Serving (approx):
Calories 590
Carbohydrate 46 gm

Protein 252 gm
Sodium 867 mg

Fat 64 gm
Cholesterol 200 mg

Mixed Turkey Grill
with Two-Alarm Barbecue Sauce

Select a variety of turkey sausages—Polish style, smoked, and Italian style—
to make this a truly "mixed" grill.

1 bottle (12 ounces) chili sauce
2 cups catsup
1 can (15 ounces) thick tomato
 sauce
1/2 cup firmly packed
 brown sugar
3 tablespoons chili powder
2 tablespoons Worcestershire
 sauce

2 tablespoons lemon juice
1 tablespoon ground coriander
3 cloves garlic, minced
Approximately 3 pounds
 turkey thighs
Olive oil
2 pounds assorted turkey
 sausages

Whisk together chili sauce, catsup, tomato sauce, brown sugar, chili powder, Worcestershire sauce, lemon juice, coriander and garlic.

Prepare medium-hot charcoal fire. Brush turkey thighs with olive oil. Grill sausages and thighs until sausages are cooked through and thighs register 175 degrees on meat thermometer. Baste thighs with barbecue sauce during final 15 minutes of cooking.   Makes 10 to 12 servings.

Per Serving (approx):
Calories 360
Carbohydrate 21 gm   *Protein 35 gm*   *Fat 15 gm*
                         Sodium 1120 mg   *Cholesterol 110 mg*

Turkey Kabobs

1 pound turkey breast fillets,
    cut into 1-inch-wide strips
1/2 pound sliced turkey bacon,
    slices halved
1 red bell pepper, cut into
    2-inch squares

1/3 cup lemon juice
1/3 cup honey
2 tablespoons soy sauce
1/4 teaspoon black pepper
1 clove garlic, minced
1 teaspoon cornstarch

Thread turkey, bacon slices and bell pepper onto wooden skewers. In shallow dish combine lemon juice, honey, soy sauce, black pepper and garlic. Add prepared skewers; marinate for at least 15 minutes. Reserve marinade at room temperature.

Grill or broil skewers about 5 minutes on each side or until turkey and bacon are cooked through. To make dipping sauce, stir cornstarch into marinade; heat until sauce boils and thickens slightly.

        Makes 14 to 18 kabobs, 4 to 6 servings.

Per Serving (approx):
Calories 257
Carbohydrate 19 gm

Protein 23 gm
Sodium 868 mg

Fat 10 gm
Cholesterol 70 mg

Fear of Flying

Domesticated turkeys cannot fly. Wild turkeys can fly for short distances up to 55 miles per hour and can run 25 miles per hour.

Oriental Turkey Fillets

1 pound turkey breast fillets
1/4 cup peanut oil
1/4 cup soy sauce

2 cloves garlic, minced
2 tablespoons grated fresh ginger
Salt and pepper to taste

Place fillets in shallow baking dish. In small bowl whisk together oil, soy sauce, garlic, ginger, salt and pepper. Pour over fillets, turning to coat well. Cover and refrigerate for 1 hour or longer.

Prepare grill for direct-heat cooking.* Remove fillets from marinade; discard marinade. Grill, uncovered, 6 inches over medium-hot coals, for 3 to 5 minutes on each side or until cooked through.

Makes 2 or 3 servings.

*Note: For information on direct-heat cooking, see page 284.

Per Serving (approx):
Calories 293
Carbohydrate 2 gm

Protein 26 gm
Sodium 1175 mg

Fat 20 gm
Cholesterol 61 mg

Peppery Turkey Fillets

1 pound turkey breast fillets
1/4 cup Worcestershire sauce
1 tablespoon Dijon mustard

1 tablespoon oil
2 teaspoons cracked black
 pepper

Place fillets in shallow baking dish. In small bowl combine Worcestershire, mustard and oil. Pour over fillets, turning to coat well. Cover and refrigerate for 1 hour or longer.

Prepare grill for direct-heat cooking.* Remove fillets from marinade; sprinkle with pepper to taste. Grill, uncovered, 5 to 6 inches over medium-hot coals for 3 to 5 minutes on each side or until cooked through.

Makes 2 to 3 servings.

*Note: For information on direct-heat cooking, see page 284.

Per Serving (approx):
Calories 185
Carbohydrate 1 gm

Protein 27 gm
Sodium 192 mg

Fat 8 gm
Cholesterol 69 mg

Turkey Zanzibar

1 pound turkey breast
   tenderloins
1 tablespoon oil
1 teaspoon curry powder

1/2 teaspoon ground cumin
Salt and pepper to taste
1/2 small lemon or lime
Mango chutney (optional)

Brush tenderloins on both sides with oil and rub with seasonings. Squeeze lemon over turkey; set aside.

Prepare grill for direct-heat cooking* or preheat broiler. Grill or broil tenderloins 5 to 6 inches from heat source for 5 to 8 minutes on each side or until cooked through. Serve with mango chutney (if desired) and Cool Cucumber Salad.   **Makes 4 servings.**

COOL CUCUMBER SALAD:
In medium size bowl combine 1 cup plain low-fat yogurt, 2 tablespoons thinly sliced green onion, 1 tablespoon vegetable oil, 1 tablespoon lemon or lime juice and 1 tablespoon minced parsley. Stir in 1 teaspoon honey or sugar; season to taste with salt, black pepper and paprika. Add 1 1/2 cups thinly sliced cucumber and toss gently. Serve on lettuce leaves.

*Note: For information on direct-heat cooking, see page 284.

Per Serving (approx) (excluding salad):
Calories 161   *Protein 28 gm*   *Fat 4 gm*
Carbohydrate 1 gm   *Sodium 57 mg*   *Cholesterol 70 mg*

Fruited Turkey Kabobs

1 pound turkey breast tenderloins   1 orange
1 green bell pepper   1/4 fresh pineapple

Cut turkey into 1-inch cubes. Combine marinade ingredients in large bowl; add turkey and let stand for 15 minutes. Cut bell pepper, orange and pineapple each into 8 chunks. leaving rind on pineapple and orange. Alternate with turkey on skewers.

Grill 4 inches from hot coals for about 20 minutes, turning frequently. Bring remaining marinade to a boil. Serve with rice and marinade on the side. Boil the marinade before you serve it.   Makes 4 servings.

MARINADE:
Combine 1/2 cup lemon juice, 1/2 cup oil, 3/4 teaspoon dried oregano, 1/8 teaspoon black pepper and 1/8 teaspoon garlic powder.

Per Serving (approx):
Calories 620
Carbohydrate 51 gm   *Protein 30 gm*   *Fat 33 gm*
                              Sodium 65 mg   *Cholesterol 69 mg*

Hot-n-Spicy Barbecued Drumsticks

These drumsticks are definitely different! Their piquant and spicy glaze will truly wake up your taste buds.

4 large turkey drumsticks
   (about 1 1/2 pounds each) or
   8 small turkey drumsticks
   (about 3/4 pound each)
1 can (8 ounces) tomato sauce
Juice of 1 lemon

4 large cloves garlic, crushed
2 tablespoons sugar
1 teaspoon chili powder
Salt and pepper to taste
1 teaspoon Worcestershire sauce
1/4 teaspoon hot pepper sauce

Wrap each drumstick in heavy-duty aluminum foil, leaving room for steam expansion and keeping dull side of foil out. Grill over single layer of slow coals, 1 hour for large drumsticks and 45 minutes for small drumsticks, turning every 15 minutes and adding additional charcoal as needed to maintain temperature.

Meanwhile, prepare barbecue sauce by combining tomato sauce, lemon juice, garlic, sugar, chili powder, salt, pepper, Worcestershire sauce and hot pepper sauce in small bowl.

Remove aluminum foil from drumsticks and continue grilling for an additional 30 minutes over slow coals, basting twice on each side with sauce and turning drumsticks after 15 minutes.   Makes 8 servings.

Per Serving (approx):
Calories 273
Carbohydrate 6 gm

Protein 35 gm
Sodium 270 mg

Fat 12 gm
Cholesterol 104 mg

Grilled Turkey Breast
with Cherry Sauce

1 turkey breast, bone in
   (approximately 5 pounds)
1 can (21 ounces) cherry pie
   filling

2 tablespoons soy sauce
2 tablespoons cooking sherry
1/2 teaspoon ground ginger
1/2 teaspoon ground allspice

Preheat grill for indirect-heat cooking.*

Place turkey, skin side up, on grill rack over drip pan. Cover grill and cook for 60 to 90 minutes or until meat thermometer inserted in thickest portion of turkey breast registers 170 degrees.

In small saucepan over low heat, combine cherry filling, soy sauce, sherry, ginger and allspice. Simmer for 5 minutes to blend flavors. In blender container puree 1/2 cup sauce. Brush pureed sauce over turkey breast during last 10 minutes of grilling time.

Remove turkey breast from grill and let stand for 15 minutes. To serve, slice breast, arrange slices on platter and top with remaining warm sauce.

Makes 10 to 12 servings.

*Note: For information on indirect-heat cooking, see page 255.

Per Serving (approx):
Calories 234
Carbohydrate 18 gm

Protein 31 gm
Sodium 274 mg

Fat 4 gm
Cholesterol 71 mg

Herbed Turkey and Vegetable Kabobs

2 turkey tenderloins
(approximately 1 1/2 pounds)
1 medium onion
12 mushrooms, 1 1/2 inches
in diameter
1 large green bell pepper
3 medium zucchini
12 cherry tomatoes

1 cup margarine
1/4 cup chopped parsley
1 teaspoon dried thyme
1 teaspoon dried marjoram
1/2 teaspoon salt
1/8 teaspoon black pepper
1 teaspoon lemon juice
1 small clove garlic

To make kabobs use 12 metal skewers about 9 inches each. Cut each turkey tenderloin in half lengthwise; cut each half into 6 chunks, for total of 24 chunks. Quarter onion; separate pieces. Cut stems of mushrooms even with caps. Cut bell pepper into 12 chunks. Cut each zucchini into 1-inch chunks, to make total of 18 chunks.

To build turkey-zucchini kabobs, use 4 turkey chunks and 3 zucchini chunks for each of 6 skewers. Alternate turkey and zucchini chunks, beginning and ending with turkey.

To build vegetable kabobs, arrange as follows: 1 mushroom, 1 bell pepper chunk, 1 onion piece, 1 cherry tomato, 1 bell pepper chunk, 1 onion piece, 1 cherry tomato and 1 mushroom.

Prepare herbed butter by melting margarine in small saucepan; remove from heat. Stir in parsley, thyme, marjoram, salt, pepper and lemon juice; add garlic clove.

Prepare grill for direct-heat cooking.* Place turkey-zucchini kabobs over hot, glowing coals; baste with herbed butter. Cook for 10 minutes; turn and baste again. Add vegetable kabobs to grill and baste; cook an additional 10 minutes or until turkey and vegetables are done as desired.

Makes 6 servings.

*Note: For information on direct-heat cooking, see page 284.

Per Serving (approx):
Calories 322
Carbohydrate 8 gm

Protein 3 gm
Sodium 562 mg

Fat 31 gm
Cholesterol 320 mg

Herb Grilled Turkey and "Sweets"

3 to 4 tablespoons olive oil
1/4 cup white wine
2 tablespoons
  Worcestershire sauce
1 tablespoon honey
1 teaspoon salt
1 teaspoon crushed dried rosemary

1/2 teaspoon dried thyme
1/4 teaspoon black pepper
1 clove garlic, minced
1 boneless turkey breast
  (approximately 1 1/2 pounds)
4 small sweet potatoes,
  scrubbed and cut in half
  lengthwise

In shallow baking dish combine oil, wine, Worcestershire sauce, honey, salt, rosemary, thyme, pepper and garlic. Mix well, reserving 2 tablespoons. Add turkey to herb marinade, coating both sides. Cover and let marinate in refrigerator for 3 hours or overnight.

Prepare coals in covered grill at least 30 minutes before grilling, placing grill 6 to 8 inches above coals. Reserving marinade, place turkey on grill over medium-hot coals. Cover and grill for 20 to 30 minutes per pound, brushing often with marinade and turning several times.

Meanwhile, brush cut sides of potatoes with reserved 2 tablespoons marinade. Place potatoes at edge of grill around roast and cook for 30 to 40 minutes; turn several times and brush with marinade. To serve, slice turkey and accompany with potatoes.   Makes 6 servings.

Per Serving (approx):
Calories 306
Carbohydrate 25 gm

Protein 28 gm
Sodium 497 mg

Fat 10 gm
Cholesterol 70 mg

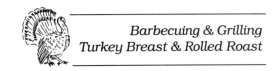

Turkey Breast Dijon

This tender, boneless white meat should be sliced on an angle and served like London Broil.

1 boneless turkey breast
   (1 1/2 pounds)
1/2 cup Dijon mustard
6 tablespoons chopped green onion
2 tablespoons soy sauce

4 tablespoons fresh lemon juice
1/2 teaspoon cayenne pepper
   (optional)
4 tablespoons oil

Place turkey breast in wide shallow bowl. In small bowl combine remaining ingredients except oil; whisk in oil. Pour half of mixture over turkey, cover and refrigerate for 1 hour or longer. Reserve remaining mixture for basting.

Prepare covered grill for indirect-heat cooking.* When coals are hot, arrange in double layer around drip pan. Remove breast from marinade, discard marinade, and place turkey on grill over drip pan. Open all vents, cover and grill over medium-hot coals for 20 minutes per pound or until cooked through, turning and basting 2 or 3 times with reserved marinade. Makes 4 to 6 servings.

*Note: For information on indirect-heat cooking, see page 255.

Per Serving (approx):
Calories 272
Carbohydrate 3 gm

Protein 26 gm
Sodium 897 mg

Fat 17 gm
Cholesterol 61 mg

Cajun Grilled Turkey

To convert Cajun Grilled Turkey to a "smoked" recipe, add water-soaked aromatic wood chips or herbs to the coals while cooking.

1 turkey half breast (2 to 3 pounds)	1 teaspoon paprika
2 tablespoons oil	1/2 teaspoon cayenne pepper
1 tablespoon Worcestershire sauce	1/2 teaspoon black pepper
1 large clove garlic, minced	1/4 teaspoon salt
1 teaspoon dried Italian seasoning	

Prepare covered grill for indirect-heat cooking.* Place turkey in shallow roasting pan. In small bowl combine remaining ingredients. Carefully loosen skin from breast to form pocket. Rub half seasoning mixture under skin and remainder over outside of breast. Cover and refrigerate until coals are ready.

Bank hot coals in double layer around drip pan with 6 to 8 unlit coals at outer edge of fire. Add 1 cup water to drip pan. Open all vents on grill. Place turkey on grill, skin side down, 5 to 6 inches over drip pan. Grill, covered, for 20 to 30 minutes per pound or until meat thermometer inserted in the thickest part of breast registers 170 to 175 degrees. Turn 3 times during cooking. Makes 4 to 6 servings.

*Note: For information on indirect-heat cooking, see page 255.

Per Serving (approx):

Calories 257	*Protein 30 gm*	*Fat 15 gm*
Carbohydrate 1 gm	*Sodium 176 mg*	*Cholesterol 87 mg*

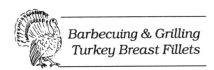

Hawaiian Turkey Fillets

1/4 cup soy sauce
1/4 cup pineapple juice
1 tablespoon brown sugar
1/4 teaspoon ground ginger
1 clove garlic, finely chopped

1/8 teaspoon cayenne pepper
  (optional)
1 pound turkey fillets
1/2 teaspoon cornstarch
Fresh pineapple wedges

In medium bowl or plastic food bag, combine soy sauce, pineapple juice, brown sugar, ginger, garlic and cayenne (if used). Add turkey; let marinate for several hours or overnight in refrigerator.

Remove turkey from marinade; reserve marinade. Grill or broil turkey for about 4 to 6 minutes on each side or until turkey is no longer pink.

In small saucepan mix cornstarch with reserved marinade. Cook, stirring occasionally, until sauce boils and slightly thickens. Serve sauce with turkey. Garnish with pineapple.   Makes 3 to 4 servings.

Per Serving (approx):
Calories 176
Carbohydrate 6 gm

Protein 28 gm
Sodium 1093 mg

Fat 5 gm
Cholesterol 69 mg

Tenderloins with Plum Sauce

1 pound turkey breast tenderloins
1 can (16 ounces) purple plums
1/2 cup apple juice

4 teaspoons cornstarch
1/4 teaspoon ground allspice

Place turkey on broiler pan. Move oven rack so top of turkey is 5 inches from heat. Broil 10 minutes; turn. Broil for 10 minutes on each side. Meanwhile, drain plums, reserving syrup. Combine syrup, apple juice and cornstarch in saucepan. Cook over medium heat, stirring constantly until thickened. Meanwhile, pit and coarsely chop plums. Add plums and allspice to sauce. Cook for 1 minute more. Serve over turkey.

Makes 4 servings.

MICROWAVE METHOD:
Place turkey in glass baking dish. Cover with plastic wrap, turning back cover to vent. Microwave on high for 4 minutes. Turn turkey over. Cover. Microwave on high for 5 minutes or until no longer pink. Combine plum syrup, apple juice and cornstarch in 2-cup glass measure. Microwave on high for 3 to 4 minutes, stirring once every minute. Meanwhile, pit and coarsely chop plums. Add plums and allspice to sauce. Microwave on high for 1 minute. Serve over turkey.

Per Serving (approx):
Calories 225
Carbohydrate 21 gm

Protein 28 gm
Sodium 65 mg

Fat 5 gm
Cholesterol 69 mg

Tangy Turkey Tenders

1 1/2 cups lemon-lime soda
1/4 cup soy sauce
1/4 cup oil
1 teaspoon horseradish powder

1 teaspoon garlic powder
1 pound turkey breast
 tenderloins, butterflied

In plastic bag combine soda, soy sauce, oil, horseradish powder and garlic powder. Add turkey. Seal bag and refrigerate for at least 2 hours or overnight. Preheat grill for direct-heat cooking.* Remove turkey from plastic bag; discard marinade. Grill turkey 5 to 6 minutes per side or until meat is no longer pink in center.

Makes 4 servings.

*Note: For information on direct-heat cooking, see page 284.

Per Serving (approx) excluding roll:
Calories 157
Carbohydrate 2 gm

Protein 27 gm
Sodium 242 mg

Fat 4 gm
Cholesterol 70 mg

Midwestern Turkey Barbecue

2 pounds turkey thighs or drumsticks

Wrap turkey in heavy-duty foil. Cook for 45 minutes in covered kettle grill 4 inches from medium-hot coals; turn. Cook for 45 minutes more. (Add coals during cooking to maintain heat.)

Meanwhile, prepare Midwest Sauce. Remove turkey from foil. Brush with sauce and grill 10 minutes more, turning occasionally. Serve with remaining sauce.   Makes 4 servings.

OVEN METHOD: Place turkey in casserole or Dutch oven; add 1 cup water. Cover. Bake in 350 degree oven for 2 hours. Pour off liquid; increase oven temperature to 400 degrees. Combine sauce ingredients and pour over turkey. Bake uncovered for 30 minutes more.

MIDWEST SAUCE:
In saucepan combine 1/4 cup catsup, 3 tablespoons chili sauce, 1 tablespoon brown sugar, 1 tablespoon chopped onion, 2 teaspoons butter, 2 teaspoons Worcestershire sauce, 2 teaspoons prepared mustard, 1/2 teaspoon celery seed, 1/4 teaspoon garlic powder, and dash of hot pepper sauce. Bring to a boil; reduce heat and simmer for 10 minutes.

Per Serving (approx):
Calories 332   *Protein 46 gm*   *Fat 13 gm*
Carbohydrate 7 gm   *Sodium 369 mg*   *Cholesterol 145 mg*

311

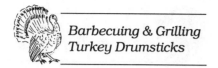
Barbecuing & Grilling
Turkey Drumsticks

Turkey Normande

2 pounds turkey drumsticks

Rinse turkey; pat dry. Wrap each drumstick in heavy-duty foil. Cook for 45 minutes in covered kettle grill, 4 inches from medium-hot coals; turn. Cook for 45 minutes more. (Add coals during cooking to maintain heat.)

Meanwhile, prepare sauce. Remove turkey from foil. Brush with sauce and grill for 10 minutes more, turning occasionally. Heat remaining sauce and serve with turkey.   Makes 4 to 6 servings.

TO MAKE AHEAD:
Rinse turkey; pat dry. Place in skillet with 1 cup water. Bring to a boil; reduce heat, cover and simmer for 2 hours. Pour off liquid. Cover and refrigerate.

Before serving, grill turkey 4 inches from medium-hot coals for 30 minutes, turning occasionally. Brush with Normande Sauce and grill for 10 minutes more.

NORMANDE SAUCE:
Combine 1 cup apple butter and 2 tablespoons soy sauce.

Per Serving (approx):
Calories 319   *Protein 30 gm*   *Fat 11 gm*
Carbohydrate 25 gm   *Sodium 425 mg*   *Cholesterol 90 mg*

MICROWAVE COOKING

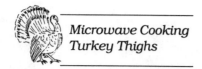
Turkey Bourguignon

Beef Bourguignon is one of France's most traditional dishes. It comes from the Burgundy region and has many variations. This version makes two thoroughly modern substitutions: turkey for health, microwaving for speed.

3 slices bacon, diced
1 medium onion, thinly sliced
3 tablespoons flour
12 small white onions, peeled
1/2 teaspoon dried thyme
3/4 cup Burgundy or other dry
   red wine

1/4 cup hot water
1 bay leaf
1 3/4 pounds turkey thighs,
   skin removed
1 cup sliced mushrooms

In 3-quart microwave-safe utensil, place bacon; cover with paper towel. Microwave on high for 3 to 4 minutes or until crisp, stirring twice. Stir in onion, flour, white onions, thyme, wine and water; add bay leaf.

Place thighs, smooth side down, on top of mixture; cover with plastic wrap. Microwave on high for 5 minutes. Reduce power to medium-high; microwave for 30 minutes, turning thighs halfway through cooking time and adding mushrooms during last 5 minutes. Let stand, covered, for 10 minutes.   Makes 2 or 3 servings.

Per Serving (approx):
Calories 580
Carbohydrate 37 gm

Protein 60 gm
Sodium 287 mg

Fat 17 gm
Cholesterol 170 mg

Turkey Cordon Bleu

1/4 cup butter
1 pound turkey breast steaks
1 1/2 cups seasoned croutons, crushed
1/4 teaspoon paprika

2 slices (1 ounce each) turkey ham
2 slices (1 ounce each) Swiss cheese
4 teaspoons Dijon mustard

Place butter in glass baking dish. Microwave on high for 45 to 60 seconds.

Pound turkey between pieces of plastic wrap to uniform thickness. Combine crumbs and paprika. Dip turkey in melted butter, then in crumb mixture. Place 1/2 slice turkey ham and 1/2 slice cheese on each turkey steak; spread each with 1 teaspoon mustard. Roll up and secure with toothpicks.

Arrange rolls in circle in glass baking dish. Cover with waxed paper and microwave on high for 5 minutes. Rearrange uncooked portions toward outer edge of dish. Microwave on high for 5 to 7 minutes more. Remove toothpicks before serving.   Makes 4 servings.

Per Serving (approx):
Calories 485
Carbohydrate 26 gm

Protein 39 gm
Sodium 950 mg

Fat 25 gm
Cholesterol 121 mg

Tom Turkey at Work

Q. How many poults can one Tom turkey father?

A. A Tom turkey can produce as many as 1500 poults during a hen's 6-month production cycle.

315

Fettuccine Alfredo Plus

If you're too busy to go to Rome and have fettuccine at Alfredo's, make this at home, put some opera on the stereo and enjoy!

3 tablespoons butter or margarine	1 cup sliced mushrooms
2 tablespoons flour	1 medium onion, sliced
1 1/2 cups milk	1 cup diced cooked turkey
1 cup grated Parmesan cheese	8 ounces fettuccine, cooked
	1/4 cup sliced almonds

In 4-cup glass measure, place 2 tablespoons of the butter. Microwave on high for 40 seconds. Blend in flour until smooth; gradually stir in milk. Microwave on high for 3 1/2 to 4 1/2 minutes, stirring every minute until thick and bubbly. Add Parmesan cheese; stir to blend. Cover with plastic wrap and set aside.

In 2-quart microwave-safe utensil, combine remaining butter, mushrooms and onion. Cover with plastic wrap; microwave on high for 4 minutes, stirring twice. Add turkey and re-cover with plastic wrap; microwave for 2 minutes. Stir in cheese sauce and pour over pasta, tossing to combine. Serve sprinkled with almonds.   Makes 4 servings.

Per Serving (approx):
Calories 474
Carbohydrate 29 gm

Protein 30 gm
Sodium 720 mg

Fat 27 gm
Cholesterol 301 mg

Turkey Manicotti

1 pound ground turkey
1/2 cup finely chopped onion
1 teaspoon garlic powder
1/2 teaspoon dried Italian seasoning
1/4 teaspoon black pepper
1 1/2 cups cottage cheese
1 package (10 ounces) frozen chopped
    spinach, thawed and squeezed dry

1/2 cup grated Parmesan cheese
1 cup plain yogurt
1/4 cup egg substitute or 1 egg
1 tablespoon dried parsley flakes
12 manicotti shells, uncooked
4 cups spaghetti sauce
1 1/2 cups grated mozzarella
    cheese

In 1-quart microwave-safe dish, combine turkey, onion, garlic powder, Italian seasoning and pepper. Microwave on high for 4 to 5 minutes or until no longer pink, breaking up turkey halfway through cooking time.

In large bowl combine cottage cheese, spinach, Parmesan cheese, yogurt, egg substitute, parsley and turkey mixture. Stuff uncooked manicotti shells with turkey mixture. In bottom of 9- x 13-inch microwave-safe baking dish, spoon 2 cups of the spaghetti sauce. Layer manicotti shells over sauce. Top manicotti shells with remaining turkey mixture and spaghetti sauce. Cover baking dish with vented plastic wrap. Microwave on high for 10 minutes, turning dish halfway through microwave time. Microwave on medium-high for 17 minutes, turning dish halfway through microwave time.

Uncover dish and sprinkle mozzarella cheese over manicotti during last 3 minutes of microwave time. Let stand for 15 minutes before serving.

Makes 6 servings.

Per Serving (approx):
Calories 457
Carbohydrate 25 gm

Protein 36 gm
Sodium 1654 mg

Fat 24 gm
Cholesterol 96 mg

Turkey Crust Pie

Here is another way to use stuffing as a pie shell.

1 pound ground turkey
1/4 cup seasoned dry bread
   crumbs
1/4 cup milk
1 teaspoon garlic salt
1/2 teaspoon crushed dried
   oregano
1/4 teaspoon black pepper

1/2 cup tomato paste
1/2 cup sliced mushrooms
1/2 cup grated mozzarella
   cheese
2 tablespoons chopped
   green bell pepper
2 tablespoons sliced olives

In 9-inch microwave-safe pie plate, combine turkey, bread crumbs, milk, garlic, oregano and black pepper. Mix well. Press mixture evenly over bottom and up sides of pie plate. Cover with waxed paper. Microwave on high for 3 minutes. Rotate plate a half turn; microwave for 1 to 3 minutes more or until turkey is no longer pink.

Carefully drain any excess juices. Spread tomato paste evenly over turkey "crust." Top with mushrooms, cheese, bell pepper and olives. Cover, and microwave on high for 1 1/2 minutes or until cheese is melted. Let stand for 5 minutes. Cut into wedges. Makes 6 servings.

Per Serving (approx):
Calories 181
Carbohydrate 8 gm

Protein 17 gm
Sodium 191 mg

Fat 9 gm
Cholesterol 64 mg

Turkey Marengo

Legend has it that Napoleon Bonaparte's chef invented Chicken Marengo in 1800 to celebrate the Battle of Marengo. We thought it was time for an update, so we used turkey instead of chicken and a microwave oven instead of a campfire.

1 pound turkey steaks
1 can (8 ounces) tomatoes, cut up, juice reserved
1 cup sliced mushrooms
1 small onion, chopped
1/4 cup dry red wine

1 clove garlic, minced
3/4 teaspoon dried Italian seasoning
1/2 tablespoon cornstarch
2 tablespoons cold water

Cut turkey steaks in half and place in 10- x 7-inch microwave-safe dish. In medium bowl combine tomatoes with their juice, mushrooms, onion, wine, garlic and Italian seasoning. Pour over turkey. Cover with plastic wrap; microwave on medium-high for 20 minutes. Halfway through cooking time, rearrange turkey, moving parts at center of dish to outside; re-cover and complete cooking. Remove turkey to serving plate; cover with aluminum foil and let stand for 5 minutes.

Combine cornstarch and water; slowly stir into tomato mixture. Microwave on high for 2 minutes or until thickened and bubbly. Serve turkey topped with sauce.   Makes 4 servings.

Per Serving (approx):
Calories 156
Carbohydrate 6 gm

Protein 28 gm
Sodium 153 mg

Fat 2 gm
Cholesterol 70 mg

The larger the turkey the more meat there is in proportion to bone. Large turkeys are a better buy.

Turkey Tacos

1 pound ground turkey
2 tablespoons dried onion
1 tablespoon chili powder
1 teaspoon paprika
1/2 teaspoon ground cumin
1/2 teaspoon dried oregano
Salt to taste
1/4 teaspoon garlic powder

1/8 teaspoon black pepper
10 taco shells
1 to 2 tomatoes, chopped
2 to 3 cups shredded lettuce
2/3 cup grated Cheddar cheese
Taco sauce, sour cream, guacamole, chopped or sliced
  olives and chopped onions

In 1-quart microwave-safe container, combine turkey, onion, chili powder, paprika, cumin, oregano, salt, garlic powder and pepper. Cover and
microwave on high for 5 to 6 minutes or until meat is no longer pink,
stirring 1 or 2 times during cooking. Spoon into taco shells; top each
taco evenly with tomato, lettuce, cheese, and other toppings, if desired.

Makes 5 servings.

Per Serving (approx):
Calories 320
Carbohydrate 20 gm

Protein 23 gm
Sodium 276 mg

Fat 17 gm
Cholesterol 82 mg

Nacho Special

1 to 1 1/4 pounds ground turkey
1 package taco seasoning mix
1/4 cup water
2 ounces shredded mild
  Monterey jack cheese
1 can (16 ounces) refried beans
2 tablespoons chopped green chilies

2 cups shredded or chopped
  lettuce
3 to 4 tomatoes, chopped
1 package (8 ounces) unsalted
  tortilla chips
1 cup prepared guacamole
1/2 cup sour cream

Place turkey in microwave-safe casserole; cover with waxed paper. Microwave on high for 4 minutes, stirring after 2 minutes. Stir in seasoning mix and water. Microwave on high for 2 minutes. In shallow microwave-safe baking dish, combine meat mixture and cheese; shape into
rings. Spoon beans on top and sprinkle with chilies; cover with waxed
paper and microwave on medium-high for 2 to 3 minutes. Around meat
mixture, arrange shredded lettuce. Top with tomatoes and tortilla chips.
Mound guacamole in center; top with sour cream.   Makes 8 servings.

Per Serving (approx):
Calories 440
Carbohydrate 37 gm

Protein 22 gm
Sodium 824 mg

Fat 24 gm
Cholesterol 53 mg

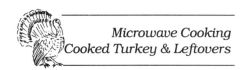

Turkey Chili with Black Beans

For full blending of flavors, make this dish one day prior to serving.

1 cup chopped onion
1 red bell pepper, cut in
    1/4-inch cubes
2 cloves garlic, minced
2 jalapeño peppers, seeded
    and minced
1 can (28 ounces) tomatoes,
    coarsely chopped, liquid reserved
1 tablespoon chili powder
1 1/2 teaspoons ground
    cumin
1 1/2 teaspoons ground
    coriander

1/2 teaspoon dried oregano
1/2 teaspoon dried marjoram
1/4 teaspoon red pepper flakes
1/4 teaspoon ground cinnamon
1 can (16 ounces) black beans,
    rinsed and drained
2 cups cooked turkey
    cut in 1/2-inch cubes
1/2 cup coarsely chopped
    cilantro
4 tablespoons shredded
    reduced-fat Cheddar cheese

In 3-quart microwave-safe dish, combine onion, bell pepper, garlic, jalapeño peppers and tomatoes. Stir in chili powder, cumin, coriander, oregano, marjoram, red pepper flakes and cinnamon. Cover dish. Microwave on high for 10 minutes; stir halfway through. Stir in beans and turkey; re-cover dish. Microwave on high for 4 minutes; stir in cilantro. To serve, ladle into bowls and garnish with cheese.

Makes 4 to 6 servings.

Per Serving (approx):
Calories 278
Carbohydrate 26 gm

Protein 30 gm
Sodium 632 mg

Fat 6 gm
Cholesterol 60 mg

Meatball Rigatoni

1 to 1 1/4 pounds ground
  turkey
3/4 cup finely chopped onion
1/2 cup seasoned dry bread
  crumbs
1/4 cup grated Parmesan cheese,
  plus more for sprinkling

1 can (6 ounces) tomato paste
1 teaspoon dried Italian
  seasoning
1 jar (30 ounces) chunky vegetable spaghetti sauce
8 ounces small rigatoni,
  cooked and drained

In medium bowl mix turkey, onion, bread crumbs, the 1/4 cup grated Parmesan, 3 tablespoons of the tomato paste and the Italian seasoning. Shape mixture into 12 meatballs.

In 10-inch microwave-safe pie plate, arrange meatballs in circle; cover with waxed paper. Microwave on high for 6 minutes. Rearrange and turn meatballs. Re-cover and microwave on high for 4 to 6 minutes longer.

Meanwhile, in medium bowl combine spaghetti sauce and remaining tomato paste; add cooked meatballs. Discard juices from pie plate. Place rigatoni in plate; spoon in meatballs and sauce to combine. Cover with waxed paper. Microwave on high for 5 minutes or until sauce is bubbly. Sprinkle with additional Parmesan; cover and let stand for 5 minutes before serving.   Makes 4 to 6 servings.

Per Serving (approx):
Calories 405   *Protein 22 gm*   *Fat 15 gm*
Carbohydrate 46 gm   *Sodium 929 mg*   *Cholesterol 71 mg*

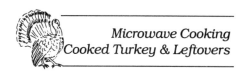

Divine Cheddar Divan

If you prefer, use broccoli in place of the asparagus.

2 tablespoons butter or
  margarine
2 tablespoons flour
1 cup milk
2 teaspoons Dijon mustard
1/8 teaspoon cayenne pepper,
  or to taste

8 slices cooked turkey
2 cups asparagus spears,
  partially cooked
1/2 cup shredded sharp
  Cheddar cheese

In 4-cup glass measure, place butter; microwave on high for 40 seconds. Stir in flour; gradually stir in milk. Microwave on high for 3 to 4 minutes, stirring every minute until thick. Stir in mustard and cayenne.

In shallow 2 1/2-quart microwave-safe utensil, place turkey. Arrange asparagus on top with tips to center. Pour sauce over top; cover with waxed paper. Microwave on medium for 7 to 8 minutes; sprinkle cheese over top. Microwave on medium for 2 to 3 minutes more. Allow to stand, covered, for 5 minutes before serving.   Makes 4 servings.

Per Serving (approx):
Calories 247
Carbohydrate 7 gm

Protein 23 gm
Sodium 258 mg

Fat 14 gm
Cholesterol 76 mg

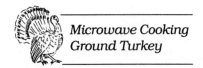

Easy Microwave Turkey Lasagne

1 pound ground turkey
1 clove garlic, chopped
1 cup chopped onion
1 can (14 1/2 ounces) tomatoes, chopped, liquid reserved
1 can (6 ounces) tomato paste

2 1/2 teaspoons dried Italian seasoning or dried oregano
8 uncooked lasagna noodles
1 container (12 ounces) low-fat cottage cheese
2 cups (8 ounces), shredded part-skim mozzarella cheese

In 2-quart, microwave-safe casserole, combine ground turkey, garlic and onion; cover. Microwave on high for 5 minutes, stirring halfway through cooking time. Stir in tomatoes, including juice, tomato paste and seasoning. Microwave, uncovered, on high for 5 minutes.

Lightly grease 2-quart oblong microwave-safe casserole. Spoon one-third of sauce (about 1 1/3 cups) over bottom of dish. Top with 4 lasagna noodles, breaking noodles to fit. Spoon cottage cheese over noodles. Sprinkle mozzarella over top of cottage cheese. Spoon one-third more sauce over cheese; top with remaining noodles. Spoon remaining sauce over noodles and cover with vented plastic wrap.

Place several layers of paper toweling in bottom of microwave oven to absorb any spills. Microwave on high for 5 minutes. Reduce power to medium; microwave for 20 to 25 minutes or until noodles are tender.

Makes 8 servings.

Per Serving (approx):
Calories 325
Carbohydrate 29 gm

Protein 27 gm
Sodium 616 mg

Fat 11 gm
Cholesterol 56 mg

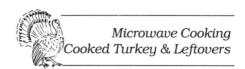

Easy Elegant Cream Soup with Tarragon

This soup, a salad and a dessert are a perfect combination for a luncheon party.

3 tablespoons butter or
    margarine
1/4 cup minced shallot
    or green onion
1/3 cup flour
3 cans (13 3/4 ounces each)
    chicken broth or about 5 cups
    homemade turkey broth

2 cups finely diced cooked
    turkey
1 cup whipping cream
1 tablespoon minced fresh
    tarragon or basil
Salt and pepper to taste

In 3-quart microwave-safe utensil, place butter. Microwave on high for 1 minute. Add shallot; microwave on high for 2 to 3 minutes, stirring once. Blend in flour; gradually add broth, stirring to blend. Cover with plastic wrap; microwave on high for 10 minutes, stirring every 2 minutes. Stir in turkey and cream. Microwave on medium-high for 5 minutes, stirring twice. Stir in tarragon and season with salt and pepper to taste.   Makes 6 servings.

Per Serving (approx):
Calories 320   *Protein 18 gm*   *Fat 24 gm*
Carbohydrate 9 gm   *Sodium 236 mg*   *Cholesterol 90 mg*

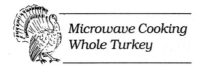

The Whole Turkey

1 turkey (10 pounds)
8 tablespoons butter, softened
1 teaspoon paprika
1 medium onion, diced
1 medium carrot, diced
1 medium rib celery, diced

1 1/4 teaspoons dried poultry
  seasoning
2 cups homemade turkey
  stock
3 tablespoons flour
Salt and freshly ground pepper
  to taste

Rub turkey with 5 tablespoons of the butter, and sprinkle with paprika. In bowl combine onion, carrot, celery and poultry seasoning. Place in body cavity. Or use your favorite stuffing in place of the vegetables. Tie drumsticks together with string. Place turkey, breast side down, on microwave-proof rack and roasting pan. Tent pan with waxed paper.

Estimate entire cooking time at 1 1/2 to 2 hours, allowing 10 to 11 minutes per pound in 700-watt oven, more or less if yours is larger or smaller. Microwave on high for 10 minutes. Reduce setting to medium and continue cooking for 30 minutes, or to halfway point of estimated cooking time. Turn turkey breast side up. Pour off accumulated juices and reserve. Continue cooking on medium, covered with waxed paper, until entire time is up, about 45 minutes. Remove turkey from oven, cover with foil and let stand for 20 minutes. Turkey is done when meat thermometer inserted in thickest part of thigh, not touching bone, reaches 180 degrees.

To make gravy, combine cooking juices in 1-quart microwave-proof bowl and let stand for 5 minutes. Skim off clear yellow fat. Add enough stock to measure 2 1/2 cups. Microwave on high until boiling, 3 minutes.

In 1-quart microwave-proof bowl, microwave remaining butter on high until melted. Whisk in flour and microwave on high until light brown, about 2 minutes. Whisk in hot cooking liquid and microwave on high until thickened, about 2 minutes. Season with salt and pepper to taste.

Makes 8 to 12 servings.

Per Serving (approx):
Calories 703
Carbohydrate 7 gm

Protein 85 gm
Sodium 593 mg

Fat 37 gm
Cholesterol 266 mg

Layered Meat Loaf Ring

A very attractive presentation!

3/4 pound mushrooms
1 to 1 1/4 pounds ground turkey
2 slices bread, torn into small pieces
1/4 cup catsup
1 egg, lightly beaten

1/2 teaspoon salt
1/4 teaspoon black pepper
4 green onions, chopped
1 can (8 ounces) tomato sauce
1 teaspoon Worcestershire sauce

Set aside 10 whole mushrooms; finely chop remaining mushrooms. In large bowl combine chopped mushrooms, turkey, bread, catsup, egg, salt and pepper; mix to blend.

In center of 9-inch microwave-safe pie plate, place inverted 6-ounce custard cup. Pack half of meat mixture in pie plate, forming circle around cup. Cut 5 remaining mushrooms lengthwise in half; place on top of meat mixture. Spoon chopped green onions over mushrooms and meat; top with remaining meat mixture.

Pat meat loaf and press edges firmly to seal; cover with waxed paper. Microwave on high for 5 minutes; reduce power to medium and microwave 20 minutes longer. Let stand, covered, for 5 minutes.

Slice remaining 5 mushrooms and place in 2-cup glass measure. Stir in tomato sauce and Worcestershire sauce. Microwave on high for minutes, stirring once.

To serve, place meat loaf on serving plate, remove custard cup and spoon sauce around top. Makes 4 to 6 servings.

Per Serving (approx):
Calories 184   *Protein 17 gm*   *Fat 7 gm*
Carbohydrate 13 gm   *Sodium 672 mg*   *Cholesterol 91 mg*

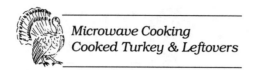

Microwave Cooking
Cooked Turkey & Leftovers

Holiday Strata

2 cups chopped cooked turkey
2 packages (8 ounces each) frozen
  hash brown potatoes, thawed
2 cups shredded Cheddar cheese
1 cup chopped onion
1 cup chopped red and green
  bell pepper

4 eggs
3/4 cup milk
1 clove garlic, crushed
1/2 teaspoon salt
White pepper to taste

In greased shallow 2 1/2-quart microwave-safe baking dish, layer half each of turkey, hash browns, cheese, onion and bell pepper. Repeat layers.

In 4-cup glass measure, beat together eggs, milk, garlic, salt and white pepper. Microwave on medium for 3 to 5 minutes or until mixture begins to cook around edges; stir 3 or 4 times during cooking.

Pour egg mixture over layered ingredients; cover lightly with plastic wrap. Microwave on medium for 15 to 20 minutes, rotating dish once. Allow to stand, covered, for 5 minutes. Serve hot.   Makes 6 to 8 servings.

Per Serving (approx):
Calories 282
Carbohydrate 14 gm

Protein 23 gm
Sodium 329 mg

Fat 15 gm
Cholesterol 166 mg

Turkey Favored for Holiday Table

In 1991, about 300 million turkeys were raised. We "guesstimate" that 45 million of those turkeys were eaten at Thanksgiving, 23 million at Christmas and 19 million at Easter.

Persian Pita Turkey

This is a truly exciting, exotic dish!

1 tablespoon olive oil
1 red onion, sliced into thin
   rings
1 pound turkey breast tenderloins,
   sliced and cut into thin strips
1/2 teaspoon ground cumin
Salt and pepper to taste
1/8 teaspoon ground cinnamon
1/2 cup dried apricot halves,
   each snipped in half

1/4 cup golden raisins
1 small head escarole, torn
   into pieces and divided
1 can (16 ounces) garbanzo
beans,
   drained and rinsed
6 whole wheat pita breads,
   each cut in half
1/2 cup plain low-fat yogurt
   (optional)

In 3-quart microwave-safe dish, combine olive oil and onion slices; cover with plastic wrap. Microwave on high for 2 minutes, stirring once. Add turkey, cumin, salt, pepper and cinnamon. Stir to combine.

Arrange mixture to form ring against sides of dish. Cover and microwave on medium-high for 3 minutes, stirring twice. Stir in apricots and raisins. Cover and microwave on medium-high for 2 minutes. Add half the escarole and all the garbanzo beans. Cover and microwave on high for 1 1/2 minutes. Let stand, covered, for 5 minutes.

To serve, line pitas with remaining escarole and fill with hot turkey mixture. Top with yogurt, if desired.   **Makes 4 servings.**

Per Serving (approx):
Calories 575   *Protein 42 gm*   *Fat 8 gm*
Carbohydrate 86 gm   *Sodium 770 mg*   *Cholesterol 70 mg*

Sweet-n-Sour Turkey

Sweet and sour pork is a staple on the menus of most Chinese restaurants. We've re-created it with turkey, and speeded things up by cooking it in a microwave oven.

1 medium onion, chopped
1/2 cup chopped celery
2 teaspoons water
1 cup chili sauce
1/2 cup firmly packed brown
   sugar

1/4 cup lemon or lime juice
2 tablespoons cider vinegar
1 1/2 pounds boneless turkey
   thighs, cut into 1-inch chunks
1 tablespoon cornstarch
1 tablespoon water

In 4-cup glass measure, combine onion, celery and the two teaspoons water. Cover with plastic wrap; microwave on high for 3 minutes. Add chili sauce, brown sugar, lemon juice and vinegar; stir. Cover and microwave on high for 5 minutes.

In 3-quart microwave-safe casserole, place turkey; pour hot sauce over top. Cover with plastic wrap; microwave on high for 17 minutes, stirring 3 times.

In cup, mix cornstarch and the 1 tablespoon water. Stir into turkey mixture; re-cover and microwave on high for 5 minutes or until sauce is thick. Let stand, covered, for 5 minutes.   Makes 6 servings.

Per Serving (approx):
Calories 246
Carbohydrate 32 gm

Protein 20 gm
Sodium 701 mg

Fat 4 gm
Cholesterol 71 mg

Sweet and Sour Meatballs

1 pound ground turkey
1 egg
1/2 cup seasoned bread crumbs
1/2 cup water
1 tablespoon dried onion

1 tablespoon green bell peppers,
   chopped
1/8 teaspoon black pepper
2 tablespoons catsup

Combine all ingredients and mix thoroughly. Shape into 1 1/2-inch meatballs. Prepare Sweet and Sour Sauce.

Add meatballs to Sweet and Sour Sauce. Cover and microwave on high for 6 to 7 minutes or until meatballs are no longer pink inside. Gently stir in pineapple chunks. Microwave, uncovered, on high for 2 minutes.

Makes 6 servings.

SWEET AND SOUR SAUCE:
Combine 1/2 cup brown sugar and 3 tablespoons cornstarch in deep 2-quart microwave-safe casserole dish. Stir in juice from 1 can (20 ounces) pineapple chunks (chunks reserved), 6 tablespoons water, 3 tablespoons vinegar, and 1 tablespoon soy sauce. Microwave on high for 5 minutes, stirring twice. Stir in 1 large green bell pepper, chopped.

Per Serving (approx):
Calories 326
Carbohydrate 46 gm

Protein 17 gm
Sodium 585 mg

Fat 9 gm
Cholesterol 99 mg

Medically Oriented

Q. Are turkeys fed hormones or drugs?

A. No. Turkeys are not fed hormones. They are federally banned for used in poultry. For treatment of disease or illness, drugs are used at therapeutic levels under FDA regulations.

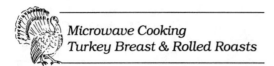
Turkey Breast a la King

4 tablespoons butter or margarine
1/4 teaspoon paprika
1 boneless turkey breast
  (approximately 1 1/2 pounds)
4 tablespoons flour
10 can (10 3/4 ounces) chicken broth

1/4 cup chopped green bell
  pepper
2 tablespoons chopped pimiento
1 cup sliced mushrooms
1/4 teaspoon salt
Dash black pepper

Place 1 tablespoon of the butter in 1-cup glass measure; microwave on high for 20 seconds or until melted. Blend in paprika. Place turkey breast skin side down on microwave-safe roasting rack or utensil. Cover with loose tent of waxed paper. Estimate total cooking time based on 10 minutes per pound; divide time in half. Microwave on high for 5 minutes. Reduce power to medium-high and microwave for remainder of first half of time.

Turn breast over and brush with butter and paprika mixture. Re-cover turkey roast with waxed paper. Microwave on medium-high for remaining time. Remove breast to platter; cover with aluminum foil and let stand for 10 minutes.

In 4-cup glass measure, place remaining butter. Microwave on high for 45 seconds or until melted. Blend in flour, then slowly add chicken broth. Microwave on high for 3 minutes, stirring twice. Add bell pepper, pimiento and mushrooms; continue to microwave for 2 to 4 minutes longer, stirring twice. Sauce should be thick and peppers tender. Stir in salt and pepper. Slice turkey and serve with sauce.   Makes 6 servings.

Per Serving (approx):
Calories 237
Carbohydrate 5 gm

Protein 30 gm
Sodium 564 mg

Fat 10 gm
Cholesterol 92 mg

Golden Breaded Turkey Tenderloins

Some folks call this Wienerschnitzel.

1 egg, beaten
2 tablespoons butter or
   margarine, melted
1 1/2 teaspoons curry powder
1 cup buttery cracker crumbs
   (about 25 crackers)

1 pound turkey breast
   tenderloins, each cut into
   6 to 8 chunks
Chutney

In small bowl, combine egg and butter. On waxed paper blend curry powder and cracker crumbs. Dip turkey into egg mixture and then into crumbs. On microwave-safe roasting dish, arrange tenderloins with thicker parts toward outside. Cover with waxed paper. Reserve remaining crumbs.

Microwave on medium-high for 12 minutes per pound. Halfway through cooking, turn tenderloins and sprinkle with remaining crumbs. Cover with double thickness of paper towels. Cook, removing paper towels during last 2 minutes. Let stand, uncovered, for 5 minutes. Serve with chutney. Makes 4 servings.

Per Serving (approx):
Calories 311
Carbohydrate 15 gm

Protein 30 gm
Sodium 338 mg

Fat 15 gm
Cholesterol 139 mg

333

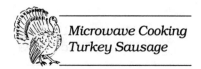

Pasta Pie

8 ounces spaghetti, cooked
  and drained
1/4 cup grated Parmesan cheese
1 tablespoon butter or margarine
1 pound sweet or hot Italian
  turkey sausage
1/2 cup chopped onion
1 bell pepper, chopped

1 can (15 ounces) herbed
  tomato sauce
1 clove garlic, minced
1 tablespoon chopped parsley
1/2 teaspoon dried basil
1/2 teaspoon dried oregano
4 ounces shredded mozzarella
  cheese

In 10-inch microwave-safe pie plate, place spaghetti. Add Parmesan cheese and butter; toss until evenly coated. Arrange pasta on bottom and up sides of plate to form pasta crust; cover with aluminum foil and set aside.

In 2 1/4-quart microwave-safe utensil, arrange sausage; cover with waxed paper. Microwave on high for 4 minutes. Cut sausage into thin slices. Stir in onion and bell pepper; cover with waxed paper and microwave on high for 3 to 4 minutes, stirring twice. Drain off pan juices. Stir tomato sauce, garlic, parsley, basil and oregano into meat mixture; pour into pasta shell.

Sprinkle mozzarella cheese in circle over sauce. Microwave, uncovered, on high for 1 to 2 minutes or until cheese is melted. Cover with foil and let stand for 5 minutes.   Makes 4 to 6 servings.

Per Serving (approx):
Calories 266
Carbohydrate 19 gm

Protein 16 gm
Sodium 1096 mg

Fat 14 gm
Cholesterol 60 mg

SANDWICHES, BURGERS, HOAGIES & SLOPPY JOES

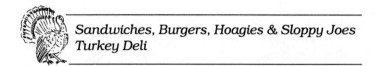

Muffaletta

This Sicilian sandwich is the perfect solution for feeding eight or more and you can make it the day before.

1 jar (5 ounces) pimiento stuffed olives, chopped

1 can (3 1/4 ounces) pitted black olives, chopped

2 tablespoons olive oil

3 tablespoons minced parsley

1 tablespoon drained capers

1 1/2 teaspoons minced garlic

1/2 teaspoon dried oregano

1 loaf (1 pound) round Italian or French bread

1/2 pound turkey salami slices

4 ounces provolone cheese, thinly sliced

In medium bowl combine olives, oil, parsley, capers, garlic and oregano.

With serrated bread knife slice bread in half lengthwise. Hollow out each bread half, leaving 3/4 inch outside shell. Reserve removed bread for another use.

Over bottom half of bread shell, spread half the olive mixture. Evenly arrange 4 ounces turkey salami over olive mixture. Top with cheese and remaining turkey salami.

In top half of bread shell, spread remaining olive mixture. Invert top bread shell over bottom bread half and press down firmly. Wrap muffaletta in foil. Refrigerate overnight.

To serve, cut muffaletta into 8 wedges. Makes 8 servings.

Per Serving (approx):
Calories 248
Carbohydrate 18 gm

Protein 11 gm
Sodium 1008 mg

Fat 15 gm
Cholesterol 22 mg

Barbecue on a Bun

Here's another "prepare-a-day-ahead" recipe to feed a hungry crowd. This dish may be made in a slow cooker.

2 cups tomato-vegetable juice
1 cup diet cola
1 tablespoon prepared mustard
1 tablespoon bottled hot sauce
1 tablespoon Worcestershire
  sauce

2 cups shredded cooked
  turkey breast
8 hamburger buns
Coleslaw (optional)

In large saucepan over high heat, bring vegetable juice to a boil. Reduce heat to low and simmer juice down to half. Stir in cola, mustard, hot sauce and Worcestershire sauce; simmer for 2 to 3 minutes to combine well. Add turkey to sauce mixture and simmer for 15 minutes.

To serve, spoon approximately 1/3 cup turkey barbecue on bottom half of each bun, top with coleslaw (if desired) and remaining bun halves.

Makes 8 servings.

Per Serving (approx):
Calories 190
Carbohydrate 24 gm

Protein 14 gm
Sodium 475 mg

Fat 4 gm
Cholesterol 29 mg

Tortilla Flats

4 flour tortillas (9 inch)
1 pound ground turkey
1 egg white
1/3 cup tomato sauce
4 green onions, chopped
1/4 pound mushrooms,
　very thinly sliced
2 cloves garlic, minced
1/2 teaspoon ground allspice
1/2 teaspoon crumbled dried oregano

1/4 teaspoon freshly ground
　black pepper
12 soft sun-dried tomato halves,
　cut in strips and soaked in
　small amount of water
3/4 cup grated Monterey jack
　cheese
3 tablespoons shelled
　pistachio nuts

Lay out tortillas in single layer on 2 baking sheets. In bowl mix together ground turkey, egg white, tomato sauce, green onions, mushrooms, garlic, allspice, oregano, pepper and tomato strips. Pat mixture over surface of the tortillas, allowing 1/2-inch border around edge. Sprinkle with grated cheese and nuts.

Bake in 425 degree oven for 10 to 12 minutes or until tortillas are golden brown on edges and meat is cooked through.　　　Makes 4 servings.

Per Serving (approx):
Calories 545
Carbohydrate 46 gm

Protein 38 gm
Sodium 624 mg

Fat 23 gm
Cholesterol 154 mg

Apple-Cinnamon Sausage Sandwich

Perfect for breakfast, lunch or brunch.

1 pound turkey breakfast
  sausage
1 apple, cored and cut into 8 rings
2 tablespoons water

8 English muffins, split and
  toasted
1/3 cup apple jelly
1/2 cup plain yogurt
1/8 teaspoon ground cinnamon

Shape turkey breakfast sausage into eight 3-inch patties. Place in non-stick or lightly greased skillet. Cook over medium heat for 8 minutes, turning occasionally. Remove patties and set aside.

Place apple rings and water in same skillet. Cover; reduce heat to medium-low and cook for 3 minutes. Place sausage on apples. Cover; cook for 3 minutes more or until apples are tender.

Assemble sandwich as follows: muffin half, apple jelly, yogurt, sprinkle of cinnamon, apple ring, sausage patty, muffin half.   Makes 8 servings.

Per Serving (approx):
Calories 191
Carbohydrate 24 gm

Protein 10 gm
Sodium 409 mg

Fat 6 gm
Cholesterol 32 mg

Voted #1

Q. What is the most popular form of turkey eaten?

A. American households consume turkey more often as a sandwich than any other way, with sandwiches accounting for 44% of all turkey consumption. Low fat, convenient products like ground turkey, sausage, bacon and various turkey parts are increasingly popular.

Turkey Dinner Sandwiches

Lunch or dinner in less than twenty minutes.

1/4 cup flour
1/4 teaspoon dried poultry
   seasoning
1/8 teaspoon salt
1 pound turkey breast slices
   (4 to 6 slices)
3 tablespoons oil
8 ounces cream cheese,
   softened

1/3 cup chopped walnuts
1 tablespoon honey
4 to 6 slices multigrain bread,
   toasted
Lettuce
1/2 to 3/4 cup whole berry
   cranberry sauce

On sheet of waxed paper combine flour, poultry seasoning and salt. Dip turkey slices into mixture, coating both sides.

In large skillet over medium heat, cook turkey slices in hot oil for 4 to 6 minutes on each side or until turkey is no longer pink.

Meanwhile, in small bowl combine cream cheese, walnuts and honey. Spread half of toasted bread slices with 2 tablespoons cream cheese mixture; top with lettuce, turkey slice, 2 tablespoons cranberry sauce and toasted bread slice.   Makes 4 to 6 servings.

Per Serving (approx):
Calories 485
Carbohydrate 32 gm

Protein 23 gm
Sodium 350 mg

Fat 29 gm
Cholesterol 83 mg

Turkey Bruschetta

This Italian open-faced sandwich was traditionally made with veal cutlet. Ours is made with turkey cutlet. They even like it in Italy.

1 pound turkey breast cutlets, thinly sliced
Salt and pepper to taste
2 tablespoons olive oil
1 tablespoon dried Italian seasoning
1 to 2 cloves garlic, minced

1 small loaf Italian bread, cut in 3/4-inch-thick slices
4 ripe Italian plum tomatoes, sliced
1/2 cup shredded part-skim mozzarella cheese
6 to 8 sprigs fresh basil and/or marjoram sprigs (optional)

Preheat broiler. Sprinkle cutlets with salt and pepper; place on broiling pan. Broil 3 to 5 inches from heat source for 1 1/2 to 2 minutes per side or until cooked through.

Meanwhile, in small bowl combine oil, Italian seasoning and garlic. Brush on bread and place in broiling pan with turkey. Toast lightly on both sides. Top bread with cutlets and tomato slices; sprinkle with mozzarella.

Place under broiler just until cheese melts. Garnish with herb sprigs, if desired, and serve immediately. Makes 4 servings.

Per Serving (approx):
Calories 395
Carbohydrate 36 gm

Protein 36 gm
Sodium 490 mg

Fat 11 gm
Cholesterol 79 mg

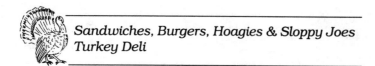

Fiesta Pinwheel Sandwiches

If these large Armenian bread rounds are not available, you can make miniature sandwiches by using pita bread instead.

1 pound cream cheese, softened	1/2 pound sliced cooked turkey breast
1/4 cup chopped parsley	1/4 pound turkey pastrami or turkey ham slices
2 rounds soft or hard Armenian cracker bread	

Combine cream cheese and parsley. Set aside.

To soften hard bread, wet both sides thoroughly; cover with towel and let stand for 10 minutes. Meanwhile, prepare Fiesta Filling. Spread cream cheese mixture and filling over bread and top each with remaining ingredients.

Roll up into log, wrap with plastic wrap and chill for at least 1 hour before slicing. Slices may be secured with toothpicks.

Makes 4 to 6 servings.

FIESTA FILLING:
Combine 1 tomato, minced, 1/2 cup chopped green bell pepper, 1/2 red onion, minced, and alfalfa sprouts or chopped fresh spinach.

Per Serving (approx):
Calories 407
Carbohydrate 10 gm

Protein 22 gm
Sodium 521 mg

Fat 30 gm
Cholesterol 122 mg

Curried Pinwheel Sandwiches

1 pound cream cheese, softened
2 teaspoons curry powder
1 tablespoon chopped fresh mint
1/4 cup chopped parsley

2 rounds soft or hard Armenian
  cracker bread
1/2 pound sliced cooked turkey

Combine cream cheese, curry powder, mint and parsley. Set aside.

To soften hard bread, wet both sides thoroughly; cover with towel and let rest for 10 minutes. Meanwhile, prepare Indian Curry Filling. Spread cream cheese mixture and filling over bread, and top with turkey.

Roll up into log, wrap with plastic wrap and chill for at least 1 hour before slicing. Slices may be secured with toothpicks.

Makes 4 to 6 servings.

INDIAN CURRY FILLING:
Combine 1/2 cup diced almonds, toasted, 4 green onions, chopped, and 1 cup currants.

Per Serving (approx):
Calories 456	*Protein 21 gm*	*Fat 35 gm*
Carbohydrate 15 gm	*Sodium 325 mg*	*Cholesterol 112 mg*

Pita Pockets

1/2 cup plain low-fat yogurt
1 tablespoon honey
1 tablespoon lemon juice
1 teaspoon curry powder
1/8 teaspoon black pepper
2 cups diced cooked turkey
1/2 cup diced bell pepper

1/2 cup diced celery
1/2 cup thinly sliced green
   onion
1/4 cup raisins
6 individual whole wheat pita
   breads, lightly toasted
1 cup sprouts (bean, alfalfa or
   radish)

n medium bowl, combine yogurt, honey, lemon juice, curry and black pepper. Add turkey, bell pepper, celery, green onion and raisins; toss to mix well. To serve, split pitas. Divide salad mixture among pitas; top with sprouts.   **Makes 4 to 6 servings.**

Per Serving (approx):
Calories 308
Carbohydrate 46 gm

Protein 23 gm
Sodium 292 mg

Fat 4 gm
Cholesterol 37 mg

Open-Faced Sandwiches Olé

1 1/2 to 2 cups coarsely
   chopped cooked turkey
1/2 cup prepared salsa
   or to taste
2 French rolls, split

4 thin slices Monterey jack
   cheese
Ripe avocado slices and/or
   pickled jalapeño pepper
   slices (optional)

Preheat broiler. In medium bowl combine turkey and salsa. Remove soft inside from rolls, leaving crusty "shells"; spoon in turkey mixture and top with cheese.

Broil sandwiches about 6 inches from heat source for 3 minutes or until cheese is melted and lightly browned. To serve, top sandwiches with avocado and/or jalapeno, if desired.   **Makes 2 to 4 servings.**

Per Serving (approx):
Calories 180
Carbohydrate 12 gm

Protein 18 gm
Sodium 246 mg

Fat 7 gm
Cholesterol 40 mg

Oven-Baked
Monte Cristo Sandwiches

8 slices firm-textured white
  sandwich bread
1 tablespoon Dijon mustard
8 slices cooked turkey
8 thin slices Swiss cheese
  (about 6 ounces)

1 tablespoon butter or
  margarine
1 tablespoon oil
3 eggs
3/4 cup milk
1/8 teaspoon black pepper

Spread bread slices with mustard. On each of 4 slices, layer 2 slices each turkey and Swiss cheese; top with remaining bread.

On 15 1/2- x 10 1/2-inch jelly-roll pan, combine butter and oil. Heat in preheated 400 degree oven for 3 minutes or until butter melts. Tilt pan to coat with butter mixture; pour excess into small bowl.

In shallow bowl beat eggs with milk and pepper. Dip sandwiches in egg mixture; place on hot jelly-roll pan. Drizzle remaining butter over tops of sandwiches.

Bake for 20 minutes or until golden brown, turning halfway through cooking time. Drain sandwiches on paper towels. Slice diagonally and serve immediately.   Makes 4 servings.

Per Serving (approx):
Calories 394
Carbohydrate 32 gm

Protein 28 gm
Sodium 522 mg

Fat 17 gm
Cholesterol 215 mg

Tarragon Turkey Pitas

2 cups cooked turkey breast
   cut in 1/2-inch dice
1/2 cup low-fat lemon yogurt
1 tablespoon reduced-calorie
   mayonnaise

1/4 teaspoon finely crushed
   dried tarragon
1/2 cup green grapes, halved
4 mini whole wheat pitas
4 lettuce leaves

In medium bowl combine yogurt, mayonnaise and tarragon. Fold in turkey and grapes; cover and refrigerate for at least 1 hour.

Trim tops from pita pockets. Line inside of pitas with lettuce. Carefully fill pitas with turkey mixture.   **Makes 4 servings.**

Per Serving (approx):
Calories 216
Carbohydrate 27 gm

Protein 19 gm
Sodium 771 mg

Fat 4 gm
Cholesterol 26 mg

Turkey Pistachio Sandwich

1/2 cup plain yogurt
1/4 cup chopped salted
   pistachio nuts
1 teaspoon dried dill weed

4 lettuce leaves
8 slices whole wheat bread
8 ounces cooked turkey
   breast, sliced

In small bowl combine yogurt, pistachio nuts and dill. Cover and refrigerate for at least 1 hour or overnight to allow flavors to blend.

To serve, arrange a lettuce leaf on a bread slice and top lettuce leaf with 2 ounces turkey. Spoon 2 tablespoons yogurt mixture over turkey and top with another bread slice. Turkey mixture will keep up to 4 days in refrigerator.   **Makes 4 servings.**

Per serving (approx):
Calories 265
Carbohydrate 26 gm

Protein 25 gm
Sodium 303 gm

Fat 7 gm
Cholesterol 42 mg

Turkey Burger Plus

1 pound ground turkey
1 1/2 cups seasoned
  bread crumbs
1/3 cup finely chopped onion
1 egg, beaten

1 teaspoon soy sauce
1 teaspoon Worcestershire sauce
1/2 teaspoon garlic powder
1/4 teaspoon dry mustard
4 burger buns, toasted

In large bowl combine turkey, bread crumbs, onion, egg, soy sauce, Worcestershire sauce, garlic powder and mustard. Shape mixture into 4 patties, each 1/2 inch thick. On lightly greased broiling pan about 6 inches from heat, broil burgers for 3 to 4 minutes per side or until no longer pink in center. Serve burgers on buns.   Makes 4 servings.

Per Serving (approx):
Calories 378   *Protein 28 gm*   *Fat 14 gm*
Carbohydrate 33 gm   *Sodium 807 mg*   *Cholesterol 144 mg*

South of the Border Burgers

1 pound ground turkey
1 teaspoon chili powder
1/2 teaspoon instant chicken
  bouillon

4 ounces shredded Cheddar
  cheese
4 sesame sandwich buns
6 ounces guacamole

Combine turkey, chili powder and bouillon. Shape into 4 burgers. Cook in nonstick skillet over medium heat for 12 to 15 minutes, turning occasionally. Top each burger with 1/4 cup cheese. Cover. Remove from heat and let stand for 2 minutes or until cheese melts. Meanwhile, spread buns with guacamole. Serve burgers in buns.   Makes 4 servings.

Per Serving (approx):
Calories 466   *Protein 32 gm*   *Fat 27 gm*
Carbohydrate 24 gm   *Sodium 570 mg*   *Cholesterol 117 mg*

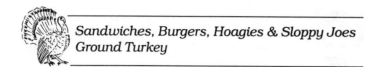

Pita Burgers

Pita burgers adapt popular pita pocket breads to a Mediterranean-style burger flavored with herbs of the Middle East.

1 to 1 1/4 pounds ground turkey
2 cloves garlic, minced
2 teaspoons paprika
1 teaspoon ground cumin
1 teaspoon ground allspice
1/2 teaspoon salt

1/4 teaspoon cayenne pepper
6 pita breads, opened and
   lightly grilled
3 plum tomatoes, thinly sliced
1 small cucumber, thinly sliced

Prepare lightly greased grill for cooking. In medium bowl combine turkey, garlic and seasonings. Form mixture into 6 patties. Grill, uncovered, 5 to 6 inches over medium-hot coals for 4 to 5 minutes on each side or until burgers are cooked through and spring back when touched.

Meanwhile, prepare Yogurt Sauce. Serve burgers in pita pockets topped with Yogurt Sauce, tomatoes and cucumbers.   Makes 4 to 6 servings.

YOGURT SAUCE:
In a small bowl combine 1 cup plain yogurt, 1 tablespoon minced parsley, 2 teaspoons minced cilantro (optional), and 1 1/2 teaspoons minced fresh mint or 1/2 teaspoon dried mint. Season with salt and pepper to taste.

Per Serving (approx):
Calories 252
Carbohydrate 26 gm

Protein 20 gm
Sodium 564 mg

Fat 8 gm
Cholesterol 60 mg

He-Man Burgers

1 to 1 1/4 pounds
 ground turkey
1/2 cup chopped green onion
1/4 to 1/3 cup prepared shrimp
 cocktail sauce

Salt and pepper to taste
4 or 5 pumpernickel or onion
 rolls split and lightly toasted
1/3 cup prepared horseradish
 sauce or sour cream

Prepare grill or preheat broiler. In medium bowl combine turkey, green onion, cocktail sauce, salt and pepper. Form into 4 or 5 burgers. Grill or broil for 4 to 6 minutes on each side or until burgers are cooked through and spring back to the touch. Spread cut side of rolls with horseradish sauce. Place burgers on lower half of rolls. Top with other half of rolls.

Makes 4 to 5 servings.

Per Serving (approx):
Calories 241
Carbohydrate 22 gm

Protein 19 gm
Sodium 481 mg

Fat 9 gm
Cholesterol 68 mg

Taco Burgers

1 pound ground turkey
1/4 cup spicy taco sauce
Salt to taste
4 slices (1 ounce each)
 reduced-fat Monterey jack cheese

4 hamburger buns
4 tablespoons guacamole
 (optional)

Remove grill rack from charcoal grill. Prepare grill for direct-heat cooking. In medium bowl combine ground turkey, taco sauce and salt. Shape into 4 burgers about 1/2 inch thick. Grease cold grill rack and position over hot coals. Grill turkey burgers for 5 to 6 minutes per side. Top each burger with slice of cheese during last minute of grilling time. To serve, place each turkey burger on bottom half of bun and top with 1 tablespoon guacamole, if desired. Place top half of bun on burger.

Makes 4 servings.

Per Serving (approx):
Calories 395
Carbohydrate 23 gm

Protein 32 gm
Sodium 541 mg

Fat 19 gm
Cholesterol 80 mg

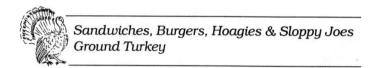

Teriyaki Turkey Burgers

Try adding Italian salad dressing and seasoned bread crumbs to ground turkey for an Italian burger. Or add taco sauce to ground turkey topped with Monterey jack cheese and guacamole dip for a taste of Mexico.

1 pound ground turkey	1 tablespoon sesame seeds,
1/2 cup finely chopped	toasted
water chestnuts	1/4 cup plum preserves
1/4 teaspoon black pepper	4 hamburger buns
2 tablespoons teriyaki sauce	

In large bowl combine turkey, water chestnuts, pepper, teriyaki sauce and 2 teaspoons of the sesame seeds. Evenly divide turkey mixture into 4 burgers, each approximately 1/2 inch thick.

On broiling pan 3 to 4 inches from heat, broil burgers for 3 to 4 minutes per side or until turkey is no longer pink in center.

In small saucepan over low heat, combine preserves and remaining 1 teaspoon sesame seeds. Heat until preserves are melted.

To serve, place a burger on bottom half of each bun, drizzle sauce over each burger and top each with other half of bun.   Makes 4 servings.

Per Serving (approx):
Calories 369
Carbohydrate 40 gm   *Protein 25 gm*   *Fat 12 gm*
                              Sodium 814 mg   *Cholesterol 85 mg*

Oriental Burgers

If you're looking for a really different flavor in a burger, try this recipe. The burgers are a bit spicy, but you can tone that down by reducing the amount of Chinese chile paste.

1 to 1 1/4 pounds ground turkey
2 to 3 tablespoons Chinese
   plum sauce*
3 green onions, chopped
1 tablespoon chopped fresh ginger

1 1/2 teaspoons Chinese chile
   paste with garlic*
1/2 teaspoon salt
4 or 5 hamburger rolls, split
   and lightly toasted

Prepare grill or preheat broiler. In medium bowl combine all ingredients but rolls. Form into 4 or 5 burgers.

Grill or broil for 4 to 6 minutes on each side until burgers are cooked through and spring back to the touch. Serve burgers warm on toasted rolls. Makes 4 or 5 servings.

*Note: Available in the Oriental food section of your grocery store.

Per Serving (approx):
Calories 254
Carbohydrate 24 gm

Protein 20 gm
Sodium 535 mg

Fat 9 gm
Cholesterol 68 mg

Turkey Burgers al Greco

1 pound ground turkey
1 1/2 cups seasoned
  bread crumbs
1/2 cup finely chopped onion
1 egg, beaten
1 teaspoon soy sauce
1 teaspoon Worcestershire sauce
1/2 teaspoon garlic powder

1/4 teaspoon dry mustard
4 mini pitas
6 tablespoons crumbled
  feta cheese
1 cup chopped tomato
1/2 cup thinly sliced cucumber
1/2 cup thinly sliced onion

In large bowl combine turkey, bread crumbs, onion, egg, soy sauce, Worcestershire sauce, garlic powder and mustard. Shape mixture into 4 patties, each 1/2 inch thick. On lightly greased broiling pan about 6 inches from heat, broil burgers for 3 to 4 minutes per side or until no longer pink in center.

To open pitas, cut off tops; insert burgers. Evenly sprinkle cheese, tomato, cucumber and onion into each pita.　　　Makes 4 servings.

Per Serving (approx):
Calories 339
Carbohydrate 16 gm

Protein 27 gm
Sodium 621 mg

Fat 18 gm
Cholesterol 175 mg

Turkish Burgers

This recipe takes the burger out of its "fast food" class and makes it a gourmet entree.

1 pound ground turkey
1 egg, lightly beaten
1/2 cup plain bread crumbs
4 pimiento-stuffed olives, chopped
1 tablespoon minced parsley
1 clove garlic, minced
1/4 teaspoon ground cinnamon

1/8 teaspoon ground nutmeg
2 2/3 tablespoons sour cream
4 hamburger buns
8 slices cucumber
4 tablespoons crumbled feta
    cheese

Preheat charcoal grill for direct-heat cooking.

In medium bowl combine turkey, egg, bread crumbs, olives, parsley, garlic, cinnamon and nutmeg. Evenly divide turkey mixture into 4 burgers, approximately 3 1/2 inches in diameter.

Grill burgers 5 to 6 minutes per side or meat is no longer pink.

To serve, spread 2 teaspoons sour cream on each bottom half of bun. Place turkey burger on each bun, top each with 2 cucumber slices, 1 tablespoon feta cheese and remaining half of bun.   Makes 4 servings.

Per Serving (approx):
Calories 439
Carbohydrate 42 gm

Protein 30 gm
Sodium 584 mg

Fat 17 gm
Cholesterol 149 mg

Mexican Turkey Burgers

1 pound ground turkey
1 1/2 cups seasoned bread crumbs
1/2 cup finely chopped onion
1 egg, beaten
1 teaspoon soy sauce
1 teaspoon Worcestershire sauce

1/2 teaspoon garlic powder
1/4 teaspoon dry mustard
4 burger buns, toasted
1 avocado, sliced (optional)
4 ounces Monterey jack cheese

In large bowl combine turkey, bread crumbs, onion, egg, soy sauce, Worcestershire sauce, garlic powder and mustard. Shape mixture into 4 patties, each 1/2 inch thick. On lightly greased broiling pan about 6 inches from heat, broil burgers for 3 to 4 minutes per side or until no longer pink in center.

Just before serving, top each burger with cheese; heat until cheese melts. Serve burgers on buns topped with sauce and, if desired, avocado.

Makes 4 servings.

SAUCE:
In small bowl combine 1/2 cup sour cream substitute, 1/4 cup chunky salsa and 1/2 teaspoon chopped cilantro.

Per Serving (approx):
Calories 548
Carbohydrate 37 gm

Protein 35 gm
Sodium 1079 mg

Fat 29 gm
Cholesterol 168 mg

For several decades after 1810 the turkey persisted in considerable numbers, especially at and beyond the frontier. However, the animal's behavior proved to be its undoing. Many of its habits which led to its successful domestication in Mexico by the Indians also contributed to its demise as a wild species.

Creamy Mushroom Turkey Burgers

1 pound ground turkey
1 1/2 cups seasoned bread crumbs
1/2 cup finely chopped onion
1 egg, beaten
1 teaspoon soy sauce
1 teaspoon Worcestershire sauce
1/2 teaspoon garlic powder
1/4 teaspoon dry mustard
1/2 pound mushrooms,
   thinly sliced

1/4 teaspoon dried thyme
2 tablespoons margarine
2 tablespoons brandy
1/2 teaspoon garlic powder
Salt to taste
1/8 teaspoon pepper
1 cup plain low-fat yogurt
4 burger buns, toasted

In large bowl combine turkey, bread crumbs, onions, egg, soy sauce, Worcestershire sauce, garlic powder and mustard. Shape mixture into 4 patties, each 1/2 inch thick. On lightly greased broiling pan about 6 inches from heat, broil burgers for 3 to 4 minutes per side, or until no longer pink in center.

While burgers are cooking, in medium skillet over medium-high heat, sauté mushrooms and thyme in margarine for 1 to 2 minutes. Add brandy, garlic powder, salt and pepper; cook for 1 minute. Stir in yogurt and heat until warm.

Serve burgers on buns topped with mushroom mixture.

Makes 4 servings.

Per Serving (approx):
Calories 361
Carbohydrate 19 gm

Protein 29 gm
Sodium 674 mg

Fat 19 gm
Cholesterol 145 mg

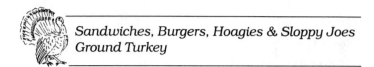

Tarragon-Mustard Burgers

1 to 1 1/4 pounds ground turkey
2 tablespoons tomato paste
1 1/2 teaspoons minced fresh
   tarragon or 1/2 teaspoon dried
Salt and pepper to taste

4 or 5 slices tomato
2 or 3 English muffins, split and
   lightly toasted
Sprigs of fresh tarragon
   (optional)

Prepare grill or preheat broiler. In medium bowl combine turkey, tomato paste, tarragon, salt and pepper. Form into 4 or 5 burgers and grill or broil for 4 to 6 minutes on each side or until burgers are cooked through and spring back to the touch.

Prepare Tarragon-Mustard Sauce. Place slice of tomato and burger on top of each English muffin half. Top with warm Tarragon-Mustard Sauce. Garnish with sprigs of fresh tarragon, if desired. Makes 4 or 5 servings.

TARRAGON-MUSTARD SAUCE:
In top of double boiler set over hot water, blend 1 1/2 tablespoons butter or margarine and 1 1/2 tablespoons Dijon mustard. Remove from heat; add 1 tablespoon tarragon vinegar. Stir in 1/4 cup reduced-fat sour cream and 1 teaspoon minced fresh tarragon or 1/4 teaspoon dried. Season with salt, black pepper and cayenne pepper to taste.

Per Serving (approx):
Calories 263
Carbohydrate 18 gm

Protein 20 gm
Sodium 477 mg

Fat 12 gm
Cholesterol 77 mg

Giant Stuffed Turkey Burger

You can also make this under your broiler or in an oven.

1 pound ground turkey
1/4 cup quick rolled oats
1 egg
1/2 teaspoon garlic powder
Dash of black pepper
1/2 cup chopped onion
1/4 cup drained dill pickle relish

2 tablespoons catsup
2 teaspoons prepared mustard
2 slices (1 ounce each) reduced-
   fat, low-sodium American
   cheese, cut into 4 equal strips
Lettuce (optional)
Tomato slices (optional)

Preheat grill for direct-heat cooking.*

In medium bowl combine turkey, oats, egg, garlic powder and pepper. Divide turkey mixture in half. On 2 pieces (each 10 by 11 inches) waxed paper, shape each half of turkey mixture into 6-inch-diameter circle. Sprinkle onion and relish over one circle of turkey mixture, leaving 1/2-inch border around outside edges; top with catsup and mustard. Arrange cheese strips, spoke fashion, over catsup and mustard. Carefully place remaining turkey mixture circle on top of cheese. Remove top layer of waxed paper from turkey mixture. Press turkey mixture edges together to seal.

Lightly grease cold grill rack and position over hot coals. Invert giant turkey burger onto grill rack; remove waxed paper. Grill burger for 8 minutes per side or until internal temperature of 165 degrees is reached on meat thermometer. To turn giant burger, slide flat baking sheet under burger and invert onto another flat cookie sheet, then carefully slide burger back onto grill rack. To serve, cut burger into fourths. Serve with lettuce and tomato slices, if desired.   Makes 4 servings.

Note: For more information on direct-heat cooking, see page 284.

Per Serving (approx):
Calories 269   *Protein 27 gm*   *Fat 14 gm*
Carbohydrate 8 gm   *Sodium 559 mg*   *Cholesterol 133 mg*

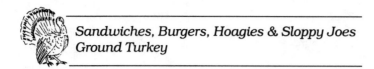
Reuben Turkey Burgers

This is an adaptation of the famous sandwich made at Reuben's restaurant in New York City.

1 pound ground turkey	1/4 teaspoon dry mustard
1 1/2 cups bread crumbs	4 slices Swiss cheese
1/2 cup finely chopped onion	(1 ounce each)
1 egg, beaten	4 burger buns, toasted
1 teaspoon soy sauce	4 tablespoons rinsed and
1 teaspoon Worcestershire sauce	drained sauerkraut
1/2 teaspoon garlic powder	4 tablespoons Russian dressing

In large bowl combine turkey, bread crumbs, onion, egg, soy sauce, Worcestershire sauce, garlic powder and mustard. Shape mixture into 4 patties, each 1/2 inch thick.

On lightly greased broiling pan about 6 inches from heat, broil burgers for 3 to 4 minutes per side or until no longer pink in center.

During last 2 to 3 minutes of cooking, top each burger with cheese; heat until cheese melts. Place burgers on buns and top with 1 tablespoon sauerkraut and Russian dressing. Heat if desired.   Makes 4 servings.

Per Serving (approx):
Calories 563
Carbohydrate 37 gm

Protein 38 gm
Sodium 1111 mg

Fat 30 gm
Cholesterol 170 mg

Norwegian Burgers

1/2 cup sour cream
1 teaspoon prepared horseradish
1/3 cup diced cucumber
1/4 teaspoon ground nutmeg
1 pound ground turkey
1/3 cup chopped mushrooms
1/3 cup chopped green onion,
  including some green tops

1/3 cup crumbled cooked bacon
1/2 teaspoon black pepper
Oil, for brushing on grill rack
8 slices pumpernickel bread,
  buttered on one side
4 slices Jarlsberg cheese
8 thin slices of large tomato

Prepare a medium-hot fire for direct-heat cooking. In small bowl combine sour cream, horseradish, cucumber and nutmeg. Set aside. In large bowl combine turkey, mushrooms, onion, bacon and pepper. Divide mixture into 4 equal portions and shape into patties the same size as pumpernickel slices.

Place patties on oiled grill and cook for 8 minutes. Turn and cook for 7 minutes longer or until done to your preference. During last few minutes of cooking, place bread slices, buttered side down, on outer edges of grill to toast lightly. During last minute or so of cooking, place cheese slice on each patty.

Spread sour cream mixture on toasted side of each bread slice. Place patties on bread slices. Arrange 2 slices tomato, overlapping, on top of each patty. Top with remaining bread slices. Slice in half on diagonal to serve.   Makes 4 servings.

Per Serving (approx):
Calories 588   *Protein 38 gm*   *Fat 26 gm*
Carbohydrate 49 gm *Sodium 611 mg*   *Cholesterol 130 mg*

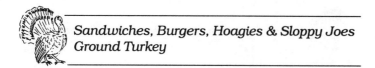

Stuffing Burgers

You can call these Thanksgiving burgers, if you like, because they taste just like a Thanksgiving turkey.

3 tablespoons butter or
  margarine
1/4 cup chopped celery
1/4 cup chopped onion
3/4 cup seasoned dry stuffing
  mix
1/4 cup chicken broth or water,
  boiling

Salt and pepper to taste
1/4 teaspoon dried sage or
  dried poultry seasoning
1 to 1 1/4 pounds ground
  turkey
1/4 cup chopped parsley
Cranberry relish (optional)

In large skillet over medium heat, melt 2 tablespoons of the butter. Add celery and onion; sauté for 5 minutes or until softened. Add stuffing, broth, salt, pepper and sage; mix well. Let mixture cool completely.

In large bowl combine turkey, stuffing mixture and parsley. Form into 4 or 5 burgers. Add remaining butter to skillet and melt over medium-high heat. Add burgers; brown for 1 minute on each side. Reduce heat to medium-low and cook for 4 to 5 minutes on each side or until burgers are cooked through and spring back to the touch. Serve with cranberry relish, if desired.   Makes 4 or 5 servings.

Per Serving (approx):
Calories 211
Carbohydrate 5 gm

Protein 17 gm
Sodium 293 mg

Fat 14 gm
Cholesterol 85 mg

> Some historians claim that the English colonists of Jamestown, Virginia, celebrated the first Thanksgiving with a traditional, ancient harvest home festival, a sort of homecoming weekend, several years before the Pilgrims.

Roumanian Turkey Burgers

1 pound ground turkey
1 or 2 cloves garlic, crushed
1/2 teaspoon dried thyme
1/2 teaspoon salt

1/4 teaspoon ground allspice
1/4 teaspoon ground cloves
1/4 teaspoon black pepper
4 burger buns, toasted

In a large bowl combine turkey, garlic, thyme, salt, allspice, cloves and pepper. Shape mixture into 4 patties, each 1/2 inch thick. On lightly greased broiling pan, broil burgers for 3 to 4 minute per side or until no longer pink in center. Serve burgers on buns.　　　Makes 4 servings.

Per Serving (approx):
Calories 299
Carbohydrate 22 gm

Protein 24 gm
Sodium 567 mg

Fat 12 gm
Cholesterol 74 mg

Bavarian Turkey Burgers

1 pound ground turkey
1 1/2 tablespoons prepared
　horseradish
1 1/2 teaspoons Dijon mustard

1 1/2 teaspoons paprika
1/4 teaspoon black pepper
1/8 teaspoon salt
4 burger buns, toasted

In large bowl, combine turkey, horseradish, mustard, paprika, pepper and salt. Shape mixture into 4 patties, each 1/2 inch thick. On lightly greased broiling pan about 6 inches from heat, broil burgers for 3 to 4 minutes per side or until no longer pink in center. Serve burgers on buns.　　　Makes 4 servings.

Per Serving (approx):
Calories 303
Carbohydrate 23 gm

Protein 24 gm
Sodium 347 mg

Fat 13 gm
Cholesterol 74 mg

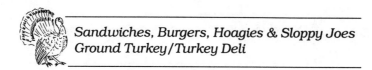

Meatball Parmigiana Hoagie

1 pound ground turkey
1 cup dry bread crumbs
1/3 cup chopped parsley
1 teaspoon dried Italian
   seasoning
1 egg

3 tablespoons grated
   Parmesan cheese
1 jar (14 ounces) spaghetti sauce
6 French rolls
1/2 cup grated mozzarella
   cheese

Combine turkey, bread crumbs, parsley, Italian seasoning, egg and
Parmesan. Mix well, then let stand for 5 minutes. Form into 1-inch meatballs; place in lightly greased baking dish 13 x 9 x 2 inches. Cover and
bake in preheated 350 degree oven for about 15 minutes or until meatballs are no longer pink. Stir in spaghetti sauce; heat for 10 minutes
longer. Spoon meatball mixture onto sliced rolls; sprinkle with grated
mozzarella cheese.   Makes 6 servings.

Per Serving (approx):
Calories 363
Carbohydrate 38 gm

Protein 24 gm
Sodium 945 mg

Fat 13 gm
Cholesterol 101 mg

Turkey Hoagies for a Crowd

2 tablespoons oil
2 teaspoons red wine vinegar
1/2 teaspoon dried oregano
1 loaf (1 pound) French bread
2 cups shredded lettuce
1 large tomato, thinly sliced

1 medium onion, thinly sliced
   and separated into rings
3/4 to 1 pound varied
   turkey deli slices
1 package (8 ounces)
   provolone cheese, sliced

In small bowl combine oil, vinegar and oregano; set aside. Cut bread in
half lengthwise and arrange lettuce, tomato and onion over bottom half.
Drizzle oil and vinegar mixture over vegetables. Top with turkey and
cheese slices. Cover with remaining bread half. To serve, cut hoagie into
8 slices.   Makes 8 servings.

Per Serving (approx):
Calories 371
Carbohydrate 34 gm

Protein 20 gm
Sodium 923 mg

Fat 17 gm
Cholesterol 40 mg

Turkey Joe #1

1 pound ground turkey
2 tablespoons oil
1 1/2 cups chopped onion
1 1/2 cups chopped celery
Dash of black pepper
1/2 cup chopped green bell
   pepper

1 can (10 1/2 ounces)
   condensed tomato soup
1 tablespoon barbecue sauce
   (optional)
1 teaspoon salt
12 buns, toasted and buttered

Brown turkey in oil. Stir in chopped vegetables and cook just until tender. Add black pepper, bell pepper, soup, barbecue sauce (if used) and salt. Simmer for 30 minutes. Serve in buns.   Makes 12 servings.

Per Serving (approx):
Calories 224
Carbohydrate 27 gm

Protein 11 gm
Sodium 632 mg

Fat 8 gm
Cholesterol 30 mg

Turkey Joe #2

1 pound ground turkey
1 medium onion, chopped
2 tablespoons oil

1 cup barbecue sauce
1 tablespoon sweet pickle relish
6 hamburger buns

Cook turkey and onion in skillet in hot oil over medium heat for 8 to 10 minutes or until turkey is no longer pink, stirring and separating turkey as it cooks. Stir in barbecue sauce and relish. Cook for 2 to 3 minutes more. Serve in buns.   Makes 6 servings.

Per Serving (approx):
Calories 275
Carbohydrate 30 gm

Protein 18 gm
Sodium 615 mg

Fat 9 gm
Cholesterol 57 mg

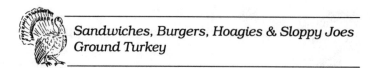

*Sandwiches, Burgers, Hoagies & Sloppy Joes
Ground Turkey*

Really Rapid Pizza

Two favorite foods, pizza and turkey, team up in this quick and easy recipe, which takes just 30 minutes to prepare.

1 package (8 ounces) refrigerated
   crescent rolls
1 1/2 tablespoons oil
1 to 1 1/4 pounds ground turkey
Salt to taste
1 teaspoon crumbled dried basil

1 can (6 ounces) pizza sauce
4 ounces sliced mozzarella or
   Monterey jack cheese
2 tablespoons grated Parmesan
   cheese

Unroll and separate rolls. Arrange together in lightly greased 11-inch pizza pan to form crust; pinch seams together well. Brush with 1 1/2 teaspoons of the oil. Bake on lowest rack of hot oven at 425 degrees for 8 to 10 minutes or until edges brown lightly.

Meanwhile, heat remaining tablespoon oil in skillet. Add turkey and brown lightly, stirring to break up into chunks. Season with salt and basil. When crust is about half baked, remove from oven and spread with 2 tablespoons pizza sauce. Top with turkey and spoon on remaining sauce. Cover with sliced cheese and sprinkle with grated Parmesan. Return to oven and bake for about 20 minutes longer or until cheese is melted and edges are well browned. Let stand for 3 to 4 minutes, then cut into wedges to serve.   Makes 4 to 6 servings.

Per Serving (approx):
Calories 497
Carbohydrate 38 gm

Protein 33 gm
Sodium 1060 mg

Fat 24 gm
Cholesterol 109 mg

Breakfast Pizza

This is a great crowd pleaser, particularly with the younger set.

1 pound turkey breakfast sausage
1 package (8 ounces)
    refrigerated crescent rolls
1 cup frozen hash brown
    potatoes, thawed
1 cup reduced-fat Cheddar
    cheese, shredded

5 medium eggs, beaten
1/4 cup milk
1/2 teaspoon salt
1/4 teaspoon black pepper
2 tablespoons grated Parmesan
    cheese

In medium skillet over medium heat, sauté sausage for 6 to 10 minutes or until no longer pink.

Unroll crescent rolls and separate dough. In 12-inch round pizza pan, arrange crescent rolls with points toward center. Press rolls over bottom and up sides of pan to form pizza crust, sealing perforations. Top crust with sausage, potatoes and Cheddar cheese.

In small bowl combine eggs, milk, salt and pepper. Pour egg mixture very slowly over sausage and potato mixture. Top with Parmesan cheese. Bake for 25 minutes in preheated 375 degree oven.

To serve, slice pizza into 8 wedges.   Makes 8 servings.

Per Serving (approx):
Calories 328
Carbohydrate 18 gm

Protein 20 gm
Sodium 704 mg

Fat 18 gm
Cholesterol 205 mg

Greek Pizza

1 package (10 ounces) refrigerated
  pizza dough
2 tablespoons olive oil
2 teaspoons garlic powder
1 teaspoon dried tarragon
1 teaspoon crushed dried rosemary
1 pound ground turkey
1/2 cup chopped onion

2 ounces feta cheese, crumbled
1 1/4 cups grated Monterey
  jack cheese with jalapeño
  peppers
1/2 cup sliced black olives
2 tablespoons chopped fresh
  chives

In 12-inch pizza pan, press dough to fit. Brush dough with oil and sprinkle with garlic powder, tarragon and rosemary. Bake dough at 400 degrees for 8 to 10 minutes or until lightly browned. Remove pizza crust from oven.

In large nonstick skillet over medium heat, sauté turkey and onion for 5 to 6 minutes or until turkey is no longer pink.

Evenly spread turkey mixture over pizza crust. Sprinkle feta and Monterey jack cheeses, olives and chives over turkey. Bake at 400 degrees for 10 to 15 minutes or until cheese is melted.

To serve, cut pizza into 8 slices.   Makes 8 servings.

Per Serving (approx):
Calories 300
Carbohydrate 23 gm   *Protein 15 gm*   *Fat 16 gm*
                                Sodium 478 mg   *Cholesterol 63 mg*

MORE STUFFINGS & SAUCES

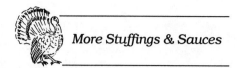

More Stuffings & Sauces

California-Style Stuffing I

1 cup chopped onion
1 cup chopped celery
1 cup chopped peeled
   tart apple
3/4 cup butter or margarine
1 1/2 cups broth or water

2 packages (6 ounces each)
   regular seasoned stuffing
   mix or seasoned
   corn bread stuffing mix
1/4 cup finely chopped
   parsley

Sauté onion, celery and apple in butter for about 10 minutes. Combine with broth. Add stuffing mix and parsley and mix well. Turn into buttered 2-quart casserole. Cover and place in 325 degree oven.

Bake for 45 minutes, removing cover during last 10 minutes of baking to crisp top.   Makes 10 servings.

Per Serving (approx):
Calories 237
Carbohydrate 24 gm

Protein 4 gm
Sodium 730 mg

Fat 14 gm
Cholesterol 35 mg

California-Style Stuffing II

1 pound turkey sausage
1/4 cup chopped onion
1 can (8 ounces) mushroom
   stems and pieces, drained
2 1/2 cups French bread cut
   in 1/2-inch cubes

1/4 cup pine nuts, toasted
1 egg
1/8 teaspoon cayenne pepper
2 tablespoons Pesto Sauce
   (see page 264)

In large skillet over medium-high heat, sauté sausage and onion, stirring to break up meat, until meat is no longer pink and onion is translucent. Drain and set aside. In large bowl combine sausage mixture, mushrooms, bread, nuts, egg, cayenne pepper and Pesto Sauce.

Makes 6 to 8 servings.

Per Serving (approx):
Calories 215
Carbohydrate 20 gm

Protein 13 gm
Sodium 458 mg

Fat 9 gm
Cholesterol 58 mg

368

Green Onion and Corn Bread Stuffing

1 can (10 1/2 ounces) condensed
   French onion soup
1 soup can of water
1/4 cup margarine
1 cup celery cut into 1/4-inch
   cubes

1 cup thinly sliced green onion
1 to 1/2 teaspoons dried
   poultry seasoning
2 packages (8 ounces each)
   corn bread stuffing mix

In 5-quart saucepan combine soup, water, margarine, celery, onion and poultry seasoning. Bring to a boil and remove from heat.

Stir in corn bread stuffing mix. Bake mixture in 1 1/2-quart casserole coated with nonstick vegetable cooking spray. Bake, covered, at 350 degrees for 45 minutes or until set.   Makes 12 servings.

Per Serving (approx):
Calories 200   *Protein 5 gm*   *Fat 6 gm*
Carbohydrate 32 gm   *Sodium 683 mg*   *Cholesterol 0 mg*

We find in the Tamil language of India, a word "toka"– peacock, the primitive meaning of which refers to a train or trailing skirt. This word adopted into the Hebrew language becomes "tukki" and by a slight change of the genius of the English language becomes what we are looking for, "turkey."

Other sources say that the American Indian name for the bird was "firkee" and still others think the present name "turkey" came from the alarm call of the bird, "turc, turc, turc."

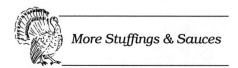

Cranberry Fruit Stuffing

3 cups herb-seasoned stuffing
   mix
2 cups chopped mixed dried fruit
1 cup chopped celery
2/3 cup chopped onion
1 cup whole cranberry sauce

1/2 teaspoon dried sage
1/2 teaspoon dried thyme
1 1/2 cups turkey broth or
   reduced-sodium chicken
   bouillon

In medium bowl combine stuffing mix, dried fruit, celery, onion, cranberry sauce, sage, thyme and turkey broth. Coat 2-quart ovenproof dish with nonstick vegetable cooking spray. Spoon dressing into dish and bake, uncovered, for 40 to 45 minutes in preheated 325 degree oven.

Makes 8 servings.

Per Serving (approx):
Calories 260
Carbohydrate 60 gm

Protein 4 gm
Sodium 420 mg

Fat 2 gm
Cholesterol 0 mg

Rye-Apple Stuffing

1 green apple, chopped
1 onion, chopped
1 celery stalk, chopped
6 tablespoons butter
5 slices dark rye bread, torn
   into small pieces

1 cup turkey or chicken broth
1 cup chopped cranberries
1 egg, lightly beaten
Salt and pepper to taste
1/4 cup apple brandy

In medium skillet sauté apple, onion and celery in 4 tablespoons of the butter for 3 minutes. Mix with bread crumbs. Add broth, cranberries, egg, salt and pepper. Mound in greased casserole.

Baste with remaining butter and apple brandy and bake at 350 degrees for 50 minutes.

Makes 6 servings.

Per Serving (approx):
Calories 285
Carbohydrate 30 gm

Protein 5 gm
Sodium 717 mg

Fat 13 gm
Cholesterol 67 mg

Mediterranean Medley

3 tablespoons olive oil
1/2 cup finely chopped onion
3 cloves garlic, minced
2 green onions, thinly sliced
   (white part plus 2 inches of
   green)
2 medium carrots,
   very finely chopped

2 medium zucchini,
   unpeeled very finely chopped
1 1/2 teaspoons lemon juice
1/2 teaspoon grated lemon zest
3 sun-dried tomatoes (oil
   packed), very finely chopped
2 tablespoons chopped fresh
   basil or 1 teaspoon dried
Salt to taste

In olive oil sauté onion and garlic over low heat until they begin to soften.
Add green onions, carrots and zucchini. Cook slowly until tender. Stir in
lemon juice, lemon zest and sun-dried tomatoes. Cook briefly, stirring to
blend flavors. Add basil at last minute. Add salt if necessary.

Makes 2 cups, 8 servings.

Turkeys in their wild state generally mated in pairs and
during the breeding season it was a case of the "survival
of the fittest." The survivor had his choice of the flock
and proudly walked away with his mate. Cases have been
recorded where a large, wild tom would fight and kill
another tom and take unto him the new mate, while his
first mate was sitting. It is owing to this rule that we
have such a fine bird today. When man tries to confine
and in-breed this great bird of the forest, nature steps in
and says, "no."

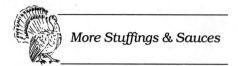

Mushroom Cream Sauce with Tarragon

From our friends at the Kendall-Jackson Winery, here is a wonderful sauce to accompany your favorite turkey dish.

1 pound button mushrooms, thinly sliced

1 stick plus 1 tablespoon unsalted butter

1 cup homemade chicken stock (unsalted or reduced-sodium)

2/3 cup whipping cream

2 tablespoons finely chopped parsley

2 tablespoons finely chopped fresh tarragon or 1 teaspoon dried

1/3 cup pine nuts

Sauté mushrooms in 1 stick butter over medium heat, stirring frequently, until tender. Add chicken stock and continue cooking, stirring occasionally, until liquid is reduced by half. Add cream and continue cooking and stirring until liquid is again reduced by half. Add parsley and tarragon and cook briefly, stirring to blend flavors. Sauté pine nuts in remaining 1 tablespoon butter over medium heat until golden brown on both sides. Sprinkle over sauce.   Makes 2 cups, 8 servings.

Curried Pineapple Glaze

Just enough curry powder is used in this glaze to give it an elusive flavor and fragrance.

2 teaspoons cornstarch
1 teaspoon curry powder
1/4 teaspoon minced instant onion
1/8 teaspoon garlic salt
2 tablespoons cold water

2 tablespoons brown sugar
1 can (8 1/4 ounces) crushed
  pineapple
1 tablespoon butter or margarine
Salt and pepper to taste

Mix cornstarch, curry powder, onion and garlic salt; stir in cold water. Heat pineapple with brown sugar. Add cornstarch mixture and stir over low heat until smooth and clear. Stir in butter, salt and pepper.

Makes about 1 cup, enough to glaze a medium turkey breast or half breast.

Sherried Cranberry Glaze

1 can (8 ounces) jellied
  cranberry sauce

1/3 cup sherry

In small saucepan combine cranberry sauce and sherry. Cook slowly, stirring, until mixture is only slighly runny.

Makes about 1 cup, enough to glaze a medium turkey breast or half breast.

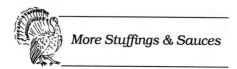

Caribbean Salsa

An interesting, spicy salsa that is good with hot or cold turkey.

2 cups mango peeled and cut
   into 1/4-inch cubes
1/2 cup cucumber peeled,
   seeded and cut into
   1/4-inch cubes
1/4 cup chopped cilantro
2 tablespoons finely chopped
   green onion

1/2 jalapeño pepper, seeded
   and finely chopped
3 tablespoons fresh lime juice
1 1/2 teaspoons brown sugar
1 teaspoon minced fresh ginger
Dash of black pepper

In medium bowl combine mango, cucumber, cilantro, green onion, jalapeño, lime juice, brown sugar, ginger and black pepper. Cover and refrigerate at least 1 hour to allow flavors to blend.

Makes 8 servings.

Today's market turkey is a "mammoth" bird, weighing about three and one-half times as much as the wild turkeys the Pilgrims ate. Moreover, the "new" turkey consumes 30 percent less feed and requires more than one month less growing time to reach market age than turkeys of 20 years ago. As an added plus, today's turkeys have about 25 percent more meat than turkeys of the 1950s.

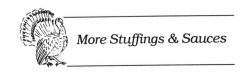

Wine and Garlic Marinade

2 cups dry white wine
1/2 cup olive oil
10 to 12 cloves garlic, crushed
6 slices lemon
2 teaspoons dried thyme
  (optional)

2 teaspoons dried basil
  (optional)
2 teaspoons salt
2 bay leaves (optional)
1 teaspoon black pepper

In wide, shallow bowl, combine all ingredients; reserve half. Add 3 to 4 pounds turkey to remaining marinade; cover and refrigerate for 1 hour or longer, turning occasionally.

To grill, drain turkey and discard used marinade. Grill turkey until cooked through, basting with reserved marinade.

Makes about 2 1/2 cups marinade.

Beer Marinade

3 tablespoons spicy brown
  mustard
3 tablespoons brown sugar
3 tablespoons oil
1 tablespoon Worcestershire
  sauce

1 teaspoon hot pepper sauce
1 teaspoon salt
1/2 teaspoon black pepper
1 can (12 ounces) beer
1 extralarge onion, sliced
  into rings

In medium bowl combine first mustard, brown sugar, oil, Worcestershire sauce, hot pepper sauce, salt and pepper. Stir in beer and onion. Use as marinade for 4 to 6 pounds turkey. Cover and refrigerate for 1 hour or longer, turning occasionally.

Onion rings may be grilled for 2 to 3 minutes on each side and served with turkey.

Makes about 2 cups marinade.

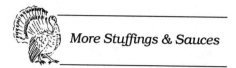

Traditional Barbecue Sauce

1 cup chili sauce
1/2 cup firmly packed
  brown sugar
1/4 cup oil
2 tablespoons cider vinegar
2 tablespoons soy sauce

1 tablespoon spicy brown
  mustard
1 1/2 teaspoons chopped fresh
  oregano (optional)
1 to 1 1/2 teaspoons liquid
  smoke (optional)

In small bowl combine all ingredients. Use as basting sauce for grilling 4 to 5 pounds turkey during last 10 to 15 minutes of cooking. Turn turkey often to avoid scorching.   Makes 1 1/2 cups barbecue sauce.

Chutney Barbecue Sauce

Prepared chutney is a shortcut to creating a delicious basting sauce. It results in deeply browned turkey.

1 jar (8 1/2 ounces) mango
  chutney
1/3 cup wine vinegar

1 tablespoon spicy brown
  mustard
1 tablespoon brown sugar
1/4 teaspoon cayenne pepper

In small bowl combine all ingredients. Use as basting sauce for grilling 4 to 5 pounds turkey during last 10 to 15 minutes of cooking. Lightly oil turkey before cooking, and turn often to avoid burning.

Makes about 1 1/2 cups basting sauce.

Index

A

Acorn Squash Soup, 29
Almond-Crusted Turkey Steaks, 214
Amish Vegetable and Noodle Soup, 28
Appetizers, 13-24
Apple-Cinnamon Sausage Sandwich, 339
Apple-Pecan Stuffing, 278
Apple Pie Turkey Salad, 76
Apple-Soy Marinade, 75
Après Ski Turkey Stew, 231
Arizona Turkey Salad, 68
Armenian Turkey Dumplings, 88
Asian & Indian, 81-108

B

Bacon and Vegetable Bread, 184
Baked Chilies Rellenos, 131
Barbecue Meat Loaf, 166
Barbecue on a Bun, 337
Barbecuing & Grilling, 283-312
Basic Turkey Schnitzel, 200
Bavarian Turkey Burgers, 362
Beer Marinade, 375
Black Bean Chili, 48
Blue Cheese Dressing, 72
Bombay Turkey, 92
Breakfast Pizza, 365
Butterflied Chile-Buttered Turkey

C

Caesar Dressing, 80
Caesar Turkey Salad, 80
Cajun Grilled Turkey, 308
Cajun Skillet Pot Pie, 174
California Meat Loaf, 161
California-Style Stuffing I, 368
California-Style Stuffing II, 368
California Turkey Chili, 44
California Turkey Puff, 173
California Turkey Schnitzel, 201
Cannellini Sauté, 246
Cantonese Turkey Steaks, 95

Cape Cod Turkey Roast, 219
Caribbean Salsa, 374
Cashew-n-Cheese Cutlets, 154
Casseroles & Meat Loaves, 145-166
Champagne-Sauced Turkey, 198
Cheese-n-Turkey Bundles, 22
Chile Butter, 276
Chile Gravy, 274
Chinese Simmered Turkey Strips, 92
Chinese Skillet Dinner, 98
Chinese Turkey Salad, 73
Chutney(s). *See* Salsa(s)
Chutney Barbecue Sauce, 376
Chutney-Curry Grill, 296
Chutney Salad Dressing, 52
Chutney Turkey Salad, 66
Colorful Turkey Pasta Salad, 62
Cooked Turkey & Leftovers
   Acorn Squash Soup, 29
   Amish Vegetable and Noodle Soup, 28
   Apple Pie Turkey Salad, 76
   Baked Chilies Rellenos, 131
   Barbecue on a Bun, 337
   Black Bean Chili, 48
   California Turkey Chili, 44
   Cheese-n-Turkey Bundles, 22
   Chinese Skillet Dinner, 98
   Chinese Turkey Salad, 73
   Colorful Turkey Pasta Salad, 62
   Country-Style Turkey Pie, 183
   Creamy Creole Turkey Bake, 156
   Curried Salad Bombay, 78
   Curried Turkey Dinner, 85
   Curried Turkey Salad Amandine, 69
   Deluxe Turkey Salad, 78
   Divine Cheddar Divan, 323
   Easy Elegant Cream Soup with Tarragon, 325
   Fettuccine Alfredo Plus, 316
   Gingery Stir-Fry Salad, 60
   Hearty Turkey-Vegetable Soup, 31
   Holiday Strata, 328
   Kansas City Salad, 74
   Mandarin Salad, 53
   Manicotti, 242

Mexican Shepherd's Pie, 175
Mini Turkey Ham Quiche, 172
New England Turkey Chowder, 33
Open-Faced Sandwiches Olé, 344
Oriental "Flower" Soup, 36
Oven-Baked Monte Cristo Sandwiches, 345
Parmesan Turkey Cubes, 21
Pasta Primavera Salad, 59
Pita Pockets, 344
Portuguese Sopa, 40
Quick Curry, 93
Rice-n-Turkey Casserole, 147
Rice Salad with Pesto Dressing, 74
Salad Niçoise #2, 55
Savory Stuffing Pie, 172
Sesame Turkey Cubes, 22
Spaghetti Pie, 251
Spicy Orange Turkey, 205
Szechuan Turkey Salad, 71
Tarragon Turkey Pitas, 346
Tetrazzini Pasta Supper, 252
Turkey and Broccoli Skillet Soufflé, 164
Turkey and Corn Bread Salad, 76
Turkey and Wild Rice Bake, 153
Turkey Chili with Black Beans, 321
Turkey Chow Mein, 84
Turkey Divan Soup, 37
Turkey Pistachio Sandwich, 346
Turkey Pumpernickel Strata, 162
Turkey Quiche in Potato Shells, 185
Turkey Tortilla Soup, 34
Vintner's Turkey Chili, 50
Waldorf Turkey Salad, 63
White Turkey Chili, 49
Cool Cucumber Salad, 301
Country Parmigiana, 114
Country Pâté, 16
Country Pot Roast, 223
Country-Style Turkey Pie, 183
Cranapple Roasted Turkey Breast I, 265
Cranapple Roasted Turkey Breast II, 266
Cranberry Fruit Stuffing, 370
Cranberry-Horseradish Sauce, 19
Cranberry Turkey, 267
Cranberry Turkey Roast, 219
Creamy Cheese Dressing, 68
Creamy Creole Turkey Bake, 156

Creamy Mushroom Turkey Burgers, 355
Creamy Turkey Piccata, 113
Crockpot Chili, 47
Crunchy Oven-Baked Turkey Drumettes, 20
Curried Pineapple Glaze, 373
Curried Pinwheel Sandwiches, 343
Curried Salad Bombay, 78
Curried Turkey Dinner, 85
Curried Turkey Pasta Salad, 52
Curried Turkey Salad Amandine, 69
Curry Mayonnaise, 69

D

Deluxe Turkey Salad, 78
Dijon Salad Dressing, 56
Divine Cheddar Divan, 323
Dressing(s). See Salad Dressing(s), Stuffing(s)
Drumstick Dinner, 230
Drumsticks with Sauerkraut, 218
Dutch Oven Pot Roast, 220

E

Easy Baked Turkey Breasts, 268
Easy Elegant Cream Soup with Tarragon, 325
Easy Microwave Turkey Lasagne, 324
Easy Turkey Chili, 46
Eggplant Turkey Stacks, 15
Empanadas Grande, 134
Enchiladas Santa Fe Style, 136

F

Family Meat Loaf, 159
Fettuccine Alfredo Plus, 316
Fiesta Pinwheel Sandwiches, 342
Firecracker Rolls, 104
Florentine Turkey Bundles, 118
Florentine Turkey Roll, 120
Foil-Baked Turkey Roast with Raspberry Sauce, 260
French Turkey Fillets, 192
Fresh Tomato Salsa, 243
Fruit and Turkey Medley, 79
Fruited Turkey Kabobs, 302
Fruitful Turkey Salad, 70

G

Garden Fresh Turkey Skillet Dinner, 222
Garlic Slow-Cooker Turkey, 225
Giant Stuffed Turkey Burger, 357
Ginger-Orange Turkey Wings, 17
Ginger-Sherry Dipping Sauce, 106
Ginger Turkey Stir-Fry, 83
Ginger Turkey Wontons, 14
Gingery Stir-Fry Salad, 60
Glazed Sesame Turkey, 294
Glazed Turkey Steaks with Apricot Nut
    Pilaf, 190
Glaze(s)
    Curried Pineapple Glaze, 373
    Orange-Apricot Glaze, 294
    Orange Glaze, 282
    Rosemary-Wine Glaze, 284
    Sherried Cranberry Glaze, 373
Golden Breaded Turkey Tenderloins, 333
Golden Delicious Turkey Roast, 261
Golden Turkey Soup, 26
Great Meatballs, 160
Greek Pizza, 366
Green Onion and Corn Bread Stuffing, 369
Green Sauce, 132
Grilled Turkey Breast with Cherry Sauce,
    304
Ground Turkey
    Armenian Turkey Dumplings, 88
    Barbecue Meat Loaf, 166
    Bavarian Turkey Burgers, 362
    California Meat Loaf, 161
    Creamy Mushroom Turkey Burgers, 355
    Easy Microwave Turkey Lasagne, 324
    Easy Turkey Chili, 46
    Empanadas Grande, 134
    Enchiladas Santa Fe Style, 136
    Family Meat Loaf, 159
    Florentine Turkey Roll, 120
    Giant Stuffed Turkey Burger, 357
    Great Meatballs, 160
    He-Man Burgers, 349
    Homemade Turkey Sausage, 194
    Individual Turkey Loaves with
        Corn Bread Stuffing, 155
    Italian Turkey Crust Pie, 178
    Layered Meat Loaf Ring, 327

Meatball Parmigiana Hoagie, 362
Meatball Rigatoni, 322
Meatballs in a Pasta Crown, 236
Meat Loaf Alaska, 148
Mediterranean Turkey and Eggplant
    Stir-Fry, 122
Mexican Turkey Burgers, 354
Morning Sausage and Apples, 194
Mushroom-Stuffed Meat Loaf, 150
Nacho Special, 320
Norwegian Burgers, 359
Oriental Burgers, 351
Party Meatballs, 19
Pesto Meatballs with Zucchini and
    Pasta, 245
Pita Burgers, 348
Really Rapid Pizza, 364
Reuben Turkey Burgers, 358
Ribbon Turkey Loaf, 157
Roumanian Turkey Burgers, 362
Santa Fe Chili, 43
Sicilian Turkey Braciola, 112
South of the Border Burgers, 347
Southwestern Turkey Hash, 141
Spicy Breakfast Sausage, 193
Spicy Cajun Hash, 193
Spicy Spanakopita, 180
Spicy Turkey Meat Loaf, 160
Stuffed Pasta Shells Italiano, 244
Stuffing Burgers, 360
Super Turkey Burger Pie, 179
Swedish Turkey Meat Loaf, 159
Sweet and Sour Meatballs, 331
Sweet-n-Sour Barbecue Turkey
    Meatballs, 158
Taco Burgers, 349
Tarragon-Mustard Burgers, 356
Teriyaki Turkey Burgers, 350
Tex-Mex Potato Boats, 137
Tex-Mex Turkey Fillets, 140
Tortilla Flats, 338
Turkey and Asparagus Terrine, 146
Turkey Burger Plus, 347
Turkey Burgers al Greco, 352
Turkey Corn Chowder, 30
Turkey Crust Pie, 318
Turkey Joe #1, 363
Turkey Joe #2, 363

Turkey Lurky Pie, 181
Turkey Manicotti, 317
Turkey Noodle Dandy, 151
Turkey Picadillo #1, 142
Turkey Picadillo #2, 143
Turkey Taco Bake, 158
Turkey Tacos, 320
Turkey Taco Salad, 58
Turkey Tortilla Stew, 234
Turkish Burgers, 353
Versatile Turkey Sauce, 238
Gypsy Cutlets, 208

H

Half Turkey
    Maple-Glazed Turkey with Apple-Pecan
        Stuffing, 278
    Teriyaki Turkey Luau, 289
    Turkey a la Jamaica, 279
Half Turkey Breast, Southwest Style, 263
Harvest Soup, 41
Hawaiian Turkey Fillets, 309
He-Man Burgers, 349
Herbed Turkey and Vegetable Kabobs, 305
Herb Grilled Turkey and "Sweets," 306
Herb-Roasted Turkey and Potatoes, 261
Herb-Sauced Turkey and Vegetables, 233
Hearty Turkey-Vegetable Soup, 31
Holiday Strata, 328
Hollywood Turkey Salad, 72
Homemade Turkey Sausage, 194
Honey Mustard Sauce, 22
Hot-n-Sour Turkey Soup, 35
Hot-n-Spicy Barbecued Drumsticks, 303
Hunan Dressing, 108
Hunan Salad, 108
Hungarian Goulash, 232

I

Individual Turkey Loaves with Corn Bread
    Stuffing, 155
Island Grilled Turkey Breasts, 294
Island Sauce, 294
Italian & Mediterranean, 109-126
Italian Stir-Fry, 119
Italian Turkey, 111
Italian Turkey Crust Pie, 178
Italian Turkey Sausage Roll, 186
Italian Turkey with Olives, 221

J

Jalapeño Corn Bread Stuffing, 280
Japanese-Style Turkey Steaks, 103

K

Kansas City Salad, 74

L

Lattice-Crust Turkey Pot Pies, 182
Layered Meat Loaf Ring, 327
Lemon Dressing, 73
Lemony Barbecued Turkey Thighs, 297
Light and Easy Turkey Tenderloin, 229
Light Teriyaki Sauce, 99

M

Madras Turkey with New Delhi Rice, 94
Mandarin Salad, 53
Mango Salsa, 90
Manicotti, 242
Maple-Basted Roast Turkey with New
    England Stuffing, 281
Maple-Glazed Turkey with Apple-Pecan
    Stuffing, 278
Marinade(s)
    Apple-Soy, 75
    Beer Marinade, 375
    Wine and Garlic Marinade, 375
Mayonnaise(s). See Salad Dressing(s)
Meatball Parmigiana Hoagie, 362
Meatball Rigatoni, 322
Meatballs in a Pasta Crown, 236
Meat Loaf Alaska, 148
Mediterranean Medley, 371
Mediterranean Turkey and Eggplant
    Stir-Fry, 122
Mesquite-Grilled Turkey, 290
Mexican & Southwestern, 127-144
Mexican Shepherd's Pie, 175
Mexican Turkey Burgers, 354
Mexico City Turkey Breast, 144
Microwave Cooking, 313-334

Mideast Fajitas, 90
Midsummer Turkey Kabobs, 295
Midwest Sauce, 311
Midwestern Turkey Barbecue, 311
Milano Turkey Roll with Tomato Basil
    Salsa, 117
Mini Turkey Ham Quiche, 172
Minted Turkey Salad, 57
Mixed Turkey Grill with Two-Alarm
    Barbecue Sauce, 298
More Stuffings & Sauces, 367-376
Morning Sausage and Apples, 194
Moroccan Crockpot Soup, 38
Moroccan Turkey Wings, 126
Muffaletta, 336
Mushroom Cream Sauce with Tarragon,
    372
Mushroom-Stuffed Meat Loaf, 150
Mustard Garlic Dressing, 65
Mustard-Topped Turkey Steaks, 293

N

Nacho Special, 320
New Delhi Rice, 94
New England Stuffing, 281
New England Turkey Chowder, 33
New Potato and Turkey Ham Salad, 61
Normande Sauce, 312
Norwegian Burgers, 359
Nouvelle Salade, 56

O

Open-Faced Sandwiches Olé, 344
Orange-Apricot Sauce, 294
Orange-Mint Dressing, 79
Oriental Burgers, 351
Oriental "Flower" Soup, 36
Oriental Turkey Breast Dinner, 105
Oriental Turkey Fillets, 300
Oven-Baked Monte Cristo Sandwiches, 345
Oven-Barbecued Turkey Wings, 227

P

Parmesan Turkey Cubes, 21
Party Meatballs, 19
Pasta Pie, 334
Pasta Primavera Salad, 59

Pastas & Grains, 235-252
Pavo Fajitas, 129
Peanut Sauce, 91
Pennies and Rice, 99
Peppercorn Turkey over Spinach
    Noodles, 250
Peppered Turkey Medallions with Chutney
    Sauce, 203
Peppery Turkey Fillets, 300
Persian Pita Turkey, 329
Pesto Meatballs with Zucchini and
    Pasta, 245
Pesto Sauce, 264
Pineapple and Turkey on Skewers, 293
Pineapple Minted Turkey Breast, 262
Pineapple-Mustard-Glazed Turkey
    Breast, 255
Pita Burgers, 348
Pita Pockets, 344
Pizzeria Salad, 67
Poached Turkey Normande, 189
Poached Turkey Tenderloins, 224
Port-Sauced Turkey, 272
Portuguese Sopa, 40
Pot Pies & Pastries, 167-186
Pot Roasts & Stews, 217-234
Pot Roast with Olives, 221
Pumpkin Turkey Bake, 165

Q

Quick Curry, 93
Quick Turkey Appetizers, 23

R

Raspberry Sauce, 260
Really Rapid Pizza, 364
Reuben Turkey Burgers, 358
Ribbon Turkey Loaf, 157
Rice(s)
    New Delhi Rice, 94
    Pennies and Rice, 99
Rich Turkey Soup, 42
Rice-n-Turkey Casserole, 147
Rice Salad with Pesto Dressing, 74
Rio Grande Turkey, 133
Roasting Breasts & Rolled Roasts, 253-268
Roasting Whole & Half Turkeys, 269-282

Roast Turkey Athena, 277
Roast Turkey Breast with Spiced Cherry
    Sauce, 257
Roast Turkey with Dried Fruit
    Stuffing, 275
Roast Turkey with Giblet Stuffing and
    Gravy, 271
Roast Turkey with Jalapeño Corn Bread
    Stuffing, 280
Roast Turkey with Oyster Stuffing, 273
Roast Turkey with Peanut Sauce, 270
Rolled Turkey Breast with Fruit Sauce, 259
Roman-Style Grilled Turkey Breast, 288
Roumanian Turkey Burgers, 362
Rye-Apple Stuffing, 370

S

Sage Corn Bread Dressing, 274
Salad Dressing(s)
    Blue Cheese Dressing, 72
    Caesar Dressing, 80
    Chutney Salad Dressing, 52
    Creamy Cheese Dressing, 68
    Curry Mayonnaise, 69
    Dijon Salad Dressing, 56
    Hunan Dressing, 108
    Lemon Dressing, 73
    Minted Mayonnaise, 57
    Mustard Garlic Dressing, 65
    Orange-Mint Dressing, 79
    Sweet & Sour Dressing, 75
    Szechuan Dressing, 71
Salad Niçoise #1, 54
Salad Niçoise #2, 55
Salsa(s)
    Caribbean Salsa, 374
    Fresh Tomato Salsa, 243
    Mango Salsa, 90
    Tomato Basil Salsa, 117
San Antonio Turkey Fajitas, 128
Sandwiches, Burgers, Hoagies & Sloppy
    Joes, 335-366
Santa Fe Chili, 43
Sauce(s)
    Chutney Barbecue Sauce, 376
    Cranberry-Horseradish Sauce, 19
    Fruit Sauce, 259

Ginger-Sherry Dipping Sauce, 106
Green Sauce, 132
Honey Mustard Sauce, 22
Light Teriyaki Sauce, 99
Midwest Sauce, 311
Mushroom Cream Sauce with
    Tarragon, 372
Normande Sauce, 312
Peanut Sauce, 91
Pesto Sauce, 264
Raspberry Sauce, 260
Sesame Scallion Sauce, 14
Sherry Orange Sauce, 14
Sour Cream Sauce, 139
Thai Peanut Sauce, 270
Thai Peanut Sauce #2, 287
Traditional Barbecue Sauce, 376
Versatile Turkey Sauce, 238
Wine-Lemon Sauce, 211
Sausage and Broccoli Quiche, 176
Sausage-Spinach Turnovers, 177
Sauté & Stir Fry, 187-216
Savory Stuffing Pie, 172
Scallopini #1, 123
Scallopini #2, 124
Schnitzel Florentine, 202
Sesame Scallion Sauce, 14
Sesame Turkey Cubes, 22
Sesame Turkey Cutlets, 87
Shanghai'd Turkey, 86
Sherried Cranberry Glaze, 373
Sherry Orange Sauce, 14
Sicilian Turkey Braciola, 112
Skillet-Simmered Turkey Thighs, 210
Smoked Turkey and Fresh Vegetable
    Salad, 64
Smoked Turkey Quesadillas, 15
Smoked Turkey Risotto, 241
Sonoma Turkey Barbecue, 286
Sour Cream Sauce, 139
Southern Fried Turkey with Gravy, 212
South of the Border Burgers, 347
Southwestern Butterflied Turkey with
    Roasted Garlic, 285
Southwestern Rice Stuffing, 282
Southwestern Turkey Hash, 141
Southwest Turkey Roast, 282
Spaghetti Pie, 251

Spanish Rice with Turkey Sausage, 240
Spicy Breakfast Sausage, 193
Spicy Cajun Hash, 193
Spicy Lime and Cilantro Turkey
 Fajitas, 139
Spicy Orange Turkey, 205
Spicy Spanakopita, 180
Spicy Turkey Meat Loaf, 160
Steaks Shanghai, 82
Stuffed Pasta Shells Italiano, 244
Stuffed Turkey Breast with Pesto
 Sauce, 264
Stuffed Turkey-Rice Roll, 243
Stuffing(s)
 Apple-Pecan Stuffing, 278
 California-Style Stuffing I, 368
 California-Style Stuffing II, 368
 Cranberry Fruit Stuffing, 370
 Dried Fruit Stuffing, 275
 Green Onion and Corn Bread
  Stuffing, 369
 Jalapeño Corn Bread Stuffing, 280
 Mushroom Stuffing, 150
 New England Stuffing, 281
 Rye-Apple Stuffing, 370
 Sage Corn Bread Stuffing, 274
 Southwestern Rice Stuffing, 282
 Vegetable and Bread Stuffing, 179
Stuffing Burgers, 360
Super Turkey Burger Pie, 179
Swedish Turkey Meat Loaf, 159
Sweet & Sour Dressing, 75
Sweet and Sour Meatballs, 331
Sweet-n-Sour Barbecue Turkey
 Meatballs, 158
Sweet-n-Sour Turkey, 330
Szechuan Dressing, 71
Szechuan Stir-Fry, 96
Szechuan Turkey Salad, 71

T

Taco Burgers, 349
Taj Kabobs, 97
Tangy Turkey Tenders, 310
Tarragon-Mustard Burgers, 356
Tarragon Turkey Pitas, 346
Tenderloins with Plum Sauce, 310

Tender-ness Turkey Stir-Fry Salad, 77
Teriyaki Turkey, 100
Teriyaki Turkey Burgers, 350
Teriyaki Turkey Luau, 289
Teriyaki Turkey Wings, 103
Tetrazzini Pasta Supper, 252
Tex-Mex Potato Boats, 137
Tex-Mex Turkey Fillets, 140
Texas Turkey Chili, 45
Thai Peanut Sauce, 270
Thai Peanut Sauce #2, 287
Thai Turkey and Mango Stir-Fry, 102
Thai Turkey Kabobs, 287
The Whole Turkey, 326
Tomato Basil Salsa, 117
Torta Rustica, 171
Tortilla Flats, 338
Traditional Barbecue Sauce, 376
Turkey a la Jamaica, 279
Turkey a l'Orange, 291
Turkey and Asparagus Terrine, 146
Turkey and Broccoli Skillet Soufflé, 164
Turkey and Broccoli Stir-Fry, 216
Turkey and Corn Bread Salad, 76
Turkey and Prosciutto Cordon Bleu, 121
Turkey and White Bean Casserole, 149
Turkey and Wild Rice Bake, 153
Turkey Bourguignon, 314
Turkey Breast a la King, 332
Turkey Breast & Rolled Roasts
 Almond-Crusted Turkey Steaks, 214
 Cajun Grilled Turkey, 308
 Cape Cod Turkey Roast, 219
 Cranapple Roasted Turkey Breast I, 265
 Cranapple Roasted Turkey Breast II, 266
 Cranberry Turkey, 267
 Cranberry Turkey Roast, 219
 Easy Baked Turkey Breasts, 268
 Foil-Baked Turkey Roast with
  Raspberry Sauce, 260
 Glazed Sesame Turkey, 294
 Golden Delicious Turkey Roast, 261
 Greek Pizza, 366
 Grilled Turkey Breast with Cherry
  Sauce, 304
 Half Turkey Breast, Southwest Style, 263
 Herb Grilled Turkey and "Sweets," 306
 Herb-Roasted Turkey and Potatoes, 261

Herb-Sauced Turkey and Vegetables, 233
Island Grilled Turkey Breast, 294
Lattice-Crust Turkey Pot Pies, 182
Mexico City Turkey Breast, 144
Oriental Turkey Breast Dinner, 105
Pineapple Minted Turkey Breast, 262
Pineapple-Mustard-Glazed Turkey
    Breast, 255
Roast Turkey Breast with Spiced
    Cherry Sauce, 257
Rolled Turkey Breast with Fruit
    Sauce, 259
Roman-Style Grilled Turkey Breast, 288
Salad Niçoise #1, 54
Scallopini #1, 123
Sonoma Turkey Barbecue, 286
Stuffed Turkey Breast with Pesto
    Sauce, 264
Turkey Breast a la King, 332
Turkey Breast Dijon, 307
Turkey Breasts Verde, 256
Turkey Breast with Southwestern
    Corn Bread Dressing, 258
Turkey Della Robbia, 254
Turkey En Croute #2, 169
Turkey Molé, 138
Turkey Pot Pies, 170
Turkey with Wild Rice, 237
Turkey Yakitori, 107
Veracruz Turkey Slices, 129
Turkey Breast Dijon, 307
Turkey Breast Fillets
    Creamy Turkey Piccata, 113
    French Turkey Fillets, 192
    Hawaiian Turkey Fillets, 309
    Mideast Fajitas, 90
    Oriental Turkey Fillets, 300
    Peppery Turkey Fillets, 300
    Teriyaki Turkey, 100
    Thai Turkey Kabobs, 287
    Turkey Fillets with Champagne-
        Mushroom Sauce, 248
    Turkey Fillets with Chutney Sauce, 89
    Turkey Framboise, 188
    Turkey Kabobs, 299
Turkey Breast Slices
    Caesar Turkey Salad, 80
    Country Parmigiana, 114
    Firecracker Rolls, 104

Fruit and Turkey Medley, 79
Fruitful Turkey Salad, 70
Ginger Turkey Stir-Fry, 83
Milano Turkey Roll with Tomato
    Basil Salsa, 117
Minted Turkey Salad, 57
Nouvelle Salade, 56
Scallopini #2, 124
Szechuan Stir-Fry, 96
Turkey Creole, 213
Turkey Creole with Mushrooms, 226
Turkey Dinner Sandwiches, 340
Turkey Jardiniere, 211
Turkey Mornay, 195
Turkey Slices Orangerie, 215
Turkey Slices with Green Peppercorn
    Sauce, 195
Turkey Spinach Salad, 75
Turkey Vegetable Tempura, 106
Turkey Breasts Verde, 256
Turkey Breast with Southwestern
    Corn Bread Dressing, 258
Turkey Bruschetta, 341
Turkey Burger Plus, 347
Turkey Burgers al Greco, 352
Turkey Cacciatore, 110
Turkey Chili with Black Beans, 321
Turkey Chow Mein, 84
Turkey Cordon Bleu, 315
Turkey Corn Chowder, 30
Turkey Creole, 213
Turkey Creole with Mushrooms, 226
Turkey Crust Pie, 318
Turkey Cutlets
    Basic Turkey Schnitzel, 200
    California Turkey Schnitzel 201
    Cashew-n-Cheese Cutlets, 154
    Curried Turkey Pasta Salad, 52
    Florentine Turkey Bundles, 118
    Gypsy Cutlets, 208
    Italian Stir-Fry, 119
    Pavo Fajitas, 129
    San Antonio Turkey Fajitas, 128
    Schnitzel Florentine, 202
    Sesame Turkey Cutlets, 87
    Stuffed Turkey-Rice Roll, 243
    Turkey and Broccoli Stir-Fry, 216
    Turkey and Prosciutto Cordon Bleu, 121
    Turkey Bruschetta, 341

Turkey Fajitas, 130
Turkey Lemon Cutlets, 207
Turkey Parmigiana, 113
Turkey Deli
    Arizona Turkey Salad, 68
    Bacon and Vegetable Bread, 184
    Cannellini Sauté, 246
    Chutney Turkey Salad, 66
    Curried Pinwheel Sandwiches, 343
    Eggplant Turkey Stacks, 15
    Fiesta Pinwheel Sandwiches, 342
    Hollywood Turkey Salad, 72
    Muffaletta, 336
    New Potato and Turkey Ham Salad, 61
    Pizzeria Salad, 67
    Quick Turkey Appetizers
    Smoked Turkey and Fresh Vegetable
        Salad, 64
    Smoked Turkey Quesadillas, 15
    Smoked Turkey Risotto, 241
    Torta Rustica, 171
    Trattoria Eggplant Turkey Rolls, 247
    Turkey Hoagies for a Crowd, 362
    Turkey Jack Appetizers, 24
    Turkey Pastrami and Cheese Strata, 163
    Tuscany Bean Salad, 66
    White Bean and Smoked Turkey
        Salad, 65
    Wild Rice and Turkey Bacon Soup, 32
Turkey Della Robbia, 254
Turkey Dinner Sandwiches, 340
Turkey Divan Soup, 37
Turkey Drumsticks
    California Turkey Puff, 173
    Country Pâté, 16
    Drumstick Dinner, 230
    Drumsticks with Sauerkraut, 218
    Hot-n-Sour Turkey Soup, 35
    Hot-n-Spicy Barbecued Drumsticks, 303
    Hunan Salad, 108
    Italian Turkey with Vegetables, 221
    Madras Turkey with New Delhi Rice, 94
    Pot Roast with Olives, 221
    Sausage-Spinach Turnovers, 177
    Turkey and White Bean Casserole, 149
    Turkey Leg Tacos with Green Sauce, 132
    Turkey Normande, 312
Turkey Eggplant Turkey Roll, 247

Turkey En Croute #1, 168
Turkey En Croute #2, 169
Turkey Fajitas, 130
Turkey Fillets
    Turkey Fillets in Mustard Cream
        Sauce, 209
Turkey Fillets in Mustard Cream Sauce, 209
Turkey Fillets with Champagne-
    Mushroom Sauce, 248
Turkey Fillets with Chutney Sauce, 89
Turkey Framboise, 188
Turkey Fricassee with Dumplings, 191
Turkey Grill, 284
Turkey Hoagies for a Crowd, 362
Turkey in an Oven-Roasting Bag, 276
Turkey in Salsa, 135
Turkey Jack Appetizers, 24
Turkey Jardiniere, 211
Turkey Joe #1, 363
Turkey Joe #2, 363
Turkey Kabobs, 299
Turkey Leg Tacos with Green Sauce, 132
Turkey Lemon Cutlets, 207
Turkey Liver Pâté, 18
Turkey Livers
    Turkey Liver Pâté, 18
Turkey Lurky Pie, 181
Turkey Manicotti, 317
Turkey Marengo, 319
Turkey Medallions Piccata, 115
Turkey Medallions with Cumberland
    Sauce, 206
Turkey Molé, 138
Turkey Mornay, 195
Turkey Navarin, 228
Turkey Noodle Dandy, 151
Turkey Normande, 312
Turkey Parts
    Rich Turkey Soup, 42
    Turkey Stock, 27
Turkey Parmigiana, 113
Turkey Pastrami and Cheese Strata, 163
Turkey Perugia, 116
Turkey Picadillo #1, 142
Turkey Picadillo #2, 143
Turkey Pistachio Sandwich, 346
Turkey Pot Pies, 170
Turkey Pumpernickel Strata, 162

Turkey Quiche in Potato Shells, 185
Turkey Salads, 51-80
Turkey Satay with Peanut Sauce, 91
Turkey Sausage
    Apple-Cinnamon Sausage Sandwich, 339
    Breakfast Pizza, 365
    Italian Turkey Sausage Roll, 186
    Pasta Pie, 334
    Spanish Rice with Turkey Sausage, 240
    Turkey Sausage Ragout on Pasta, 249
Turkey Sausage Ragout on Pasta, 249
Turkey Shish Kabobs, 125
Turkey Slices
    Steaks Shanghai, 82
Turkey Slices Orangerie, 215
Turkey Slices with Green Peppercorn
    Sauce, 195
Turkey Soups & Chilis, 25-50
Turkey Southwest Style with Sage Corn
        Bread Stuffing and Chile Gravy, 274
Turkey Spinach Salad, 75
Turkey Steaks
    Cantonese Turkey Steaks, 95
    Glazed Turkey Steaks with Apricot Nut
        Pilaf, 190
    Japanese-Style Turkey Steaks, 103
    Mustard-Topped Turkey Steaks, 293
    Pineapple and Turkey on Skewers, 293
    Turkey Cordon Bleu, 315
    Turkey Marengo, 319
    Turkey Steak Diane, 199
    Turkey Steaks Kiev, 196
Turkey Steak Diane, 199
Turkey Steaks Kiev, 196
Turkey Stock, 27
Turkey Taco Bake, 158
Turkey Tacos, 320
Turkey Taco Salad, 58
Turkey Tenderloins
    Bombay Turkey, 92
    Champagne-Sauced Turkey, 198
    Chinese Simmered Turkey Strips, 92
    Fruited Turkey Kabobs, 302
    Ginger Turkey Wontons, 14
    Golden Breaded Turkey Tenderloins, 333
    Herbed Turkey and Vegetable
        Kabobs, 305
    Light and Easy Turkey Tenderloin, 229

Mesquite-Grilled Turkey, 290
Midsummer Turkey Kabobs, 295
Peppercorn Turkey over Spinach
    Noodles, 250
Peppered Turkey Medallions with
    Chutney Sauce, 203
Persian Pita Turkey, 329
Poached Turkey Normande, 189
Poached Turkey Tenderloins, 224
Sausage and Broccoli Quiche, 176
Shanghai'd Turkey, 86
Spicy Lime and Cilantro Turkey
    Fajitas, 139
Tangy Turkey Tenders, 310
Tenderloins with Plum Sauce, 310
Tender-ness Turkey Stir-Fry Salad, 77
Turkey a l'Orange, 291
Turkey En Croute #1, 168
Turkey Medallions Piccata, 115
Turkey Perugia, 116
Turkey Satay with Peanut Sauce, 91
Turkey Teriyaki Tidbits with Pennies
    and Rice, 99
Turkey Veronique, 197
Turkey Zanzibar, 301
Turkey Teriyaki Tidbits with Pennies
    and Rice, 99
Turkey Tetrazzini, 239
Turkey Thighs
    Après Ski Turkey Stew, 231
    Cajun Skillet Pot Pie, 174
    Country Pot Roast, 223
    Crockpot Chili, 47
    Dutch Oven Pot Roast, 220
    Garlic Slow-Cooker Turkey, 225
    Golden Turkey Soup, 26
    Hungarian Goulash, 232
    Italian Turkey, 111
    Lemony Barbecued Turkey Thighs, 297
    Midwestern Turkey Barbecue, 311
    Mixed Turkey Grill with Two-Alarm
        Barbecue Sauce, 298
    Moroccan Crockpot Soup, 38
    Pumpkin Turkey Bake, 165
    Rio Grande Turkey, 133
    Skillet-Simmered Turkey Thighs, 210
    Sweet-n-Sour Turkey, 330
    Taj Kabobs, 97

Texas Turkey Chili, 45
Thai Turkey and Mango Stir-Fry, 102
Turkey Bourguignon, 314
Turkey Cacciatore, 110
Turkey in Salsa, 135
Turkey Medallions with Cumberland
    Sauce, 206
Turkey Navarin, 228
Turkey Shish Kabobs, 125
Turkey Tetrazzini, 239
Turkey Vegetable Chowder, 39
Turkey Viennese, 204
Turkey with Orange, 101
Turkey Tortilla Soup, 34
Turkey Tortilla Stew, 234
Turkey Vegetable Chowder, 39
Turkey Vegetable Tempura, 106
Turkey Veronique, 197
Turkey Viennese, 204
Turkey Wings
    Crunchy Oven-Baked Turkey Wings, 20
    Garden Fresh Turkey Skillet Dinner, 222
    Ginger-Orange Turkey Wings, 17
    Harvest Soup, 41
    Moroccan Turkey Wings, 126
    Oven-Barbecued Turkey Wings, 227
    Southern Fried Turkey with Gravy, 212
    Teriyaki Turkey Wings, 103
    Turkey Fricassee with Dumplings, 191
    Turkey Wings with Couscous
        Dressing, 152
    Zesty Grilled Turkey Wings, 292
Turkey Wings with Couscous Dressing, 152
Turkey with Orange, 101
Turkey with Wild Rice, 237
Turkey Yakitori, 107
Turkey Zanzibar, 301
Turkish Burgers, 353
Tuscany Bean Salad, 66

V

Vegetable and Bread Stuffing, 179
Veracruz Turkey Slices, 129
Versatile Turkey Sauce, 238
Vintner's Turkey Chili, 50

W

Waldorf Turkey Salad, 63
White Bean and Smoked Turkey Salad, 65
White Turkey Chili, 49
Whole Turkey
    Butterflied Chile-Buttered Turkey, 276
    Chutney-Curry Grill, 296
    Maple-Basted Roast Turkey with New
        England Stuffing, 281
    Port-Sauced Turkey
    Roast Turkey Athena, 277
    Roast Turkey with Dried Fruit
        Stuffing, 275
    Roast Turkey with Giblet Stuffing and
        Gravy, 271
    Roast Turkey with Jalapeño Corn Bread
        Stuffing, 280
    Roast Turkey with Oyster Stuffing, 273
    Roast Turkey with Peanut Sauce, 270
    Southwestern Butterflied Turkey with
        Roasted Garlic, 285
    Southwest Turkey Roast, 282
    The Whole Turkey, 326
    Turkey Grill, 284
    Turkey in an Oven-Roasting Bag, 276
    Turkey Southwest Style with Sage Corn
        Bread Stuffing and Chile Gravy, 274
Wild Rice and Turkey Bacon Soup
Wine and Garlic Marinade, 375
Wine-Lemon Sauce, 211

Z

Zesty Grilled Turkey Wings, 292

Additional copies of this book *The Great Turkey Cookbook: 385 Turkey Recipes for Every Day and Holidays,* are available at book, gift and gourmet food stores.

Or, you may order directly from the publisher by phone, fax or mail.

Each copy is $19.95, which includes shipping and handling.

By phone, call (800) 777-1048 with your Visa or Mastercard.

By fax, call 408-722-2749 with your Visa or Mastercard.

By mail, send your personal check, money order, or credit card information to: The Crossing Press, P.O. Box 1048, Freedom, CA 95019.

If you would like to receive our cookbook catalog, call toll-free (800) 777-1048, or write to us at the address above.